LEO BAECK

TEACHER OF THERESIENSTADT

LEO BAECK
TEACHER OF THERESIENSTADT

Albert H. Friedlander

THE OVERLOOK PRESS
Woodstock, New York

To Evelyn

First published in 1991 by
The Overlook Press
Lewis Hollow Road
Woodstock, New York 12498

Library of Congress Cataloging-in-Publication Data

Friedlander, Albert H.
Leo Baeck : teacher of Theresienstadt / by Albert H. Friedlander.
p.   cm.
Reprint. Originally published : New York : Holt, Rinehart, and
Winston, 1968.
Includes bibliographical references.
1. Baeck, Leo, 1873-1956.   2. Judaism—Germany—History—
20th century.   I. Title.
BM755.B32F7   1991
296.8'346'092—dc20
{B}   89-49175
ISBN 0-87951-393-4 (Cloth)   CIP
ISBN 0-87951-441-8 (Paper)

Printed in the United States of America

CONTENTS

ACKNOWLEDGMENTS

A study of this nature draws upon the scholarship of all who have preceded the writer. The debt owed to the scholars who were quoted and whose advice was utilized is freely and gratefully acknowledged.

Special mention must be made of the Leo Baeck Institute and its director, Dr. Max Kreutzberger. Without their help, this book would not have been written. The archives with their original sources were put at the disposal of the author; Dr. Kreutzberger's own knowledge of the period was freely given; and every possible assistance, including a financial grant at a crucial time, gave the fullest support to the writer.

A great deal of the research was done under the direction of Professors Joseph Blau, Jacob Taubes, and Salo W. Baron of Columbia University, where much of this material appeared as a Ph.D. dissertation. The personal counsel and friendship of these men continue to influence the writer, who expresses his grateful appreciation to his teachers and university.

The interest and concern of Arthur A. Cohen and his staff at Holt, Rinehart and Winston have been, as in previous times, an expression of creative partnership in the enterprise of scholarship too little appreciated by the general public.

Acknowledgments are also made to the publishers of studies quoted.

The final acknowledgment must be the book itself, which is an expression of gratitude and a tribute to the author's teacher: to Leo Baeck.

A. H. F.

London, England
June, 1968

1

Prelude at Terezin

Far too much refuse had been placed in the garbage wagon. It moved through the gray rain of the camp with terrible slowness, an inert and ugly mass chaining its beasts of burden to the reality of a filth from which there was no escape. Its miasma clogged their pores. Its weight cut into shoulders, arms, and legs as foot was carefully placed before trembling foot and the cart was inched on its way past the barracks. Every once in a while the cart came to a halt: to load, to unload. Filthy, tired, trembling from their exertions in the harsh winter atmosphere, the beasts of burden turned toward one another:

"But my dear professor," said one to the other, "surely you would not ignore the actions of the protagonists in the Symposium? Even the direction in which the glasses move has significance. And the stormy entrance of Alcibiades—your students at Leyden must have connected this with the text? Or do you think . . ."

"I'm sorry, Dr. Baeck," interrupted the neighbor, "but the guard is motioning us on. Wait until we've turned the corner." And the garbage cart continued on its way through the streets of Terezin, Hitler's "model" concentration camp.

Next week, Leo Baeck would be seventy years old. A tall, imposing, bearded figure, he had been judged strong enough to be one of the beasts of burden for the camp. Behind that judgment, there hid the mean hope that the work would break and destroy this man. Terezin did not gas its victims. Starvation, hardships, exposure to the elements, and fever were enough to destroy its prisoners by the thousands. For those who survived, there were periodic transports to Auschwitz and "Eastern resettlement." But special circumstances surrounded Leo Baeck. The quicker his spirit was broken, his dignity besmirched, his moral and physical strength shattered, the more certain would be the approval from Berlin and from Eichmann himself. For Leo Baeck, after all, was not just any Jew taken by the Nazis and thrown into the blazing furnace of Hitler's "Final Solution"; he was the leader of German Jewry, the last duly elected and appointed leader of a community which had come to an end after more than a thousand years of historic existence. He was one of the great scholars of his generation; what he had to say about Christianity and concerning mysticism or ancient philosophy was received with as much attention as his great writings on the essence of Judaism. Grandmaster of the German B'nai B'rith fraternal organization of Jews, the leading rabbi of the Jewish community of Berlin, professor of the last Jewish seminary in Germany still secretly ordaining young men as rabbis to a dying community, Leo Baeck had refused to leave Germany—despite the insistence of Jews all over the world, of the German leaders themselves. Now, after five arrests and much suffering, he had come to Terezin.

The days and nights of Terezin—Theresienstadt, the Germans called it—have been described by others who survived. Reports of it had already come to Leo Baeck. Three of his sisters had died there; a fourth one died shortly after he arrived. And now he was there himself, one of the many so-called important prisoners who had once been considered the great men of the age by the surrounding world. Here, they were to be mocked, to be broken, to be used as marionettes in the ghastly games of the Nazis. For there were times when the outside world was to be permitted a glimpse of the camp. The sick and dying were crammed into the upper stories of the barracks—visiting dignitaries cannot be bothered to climb a staircase—musicians were forced to play, blankets were issued for the day, and those who really did not want to know the truth could fool themselves into the belief that things were really not so bad, after all.

Baeck did not permit himself to be used. He took his place in the camp: No. 187,894, beast of burden for the refuse cart or any other task the jailers would assign. But they would not be able to stop a beast of burden from discussing philosophy with its neighbor; and they would not stop him from being himself: a rabbi, a teacher.

Metals are heated in the furnace to the point where all foreign matter is melted away, where only the essence remains. Placed into the fiery hell of the concentration camp Baeck's essence revealed itself: He was a rabbi. He would not take an active role in the inner administration of the camp, even as a member of the Council of Elders. There was power there, power which could corrupt—extra days of life were accessible to those in authority. Someone had to serve in those councils; but there were many available for that task. Another task opened itself to Baeck in those days and nights of Terezin. The sick had to be comforted; the dying had to be attended; death needed the dignity of ritual. And the living had to be taught. Terezin needed its teacher.

The beast of burden was able to turn to other tasks, to teach and to preach. Baeck served all inmates. It is sometimes forgotten how many Christians found their way into this hell—one Jewish grandparent was enough to qualify a man for admittance. These inmates lived in a particular anguish of their own. Often strong in their Christian faith, they yet found themselves bereft of religious instruction and ritual, without the comforts of their faith at a moment when these were desperately needed. They learned to come to Leo Baeck, to be instructed and comforted by him. They, too, called him rabbi.

And out of Terezin there came the word of Torah.

What did the inmates learn? And were there seeds which survived the flames and left a harvest for the days which followed, for our own times?

Wild beasts in uniforms roamed the streets of Terezin, guarded its gates, tried to stamp out the humanity still flickering in the thin gray faces of the prisoners. They could not succeed. For late at night, crowded together tightly in a small barrack hall which could not contain them all, the prisoners sacrificed vital hours of rest in order to listen to Leo Baeck and others who lectured to them on Plato, Aristotle, on Greek and Roman philosophy. Using his fantastic memory, Baeck recalled page after page of the writings of famous historians, of Thucydides and Herodotus. Darkness covered the camp, the room. Only his voice was heard, weak, melodic, low but very clear, evoking other times and places. And there must have been many present who wondered: Why are we listening to this? Why not to prayers? Why not to words of rebellion? Why listen at all?

And yet they knew. In the warm barracks of the guards, the Nazis were mocking them for what they were doing: dead men, listening to dead things. But in the crowded prison hall, there existed the awareness that the very act of listening constituted a rebellion, an uprising against the inhumanity of their captors, an assertion of their own humanity. This was no mere gesture, an attempt to maintain one's dignity—a British lord at tea among savages, French nobility dancing minuet or gavotte while waiting their turn for the guillotine. The time for gestures was over, dignity impossible to maintain where guards would break up the lines leading to the toilets in order to see old people befoul themselves. One merely existed, lived for the next day and the day after that. But as long as one knew that there was an inner core to that existence, that at the very moment of extinction the finite reaches out beyond its boundaries, defeat had been kept at bay. And so they listened to Leo Baeck; not because he was a scholar enabling them to pose as civilized people, but because he was their rabbi who taught them that their humanity need not be extinguished.

Baeck was the teacher of Terezin. He was not "the saint of Theresienstadt," as some would have it. He was a man, with flaws and weaknesses. He made mistakes. What matters is that he was true to himself, to his calling as a teacher, a rabbi. And so his life and teaching shine out of those dark days, into our own existence, in a calling, commanding manner.

The garbage wagon rolled on through the mud and snow of the alley. It turned around the corner. Somewhere in the distance, an incongruous sound hung in the heavy air—the musicians of Terezin were rehearsing the Verdi *Requiem*. It was their final rehearsal: After the performance, they would be sent to Auschwitz in one transport. Nearby, in a barracks, a child drew a picture of a butterfly on a scrap of paper, looked around, and wrote a little poem: "I never saw another butterfly." Two streets away, a tired prisoner slumped to the ground and moved no more. And, around the corner, the wagon had come to a stop. The beasts of burden again turned toward one another, and one of them continued in a soft, clear voice: "The clearest definition of love in Plato's sense may be found in the myth which is told as the climax of the Symposium."

In the darkness of Terezin, men continued to define themselves as fashioned in God's image, reaching toward the light.

I I

In the nineteenth century, men still believed in the speedy coming of the messiah. If they had stopped believing in the messiah of religion, they believed in the messiah of reason; or they believed in the messiah of social progress. Most certainly, they believed in man.

In the twentieth century, these faiths died. Franz Kafka looked at the messiah in one of his parables. With some weariness, he concluded that the messiah would only come when he would be no longer necessary. In fact, he would arrive on the day after his arrival; not on the last day, but on the very last one. Other times, and other darknesses, had viewed their pains as the birth pangs of the messiah. In our time, Jews still sang of their perfect faith in the coming of the messiah as they entered the death camps. And died. Faith in reason, faith in social progress, faith in man died in those days. Elie Wiesel wrote out of the night of Auschwitz, wrote that he looked upon the gallows and saw God hanging there. And William Hamilton, one of the leading "God-is-dead" theologians, has indicated his belief that "God died at Auschwitz and Bergen-Belsen, with the death of six million Jews."

How, then, can we understand Leo Baeck and his religious message, which came out of the same darkness, out of the very depths of human anguish? How can we look at the parable of his life which is a paradox, and at the paradox of contemporary existence which refuses to let itself be pressed into a parable? Perhaps there can be no full understanding; certainly, we do not know the answers which our time demands out of existence and which find a fragmentary way to us through the shards of daily experience. But there are ways of entering into the realities of the past, into the inner and outer dimensions of the life and teachings of Leo Baeck. For the essence of Leo Baeck is that he was a teacher; and the ability of transferring knowledge was a reality of his existence. Since we have to understand the present, and must learn from the past, we have to confront men like Leo Baeck. And since our time has noted the tragic split between human experience and the traditional teaching of religion, it becomes all the more important to reach out toward a man who was rooted in the traditions of his faith, who took the essence of Judaism into the darkness of twentieth-century experience—and who emerged out of that darkness with his faith intact. It was a changed faith, with a new emphasis on existence rather than on essence. But it was still the faith of Biblical man, a doorway to an understanding of human existence in which myth, allegory, and the sancta of religion indicate that there are dimensions of man which are only understood when man is defined as *individuum ineffabile*—man in God's image.

Leo Baeck's teachings are not easily summarized or understood. In a very real way, he is the bridge between the nineteenth and twentieth century in Jewish thought. But within the Jewish community, far less attention has been paid to his subtle theology than to that of his colleagues Martin Buber and Franz Rosenzweig. Yet it was Baeck who most clearly developed the heritage common to these three—the teachings of Hermann Cohen—and who placed Jewish thought in the mainstream of European intellectual life, moving from Dilthey and his *Einfuehlung* into a confrontation with the leading Christian thinkers of his time.

Those who think of Leo Baeck "solely" as a rabbi and communal leader ignore the intellectual dimensions of his religious leadership. Baeck was the great apologete and polemicist of the Jewish community, bringing a completely new emphasis into the Jewish-Christian dialogue. Within his own community, he was *the* systematizer of modern Jewish theology. In Jewish scholarship, he opened up new areas in the field of early Jewish preaching and in Jewish mysticism. And Christian scholarship is only now cognizant of his contribution to New Testament interpretation, where his emphasis upon Jewish traditions has received the support of recent findings. The basic difficulty in coming to terms with these various facets of Baeck's thought is that they are scattered through some four hundred articles written over a sixty-year span. Two basic texts do exist: *The Essence of Judaism,* written in 1905, and *This People Israel,* published half a century later. But the internal structure relating these works only comes into view when other writings, many of them unknown to most scholars, are placed alongside the better-known works. In turning to this task, we face the additional difficulties that little of Baeck's writings has been translated; that much of the material is scattered, and some of it lost; and that there are no full-length studies of Baeck's works, no study of his life. But there are devoted scholars of Baeck's works; as we draw their findings into a unified whole, the essence of Baeck's teachings begins to emerge.

It is necessary to start with the life of Leo Baeck. A full length biography is still vitally needed. But in our limning of the outlines of an intellectual biography of Baeck, we begin to understand Baeck and his time as we see the final attempt of the German-Jewish community to achieve a symbiosis with its German environment. With the emergence of the new Nazis in Germany, the need to understand that land and its relationship to the Jews and Judaism moves into the forefront of current issues. Baeck's life and writings are a continuous confrontation with this problem. Slowly, gradually, the texts fall into a configuration—which is not a "system"; Baeck strongly rejected any system which appeared to him as a calcification of religious thinking. If the term "system" can be applied at all, Baeck operates within the spirit and system of the Midrash (those early rabbinic sermons in which he specialized): a text is approached from constantly different points of view until, finally, the concealed meaning breaks through in all of its clarity. Apparently gentle, this method is yet ruthless in its search for absolute clarity. Thus Baeck approaches the problem of German-Jewish existence with quiet tenacity; and his life and teachings ultimately combine to give an answer which shakes us to our foundations. Again, we must be warned that Baeck's life is not a page of martyrology. Softness conceals an adamantine core. Sainthood is neither sought nor is to be bestowed. And neither life nor teaching can be fully understood apart from one another.

The study of the texts written by Baeck over the span of more than sixty years thus constantly returns us to his life. The first texts presented deal with his encounter with Adolf Harnack at the turn of the century. Much of twentieth-century theology cannot be understood until the student has learned how much of Christianity is summarized in Harnack, Baeck's great opponent. The encounter between Harnack and Barth has been duly studied and evaluated. Yet understanding of the lesser-known conflict between Harnack and Baeck—two men who shared far more than they would ever admit—is necessary for a knowledge of Western religion in the twentieth century. And in the encounter between Judaism and Christianity we also come to note conflicting forces which change both faiths and bring modern Europe into that area which lies beyond tragedy.

The basic text for our study has to be Baeck's *The Essence of Judaism*. In some way, the 1905 edition has become a "lost book," concealed behind the second edition of 1922 and its various mistranslations. The culmination of nineteenth-century thought, of Hermann Cohen's idealistic philosophy and ethical messianism, of the great commandment, the "Ought," find full expression here. But slowly, subterraneously, the twentieth century moves into the framework of neo-Kantian idealism. Revelation is no longer validated by tradition or in the realm of reason, but within the experience of the individual. Baeck's system of polarity commences: the term "paradox" introduces the Mystery which stands behind the Commandment. There is the beginning of a structure here, one which does not adapt current Christian thought to the Jewish tradition, but which stands independent of Christian systematics. As we move to Baeck's "middle writings," to his polemics against Christianity, the whole era of the twenties receives a new illumination. Bultmann, Barth, Tillich, Gogarten, and the others of that period witness how fateful the discussions of the twenties proved for the second half of the twentieth century. The Jewish participants in this theological search have been forgotten—yet what they said and wrote had its effect. Even the recognition that Baeck's critique of Christianity as the "romantic" faith has a relationship to Fritz Strich's *Klassik und Romantik* and to the deplorable Carl Schmitt's *Politische Romantik* gives us a fuller appreciation of the texture of those times when religion failed in so many ways and died in order to survive.

For students of Christian thought, much of what Baeck has to say is of haunting familiarity. He speaks the language of the Protestant era. Heinz Zahrnt's recent German study characterizes the Christian theologians in terms of the prepositions they employ. Karl Barth uses "over" —God is over, above the world; the strength of his discovery of the loving God is here vitiated by the distance which removes God out of concrete history. Rudolf Bultmann uses the "over against" to let man confront God in an existential decision. The Christian *kerygma* is thus a call to present-day life and out of it—but the Gospels lose reality and become a demand rather than a gift. And Paul Tillich uses "in"—God meets man in the reality of the world, in all being, in the immediate and unconditional aspects of his being. According to Zahrnt, this, too, has its flaw. God and world come to intermingle to the point where all is God and man can no longer recognize the world, where all is world and man can no longer find God.

Baeck's preposition is also "in"; and he resembles Tillich in important ways. The very weakness which Christians find in Tillich—the drive toward the universal which seems to them to obliterate the distinctiveness and claims of Christianity—becomes an area of meeting between the Christian theologian and the new thinking in Judaism of Baeck, Buber, and Rosenzweig. It is at that point, when we compare Tillich with Baeck, that Tillich's authentic Christianity is once more validated by the touchstone of Baeck's authentic Judaism. The shared language—tension, polarity, the middle way, correlation, apologetics—comes to mean different things in their differing frames of reference. Tillich teaches the Christian revelation of the Gospels, *logos* in its specific *kairos*. And his theology mediates between that time and contemporary man by defining man and his culture in the broadest possible ramifications as a necessary aspect of that time of salvation. The Gospels here become the symbol of the existential encounter between man and the full truth which is ever possible. Baeck, on the other hand, does not use theology "to mediate between the eternal criterion of truth as it is manifest in the picture of Jesus as the Christ and the changing experiences of individuals and groups, their varying questions and their categories of perceiving reality . . . between the mystery which is *theos* and the understanding, which is *logos*."[1] Revelation, for Baeck, is placed into the continuous experience of the Jewish people. It is not the special content of a special moment in the past which must be mediated for changing groups: It is a constant of Jewish life. *The Jewish people itself is revelation.* What there is of mediation is bound up in the mission of Israel to bring this to the rest of the world. But the mystery is not found in symbols of the past: Israel is Biblical man, an unbroken experience in which Calvary is only one incident out of many which the daughter religion has used to break away from the Jewish experience, into a world of its own where sentiment has led to an estrangement from the divine which is entered through the ethical act of daily existence. This knowledge separates Baeck from Tillich, even as it unites the two in their great confrontation of the Nazi evil. Both are children of the God of time fighting the false gods of space; but one goes to the *kairos* of Calvary, the other lives in *toldot*—the continuous existence of Israel.

Baeck's religion of polarity must be understood within the existence of the people Israel. It is a religion of experience, a humanistic theology which yet affirms God's existence unequivocally in ancient Jewish terms. Much of Baeck's writings is metaphysical poetry, an open language which strikes at the limits of theology, desirous not so much of producing a system as of indicating a direction in which an intermingling of the

[1] Paul Tillich, *The Protestant Era* (Chicago, 1957), p. ix.

rational and nonrational bring us to the knowledge of the twofoldness of human existence.

Baeck's writings, once brought together, lead us back into his life. The teacher of Terezin, writing on tiny scraps of paper constantly concealed from the Nazi guards, addressed himself to the problems of life encountered by all men. Not everyone addressed by Baeck will listen to him. Radical theology—represented by Christian death-of-God theologians like Hamilton and Vahanian and Jewish counterparts like Richard Rubenstein—has closed its ears to the type of language employed by Baeck. One suspects that these thinkers will also close their mind to the life lived by Baeck. Living under the conditions and comforts of freedom, not having been exposed to hell itself, the moral fervor of these theologians has forced some of them into a vicarious reliving of the Auschwitz period in which the rest of the landscape of existence is obscured. Something curious takes place here. A Richard Rubenstein, standing outside the death camp, defines man within its limits. For him, to the extent that Auschwitz, the *anus mundi,* fills the world, man is excrement. A Leo Baeck, living in the inner circle of that hell, can contemplate man's nature as it transcends this evil. Both point to the experience of Auschwitz which is primary for our time and cannot be ignored. But in Baeck there is a forward movement characteristic of Jewish life: Rebirth takes place; man can transcend the past and it is not destroyed while he atones. Baeck gives Israel as an example of the life which does not remain enslaved to the gods of space; and he sees Israel as the paradigm of humanity. We in turn may take Baeck as a paradigm of the Jew as God's witness in the world. And then we have to listen to the teachings of his life.

In Baeck's teachings, any life, once entered, shows itself to have limitless dimensions: Again and again, the teaching of the *individuum ineffabile* makes the finite the area in which our exploration reaches out until it touches the infinite. Our study begins at that point, as we enter into the life of Leo Baeck.

2

Between the Generations:
The Life of Leo Baeck

In his *Weltgeschichtliche Betrachtungen,* Jacob Burckhardt once wrote: "According to the proverb, 'no man is indispensable.' But the few who are so nevertheless are great." With some care, these words can be applied to Leo Baeck. The German-Jewish community which chose him to lead it through its darkest days found that there are times when a great man is needed. At that time, and in those days, Leo Baeck was both indispensable and great. He represented German Jewry and Judaism in a manner which left its imprint upon world history. There was dignity, and decency, and personal fearlessness which spoke out of a Jewish tradition deeply aware of itself at the time of the Holocaust: and all of this was summarized in Leo Baeck.

Baeck looms out of recent Jewish history as an eschatological, mythical figure; and this creates problems. For those who survived, who could and did identify with Baeck, he became a symbol not only of their survival but also of the rightness of their past. A myth was created in which Baeck became a saint. But as there are those who need a myth, there are also those who have to attack myth, who cannot accept a mythical reconstruction of the past in which all faltering and every darkness has been lost in the assertion of the good which prevailed. Facts about Baeck's life have been disputed with little evidence on either side. Questions about existence in the concentration camps have been raised which are valid as general queries about the history of those days, but which lose their value when they are placed into a frame of contentiousness centered in the present and not in the historical situation as it really was.

A full-scale biography is needed to assess these questions properly. There has never been any real question about Baeck's achievements and integrity[1]; but the complexity of his character and of his place in Jewish history can only be evaluated fully once all the historical material has become available and when a full measure of objectivity has entered this area of historiography. Meanwhile, we must learn to know him through his works.

In Rosenzweig's introduction to Hermann Cohen's *Juedische Schriften* we find the statement that "great as the philosophical work of this man stands before us . . . he himself was yet greater than his work." [165, p. xv][2] In Baeck's case, only one of his works, *The Essence of Judaism*, really had an audience; and most people have come to assume that it is Baeck's life rather than his writings which make him a significant figure in German-Jewish history. The full presentation of his thought may serve to create a more balanced picture. At the same time, a full understanding of Baeck's writings is only possible within the framework of his life. It is a life which must be seen almost as a paradigm of twentieth-century German Jewry, with all of its internal and external problems.[3] It moved within the tensions of German and European thought, amidst dying systems of thought and new approaches to the old problems of faith and knowledge in the life of man. The economic and social position of the Jew in that world had far-reaching consequences upon his way of think-

[1] Perhaps the sharpest critic of Baeck, Recha Freier [116] is careful to indicate that it is not so much Baeck who is under attack as the legend. She does question Baeck's role in the 1940s, when the Reichsvertretung became the Reichsvereinigung. Where she questions not only Baeck's judgment but also his integrity, an unfortunate fanaticism and misuse of sources is readily discernible. By contrast, Hannah Arendt has deleted an unfavorable statement on Baeck from her book on Eichmann, and (in an interview with this writer at her home, on January 7, 1966) commends Baeck for his "unquestionable courage and disregard for personal danger."

[2] Numbers in brackets refer to works listed in Bibliography at the end of this book.

[3] Cf. Baeck's teacher, Wilhelm Dilthey, *Gesammelte Schriften*, VII, Berlin 1955, p. 248: "The lifespan of a historic personality is a linking together of effects in which the individual receives impressions from the historical world, forms himself under these impressions, and then in turn has his own effect upon this historical world."

ing. Within Jewish life itself, there was the conflict between the old and the new. Traditional thought was learning to live in a new world. The "science of Judaism," once satisfied to apply the disciplines of modern scholarship to Jewish history, was now beginning to ask itself whether the nature of the material it was treating did not demand some enlargement of its methods. Baeck's own teachers, Hermann Cohen and Wilhelm Dilthey, represented different approaches. And Baeck himself, thoroughly at home in the classic Jewish sources, was just as familiar with Greek and Latin texts. All these complexities must be drawn together in a study of his life. Yet, in the end, his is a classic Jewish life, drawn out of the generations of rabbinic existence; and it is that which gives a final unity to his theology and accounts for its basic contents.

II

When Baeck died, one of his students applied to him those words which Baeck himself had used in eulogizing Franz Rosenzweig: *Malach Adonai, b'malachut Adonai* ("A messenger of Him-Who-Is, in the message of Him-Who-Is").[4] While Baeck would have rejected the honor herein intended, he would have accepted the basic concept of the rabbi fulfilling the prophetic task of serving as God's messenger. And Baeck was a rabbi. The family tradition of service to the Jewish community had produced generation after generation of rabbis. In Baeck's concept of Jewish history as *toldot* rather than *historia*, the interweavings of the generations gave greater intensity and depth to the task of the rabbinate when it assumed the dimensions of his own existence. Samuel Bäck, his father, was the rabbi of the Jewish community in Lissa (Posen), a border town between Germany and Poland. Baeck was born in Lissa on May 23, 1873. He grew up there; and he attended the well-known Gymnasium of that city. It had been founded by Amos Comenius (1592–1670), and represented the learning found in the Christian community. But the Jewish community of Lissa was mindful of a distinguished tradition of its own: the great Rabbi Akiba Eger (1761–1837) and Rabbi Jacob Lissa had been its teachers.

Life in a border town can lead to a greater openness of mind. Cultures clash—in this case there was the mingling between Eastern and

---

[4] Haggai 2:13; quoted by W. Van der Zyl in [197, p. 26].

Western European thought—and communities also can come into conflict. And the Jewish community, in a precarious position between the
Polish and German groups, was driven both toward deeper self-knowledge and to a fuller appreciation of its neighbors' tradition. In retro-
spect, the position of the German Jew was less shrouded in ambiguity
here. He remained an outsider; but there were many links between him
and the general community. The "Jew from Posen" was almost pro-
verbial in German-Jewish life, a recognized aspect of Berlin Jewry.

One of Baeck's friends, from these earliest days, was the great Jewish
historian Eugen Taeubler. Taeubler was the only Jewish scholar to have
become a full professor at Heidelberg, accepted in the Academy, and
unique in teaching ancient, medieval, and modern history at the university. Thinking back to their shared youth in Lissa, Taeubler noted
that

> Nothing was as important for the awakening and development of my
> historical and political sense as this: that in my early youth, within a small
> town that had largely remained Polish, and in which my father was a
> confidant to both parties, I could not only observe these strained relation-
> ships but would also be forced into them myself. . . . I have never lost
> the feeling and conscious knowledge that basically I am a Jew from
> Posen. [184, p. 9]

Baeck and Taeubler shared that heritage. The same problems reached
out to them, and the same tensions of German-Jewish existence brought
them to different paths which did not really converge again until the
final years of their lives: Both Leo Baeck and Eugen Taeubler became
teachers at the Hebrew Union College in Cincinnati. In between,
Taeubler had become the scholar asserting his European heritage, the
amanuensis and then the heir of the great historian Theodor Mommsen.
Baeck's Judaism, by contrast, enfolded within itself the outside culture.
First of all, Baeck was a rabbi and a teacher of rabbis. Taeubler's Judaism
was also clear and unambiguous. He had been the founder of the
"Gesammartchiv der deutschen Juden" and, when he had felt the rejection from the German community, had also come to teach at the
Lehranstalt with Leo Baeck. But in Taeubler, it was the outer culture
which was dominant. A minor but significant fact: In their final years,
in Cincinnati, both Baeck and Taeubler would rise early in the morning,
and would meet in a walk through the woods next to the seminary. Baeck

would have said his morning prayers in the traditional manner. And Taeubler—had made his entries in a small daybook, in Latin, "the only exact language in the world" as he confided to his students.

In Lissa, Baeck was also exposed to the tensions within Christianity, since both Catholicism and Calvinism had deep roots in the community. The Calvinist minister was Rabbi Samuel Bäck's landlord. A warm and intimate relationship could be noted between the two clergymen; and the young boy could observe how an enriching relationship between the two faiths was possible if each side loved its own tradition and respected the faith of his neighbor.

Within Baeck's home, there was a strong love for the Jewish tradition, which was all the stronger for being not fanatical but informed. Leo Baeck's father was a scholar. He had written a commendable history of Jewish life and literature; and he loved the rabbinic lore to which he introduced his son at an early age.

Throughout his life, Baeck maintained the traditions of his father's home in Lissa. The ceremonies of those days had not been automatic performances, but had been conducted in an atmosphere of reverence and devotion which had made them a joyous poetry of life. In his later years, Baeck and his teachings have been primarily identified with the liberal wing of Judaism; and rightly so. But where Baeck's writings show an impatience and an anger directed against the traditionalist who places the ceremony above the moral act contained in it, it is because Baeck had come to know the tradition at its best. He spoke out of love for the tradition, and not with the contentiousness of one who attacks what he has abandoned himself.

It is important to keep this traditional structure of Baeck's life in mind. In his personal life the dietary laws were observed. And no day went by without the study of Talmud.[5] His friendship with the learned Rabbi Nehemia Anton Nobel would not have been possible without this. Baeck continued his "learning," his study of Talmudic text, during his years in Berlin at the *beth hamidrash* where Rabbi Nobel also studied.[6] The traditional Jewish scholar Aviad-Wolfsberg has noted:

[5] Ernst Simon reports (interview December 23, 1965, New York) that "Baeck would begin each morning with *davvening*. Then, he would do a *blatt g'mora* (a page of the Talmud). Then, he would read one act from a Greek play in the original Greek; and then, he would be ready for the day."

[6] For one of Baeck's finest vignettes of his contemporaries, see [26, pp. 357–362].

The abilities and functions of the rabbi were therefore inherited by Baeck, nurtured by him, and he developed them carefully. His intellectual world was not satiated by just the Bible, the Aggadah, and modern Jewish writings. The Science of Judaism which he himself enriched and whose masters he undoubtedly revered, was for Baeck no substitute for the classical inheritance. Halacha, the backbone of the Oral Law, is part of this inheritance; and its role remained firm for Baeck. [196, p. 140]

But if its role remained firm for Baeck, its actual power over the forms of his life was diminished over the years. In the early years the Halacha had a direct impact upon Baeck. It shaped his daily observances. Over the years, Baeck moved into the liberal field. Halacha became an idea, a concept which he appreciated and honored but which he now saw as an abstraction and not as the reality of his life. Even in Lissa, there was a liberalism in his father's teachings which attenuated the Halacha. The outside world, the twofoldness of Jewish life in Posen, placed stresses upon the Law. But there is an elasticity to Halacha which has been able to absorb the changing outlines of all Jewish communities—as long as Halacha is recognized as the basic law of Jewish life. Had Baeck stayed within that tradition of Posen which built upon the memory of Rabbi Akiba Eger and Rabbi Jacob Lissa (actually, Lorbeerbaum, author of the *Netivoth*), the Halacha would have become his "way." But Baeck did not remain. He moved outside traditional life. At the age of seventeen, Baeck went to Breslau to enter the Jewish Theological Seminary and the university.

III

In its own turbulent history, the Breslau Seminary was a summation of Jewish thought at the end of the nineteenth century. It had been a dream of the liberal Abraham Geiger; but it became the self-realization of the more conservative Zecharias Frankel. The so-called Historical School of Judaism, on which present-day American Conservative Judaism has built, had its center in Breslau. The liberalism of the pioneer reformers of German-Jewish thought was more than tempered here. Nevertheless, Breslau was a clear break with traditional Judaism. The "science of Judaism" dominated the curriculum; and Heinrich Graetz eventually came to dominate the faculty.

Baeck entered the seminary in May, 1891, and was able to listen to Heinrich Graetz's final lectures before his death in September of that year. Marcus Brann, a disciple of Graetz, succeeded him and became Baeck's teacher. Baeck thus encountered a powerful approach to Judaism in terms of a historicism which was antiromantic, rational, and yet based upon a nationalism which contrasted with the universalism of men like Leopold von Ranke who dominated the European scene.[7] Graetz was often led astray by his strong antipathy to all romanticism; his misjudgments of Jewish mysticism and Eastern European Jewish life have been cited often enough. But he brought into Jewish historiography the reverent attention to detail, the *Quellenforschung* which mastered vast masses of material and drew together a picture of the past in which both liberalism and conservatism had their say.

Baeck here encountered the historian as creative artist. And if he disagreed with Graetz's picture of the Jew as the often martyred pilgrim in a hostile world, he could still take the basic insight of Israel as a special type, as a unique people. But where Graetz let history dominate theology, Baeck found an understanding of Israel's role in world history outside the frame of history. The same forces within the environment which set Troeltsch and Dilthey against the Historical School brought Baeck to the attack against Jewish historicism on the basis of this theology.

Baeck's favorite teacher in Breslau was Rabbi Israel Lewy, who taught him Talmud. An enduring friendship between teacher and pupil developed at that time. Dr. David Rosin, Baeck's teacher in homiletics and philosophy, was eighty years old; and he was a warm and inspiring figure whom Baeck and the other students could admire equally for his scholarship and for the integrity of his character. Baeck's main teacher was Marcus Brann, who came to inherit all courses of the older members of the faculty who passed away at that time and who edited the *Monatsschrift fuer Geschichte und Wissenschaft des Judentums.*

Nevertheless, Baeck left Breslau in the summer of 1894 for Berlin, which had more to offer. Baeck's affirmation of the "spirit of Breslau," of the need to be grounded in the traditions of Jewish experience, continued unabated. Much later, Baeck spoke of this:

> The rabbi must be a man of the Jewish way of life, and perhaps the Jewish way of life means also a bit of puritanism, a bit of asceticism. The new rabbi

[7] Salo W. Baron, *History and Jewish Historians* (Philadelphia, 1964), pp. 269–276.

does not mean the fashionable rabbi. His sermons must be a part of his own life. The rabbi must live the Jewish life; and then he will not only give sermons and speeches, but he will give himself.[8]

Baeck was very much the "new rabbi," entering into all the ramifications of modern Jewish existence, living in two cultures with many languages thronging in upon him. There was Biblical Hebrew and Aramaic, the involved wordings of the mystic texts, Glueckel of Hameln in Yiddish— and, on the other side, Baeck read Plato in Greek; Tertullian in Latin; Hobbes in English; and his German, though sometimes abstruse, had a deeply poetic quality. But the sojourn in Breslau had strengthened traditional qualities in Baeck. There were those who saw him, toward the end of his life, as "an old 'Rav' . . . a figure descended from antiquity and the Middle Ages, untouched by modern times—the *teacher of the congregation*, not the mediator between man and God." [144, p. 421]

Baeck's progression from traditional to conservative and then liberal Jewish training was never a departure from one stage to the next. Each aspect of his Jewish studies continued within the others, building the foundation for a religion of polarity and for a personality that never rejected "the other" but somehow included it within itself.

There was an organic, inner relationship between the Jewish Theological Seminary in Breslau and the Lehranstalt in Berlin. Both were established by the men of the "scientific study of Judaism." If Breslau had been Geiger's unachieved dream, Berlin was the reality (but much less than the dream).

Abraham Geiger gave his lectures on the "science of Judaism" at the Berlin school until his death in 1874. The school continued in his spirit. Yet it should not be forgotten that Solomon Schechter, later the president of the Conservative Jewish Theological Seminary in New York, was enrolled as a student from 1879 until 1883.[9] The school was different from Breslau in its emphasis upon contemporary Jewish life, comparative religion, and the systematic study of ethics (Moritz Lazarus taught in Berlin) and philosophy of religion (Heymann Steinthal became Baeck's professor in this field). But the rabbinic texts were not neglected at

[8] Leo Baeck, Lecture given at the installation celebrations honoring President Nelson Glueck at the Hebrew Union College.

[9] Adolf Kober, "Die Hochschulen fuer die Rabbinerausbildung in Deutschland" in [160, p. 23].

Berlin. The difference of emphasis between Breslau and Berlin did not constitute a real break between these progressive seminaries. The lines of opposition were established much more in the community, between the graduates of these institutions.

Baeck once again had excellent teachers, even if the facilities of the Berlin school had little to recommend them at that time. (It did not move into its own building until 1907.) His teachers were Steinthal, Martin Schreiber, and Siegmund Maybaum, whose field of midrash and homiletics was of particular interest to Baeck. Baeck studied Talmud and the post-Talmudic period with Joel Miller (died 1895), and afterward with Dr. Edward Baneth. He had immersed himself in the materials of Judaism; but Berlin joined this with the modern disciplines of scholarship. And the Baeck who was ordained in the winter semester of 1896–1897 would have taxed the understanding of Rabbi Akiba Eger or Rabbi Jacob Lissa. Baeck had become a modern rabbi, a scholar and thinker. In those years, before the turn of the century, he seemed the very prototype of the German Jew who had found his place within the outside world. But he had found it as a rabbi, as a spokesman of his people in whom the generations of the past found full expression.

I V

Was the Lehranstalt the strongest influence upon Leo Baeck during his Berlin days? Our only answer is to indicate once again that there was a twofoldness to Leo Baeck, a life in which the general and the particular culture interpenetrated one another. It must be noted that it was not so much the Lehranstalt which had attracted Baeck to Berlin as the University of Berlin. The one teacher of Leo Baeck who stood out above all the others was Wilhelm Dilthey, who taught at the University of Berlin. Unappreciated by many, he *was* the university for Leo Baeck.

The University of Berlin is a concept within itself. Franz Rosenzweig's inspired introduction to Hermann Cohen's *Jewish Writings* [165] in 1924, celebrates the concept of the German professor in the nineteenth century and the creation of the German university. There was a way which went from Jena to Goettingen to Berlin—the universities and not the cities—in which the greatness of German intellectual life found its form:

Kant . . . and Goethe . . . were joined: a wonder of world history took place. The universal philosophy celebrated its reconciliation with the national culture, the language of the poets gave body to the thoughts of the thinkers. Thus arose what has been called the German Idealism, Germany's claim for intellectual pre-eminence which it actually did exercise upon the nineteenth century. . . . And only the confluence of the two streams which emanated from these two men had established the world dominance of the German spirit. And this confluence took place in a university. [165, p. xv]

For a while, the professor of philosophy and the philosopher were one and the same person. And while this was a transitory state, some enlargement of the role of the German professor endured. He thought of himself as both thinker and teacher. The Berlin of Ranke, Savigny, Gans, Grimm, and Helmholtz established the pattern for its teachers. Rosenzweig named them "mediators between the Weltgeist and their own people, chosen to interpret the way of the Weltgeist to their people, to bring them its messages." [165, p. xvi] When Baeck came to the University of Berlin, the system was already breaking up, and the self-assurance of German thought contained its gnawing, inner doubts. But among the many who played the role of the German professor without realizing that it had become more of a role and less of a prophetic vocation, there were still some men who felt themselves the inheritors of that earlier generation and saw themselves as teachers to the nation. These were the men who were not satisfied to establish their pre-eminence over some small area of one scientific discipline, who wanted the total view of man in the world, who followed the path of Hegel. Rosenzweig recognized such a man in Hermann Cohen, the cantor's son who saw the professor's role in the fullness of its potentiality. Baeck became Hermann Cohen's disciple. But his first encounter with such a professor, a giant who in some ways could be viewed as a lesser edition of Hegel, took place when Baeck studied under Dilthey.

Dilthey had come to Berlin in 1882 when he succeeded Lotze. A year later, he published his *Einleitung in die Geisteswissenschaften* [104] in which we find the beginnings of his system of *verstehende Psychologie* which seeks to enter sympathetically into the pattern of thought underlying the literary creations of the past. Dilthey distinguished between the social and natural sciences. The first deals with the outer structure, the second with the inner content. And Dilthey's new tool is this analytic and descriptive *verstehende Psychologie* through which this inner content can be understood. Psychology here became the key to a new system which combined the knowledge of the nature of consciousness with the inner unity of individual and social life (*Strukturzusammenhang*). He saw an organic unity to life (*Lebenszusammenhang*) which appeared in artistic and religious forms as well as in scientific structures. And his studies of the great writers showed a remarkable sensitivity to the inner workings of the gifted writer which added a new dimension of understanding to the encounter with the past. [101] It was the total Gestalt which mattered to Dilthey, not the isolated elements.

Dilthey's system appealed to Baeck. When we come to the total structure of Baeck's work, we see the two major books standing at the beginning and ending of his writing—*The Essence of Judaism* [1] and *This People Israel: The Meaning of Jewish Existence* [7] to have a morphological unity, a Diltheyian Gestalt. Judaism and the Jew were one structure for Baeck, to be explored with Dilthey's *Einfuehlung*, to be understood with what becomes at times a psychology of religion. And Dilthey's *Lebensphilosophie*, which eliminates the distinction between intellect and reality (and therefore between spirit and matter), enters into Baeck's basic system of the polarities, of the mystery and the commandment, the finite within the infinite and the infinite that always reaches through what is finite. Behind Dilthey one can also sense Schleiermacher;[10] depth psychology brings with it a deeper appreciation of the phenomenon of *feeling* in religious life. But at this point, the Jewish tradition maintained its hold on Baeck. The ethical activism of rabbinic Judaism, found in the new and—to Baeck—completely convincing philosophical and ethical teachings of Hermann Cohen, controlled this aspect of Baeck's teaching. Dilthey's approach was used to find the inner life of the Jew and his faith: Baeck established his religious teachings through the psychological exploration of man's nature. Baeck did not start with doctrine, but showed how faith arose from a concern with the meaning of life. But religion could not be viewed by Baeck as Schleiermacher's feeling of absolute dependency and of sentiment. The ethical structure dominated here. Religion was ethical sentiment in which the rational aspect of man experienced and knew the will of God through the imperatives of the "Ought"; the mystery was a way to the commandment.

10 Cf. Wilhelm Dilthey's never completed *Das Leban Schleiermachers* (Berlin, 1870; new edition by Hermann Mulert, Berlin, 1922).

It might have been expected that Baeck's Ph.D. dissertation on Spinoza [11], written under Dilthey's supervision, would show the influence of the system Dilthey was then developing. Instead, we are confronted with a competent study in which the reverence for insignificant detail is not absent. Baeck looks through the earliest Spinoza literature written in Germany, and only an occasional side remark indicates his feeling for Spinoza.[11] What does appear is the beginning of his polemic against Christianity. We find here a characterization of Luther and the Reformation which appears throughout his writings: "In their strife with the spiritual sword, the Reformers had found protection given them by the worldly sword; and, grateful for this, they ever preached: 'Be subservient to the authority.' " [11, p. 8]

Much of the criticism directed against Spinoza is seen as emanating from these sources. Baeck sifts through all these criticisms with scholarship and imagination. If it is more of a traditional Ph.D. dissertation without any attempt to introduce a pioneering technique, that is natural enough. And the nature of the material studied by Baeck did not really lend itself to an attempt to blend *Erlebnis* (experience) with *Dichtung* (poetry). Yet in his analysis of German reactions to Spinoza, Baeck does not confine himself to the rational debate between different schools of thought. There is an awareness of the psychology of the German scholar, of the inner reasons which prompted the sometimes hysterical reactions to *le petit juif d'Amsterdam*. And Baeck is in agreement with his teacher Dilthey in recognizing the boundaries of psychological insight which cannot overwhelm an intellectual structure which has its own laws and integrity. The dissertation thus shows itself as the responsible work of a German scholar who has gained the necessary competence to engage in the study of intellectual history.

11 [11, p. 4] "neuer, kuehner Denker" ("a new, courageous thinker"); [p. 7], "Spinoza's Mystik bestand darin, dass er die Gesetze Gottes in die Herzen der Menschen eingeschrieben sein liess." ("Spinoza's mysticism consisted in this: he let the laws of God be inscribed in the hearts of men.") See also Baeck's *This People Israel* [8, pp. 305–308], where Baeck's appreciation of Spinoza is once again an *Ausklang*, a final note struck at the end of his life recapitulating its beginnings. Rosenzweig deals with a "spinozising" youthful work of Hermann Cohen's [165, p. lv] that has some interesting parallels; and he points out that Spinozism had been spiritualized at that time: "the century of Hegel and Ranke read Deus sive Spiritus for the Natura sive Deus of Galileo's and Newton's century." Yet Baeck follows Cohen in rejecting Spinoza—and on Cohen's grounds that man's task is not the contemplative vision of the good but the active creation of it in the ethical deeds that are commanded him.

V

Baeck was also ready to take his place in leading the Jewish community. In the two years before he was ordained, 1895 to 1897, Baeck published a number of articles in the Bohemian periodical *Juedische Chronik*, edited by Rabbi Dr. Simon Stern (who later became Baeck's brother-in-law).

In these writings, we come to realize that the pattern of Baeck's thoughts was established from earliest times. A liberalism and affirmation of science manifests itself. One essay begins with the statement that "we always count Spinoza, with pride, as one of us" [14, p. 12]—understandable enough from the Spinoza scholar, but somewhat daring when placed into the framework of a Jewish community that had its strongly conservative aspects.

Leo Baeck, from the very beginning, was absolutely fearless and secure in his individuality. A most characteristic word comes from this young man when reviewing a scholarly work in the *Juedische Chronik*. Many young writers delight in sharp criticism; but few would combine it with Baeck's grave politeness which manages to place stinging criticism into diplomatic language: "The author has not been completely just to the positions examined in his work; but his industry in collecting this material is worthy of praise." [14, p. 13]

These are minor essays. But one of these essays anticipates much of his later writings: Judaism is viewed here within the tension existing between the individual and the community; in the conflict between contemporary expression and the inheritance of antiquity; in the liberalism of thought and in the conservatism of ritual. In a very real way, the article "Orthodox or Ceremonial?" written in the winter of 1896, becomes a programmatic outline of Baeck's thoughts, comparable to the writings of the young Leopold Zunz published in the *Zeitschrift fuer Cultur und Wissenschaft der Juden* when Zunz was also at the beginning of his career as the fashioner of the *Science of Judaism*.

Basic themes are sounded. Years later, Baeck was attacked for his statement that Judaism has no dogmas. But we already find it here:

> If one does not define the concept "dogma" too broadly, the claim can be made that Judaism has no dogmas; at least, not since the unifying organization of the Sanhedrin was lost to it. For the same reason, Judaism also has no Orthodoxy. [14, p. 13]

And the polemic against Christianity does not begin with Harnack or with "romantic religion." Baeck's dissertation on Spinoza contained traces of it, and in this early essay:

> [Dogma enforced by secular power] shows itself in all its consequences within the Christian sects. These, in the first centuries, determined the validity and rightness of dogma by means of weapons. And later, after the Reformation, the principle was established that the lord of the land is also the lord of the faith. [14, p. 14]

Baeck's teaching of Judaism as a dynamic, evolving faith, as an individuality that comes to be reborn in every generation, is clearly stated here.

The young rabbi-to-be writes

> "The times change, and we change in them." This is particularly valid of religious thought; it, as nothing else, is rooted in the innermost individuality. Every epoch must seek to achieve clarity for itself concerning its beliefs and hopes; but to declare the form in which it clothes this as imperative for all time and place would be an attempt to force the next generation into its own pattern of understanding. [14]

He sees religion preserved from calcification and death only by the struggle of every generation to gain a rebirth, to find its own individuality. Even when it accepts the past, the new generation has to discover a contemporary form for it: "only thus does the teaching of faith become the truth of faith . . ." [14, pp. 15–16] The Torah is to be learned, not just obeyed. It always says "Thou shalt," but never "Thou shalt believe." That is why it remains an ever new book.

The mission of Israel is basic in Baeck, from his first writing to his final statements on Jewish existence. And here, too, we find the mission of Israel and the election of Israel established at the core of his argument:

> The concept "Jewish religion" fundamentally only contains the conviction that the teaching of the one and unique God with all its consequences, as it was preserved within Judaism, is the true religion. The idea of a special task and mission which is the obligation of the Jewish community is absolutely contained in this. To believe in a truth also means believing in the election and fate of all its adherents. [14, p. 16]

And Baeck establishes himself as a rabbi to the whole congregation of Israel by insisting that the essence of Judaism is shared by all Jewish groupings; and that the differences come to manifest themselves mainly in the observance of the ritual. Since, as we have seen, Baeck did observe the rituals to a far greater degree than most of the liberals with whom he was associated, he could stress the overall, the unity of the Jewish community, and his own relationship to that unity. In his justification of the ritual we see a foreshadowing of his later concepts of mystery and commandment:

> A religious ceremony is every action which . . . expresses a religious thought; in contrast to the actual religious commandment of duty, its purpose is thus outside of it. The observance of the dietary laws, for example, is the practicing of a ceremony . . . through which the idea of sanctification is to be presented to us. [14, p. 17]

There is a turning here to the area of Jewish experience, to the personal life, which is to become central in Baeck's later presentation. Judaism is not the clear and final revelation from one moment of time, preserved in the synagogue and brought out for the worshipper to accept. The symbols of religion are valid as a concretization of that which lies beyond:

> Religion appears within reality only as historical religion which is passed on as an inheritance through the centuries. It cannot be transmitted as pure soul, for it is too intangible; it must approach man through a process of gaining corporality, of becoming symbolized. A so-called natural religion exists only in systems, but not in life. Symbolic ceremonies fulfill this function; they are the language through which religious thought is expressed. [14, p. 17]

Baeck finds his place in *K'lal Yisrael* (the totality of Jewish life) by asserting that the ceremonials which still speak to the general community, which serve the "political" function of preserving the group, have a validity which should not be destroyed. But he preserves his liberalism for himself by indicating that the individual must judge whether other ceremonies, which do not serve the pragmatic function of maintaining the community, have a religious meaning for him or have degenerated into empty ceremonial.

In these, Baeck's first writings, we come to see the rabbi and teacher of the later days. Less than a year after writing this article, Baeck was ordained; and he went to his first pulpit, in Oppeln (Silesia). It was the only liberal pulpit in that part of the country.

VI

The liberal congregation in Oppeln gave ample opportunities for the young scholar to continue his writings, and for the young rabbi to come to terms with the manifold responsibilities of spiritual leadership. Nevertheless, at the very beginning of his career, Baeck acted in a manner which placed him solidly against all of his colleagues, and could well have meant the end of his aspirations. His action, taken at a rabbinical convention, was an absolutely fearless act in which Baeck showed himself—this was to become a significant aspect of his career—to be far in advance of contemporary Jewish thinking.

In 1897, two months before the First Zionist Congress in Basle, the five rabbis forming the executive board of the German Rabbinical Association had issued a declaration condemning Zionism "in order to safeguard the Jewish religion from political Zionism." Theodor Herzl, in the July 16, 1897, issue of *Die Welt,* had contemptuously dubbed these men *Protestrabbiner* ("protesters"). Yet the 1898 general convention of the German Rabbinical Association, meeting after the Zionist Congress had finished its meeting in Basle, supported the anti-Zionist declaration, after prolonged study, "with a practically unanimous majority."[12] While it was not placed into the minutes, it was soon general knowledge, established by competent witnesses, that two of the rabbis had opposed the declaration and had voted against it: Rabbi Saul Katz (Zabrze, Hindenburg O/S) and Rabbi Leo Baeck (Oppeln). [188, p. 56] Baeck was not a Zionist at that time. But he felt, then and in the days ahead, that conflicting approaches are part of the totality of Jewish existence; that the rabbis did not have the right to act in this fashion toward their fellow Jews; and that Zionism was achieving worthwhile goals. The stand Baeck took at that time proved to be no detriment to his career; twenty-five years later, he became the president of the same Rabbinical Association.[13]

[12] Quoted in [188, p. 55].

[13] Another incident from that era proves Baeck's consistency in favor of free speech. When Rabbi Emil Cohn of Berlin was suspended by his congregation for his Zionist activities, Baeck wrote him a note (dated Oppeln, April 30, 1908; previously unpublished and made available by Cohn's son, Rabbi Bernhard Cohn of New York) in which he expressed deep sympathy and concern for his colleague:

"What happened to you is so illiberal, so unreligious and so non-Jewish, that one can scarcely grasp how this could take place in the name of a Jewish religious

Baeck stayed on in Oppeln for ten years. It was a good place for him. There was time to study, to grow, to develop. He was married in Oppeln to Natalie Wiener; until her death, in 1937, she created a warm and harmonious home for them. She, too, came from a family of scholars (her father had published a noted book on the Jewish dietary laws); and the love of learning and of Jewish tradition filled their home. In these surroundings, Baeck came to full maturity as a rabbi and scholar.

In 1900, Harnack's *Das Wesen des Christentums* appeared. Christianity of that time was fiercely divided on Biblical and historical criticism in its bearing on the truth of the Christian revelation; science and evolution in their bearing on the doctrines of creation and providence; and the social problems created by the industrial revolution in their bearing on Christian ethics and the hope of the Kingdom of God. [138, p. 255]

Liberalism grew and spread at this time because it seemed to have clearer answers to these issues than orthodoxy. But there was also disagreement within the liberal camp. The "great debate" at the turn of the century took place between Harnack, the liberal Protestant, and Alfred Loisy, a liberal Catholic. [148] Loisy's challenge to Harnack was primarily in the field of liberal Biblical criticism. He also disagreed with him as a Catholic (at this point, Loisy still defended the Church, which later excommunicated him for his modernism): The later dogma of the Church is viewed by Loisy as founded in the Gospels. Where Baeck challenged Harnack for cutting off the Gospels from their Jewish roots, Loisy stressed the fruit of the Gospels—Church authority, the sacraments, the dogmas. Loisy joined Baeck's side of the argument by rejecting a Biblical criticism which showed itself unaware of the Gospel's Judaic background, and which suppressed the apocalyptic aspects of Jesus's teaching which did not fit into Harnack's liberal thinking. Yet all three, Harnack, Loisy, and Baeck, shared more likenesses than differences. From Ritschl and Schleiermacher they had inherited the tendency to stress the immanence of God, whether in man or in nature. Both Loisy and Baeck challenged the structure of dogma within their own faith, deriving the validity of the teaching out of the experience of human

---

community which calls itself liberal. It is just as incomprehensible to me how the rabbinical association in Berlin could keep silent . . .

"Let me express my sincerest wishes that you will be preserved for your profession. Our group is not so rich in men of individual, consistent feelings that it could simply resign itself to the fact: 'man overboard!' "

existence. But where Loisy drifted into a "religion of humanity" not unrelated to Comte [138, p. 257],[14] Baeck's Jewish roots not only gave his life its ceremonial aspects but also kept him deeply aware of the transcendent God who enters human existence as the revelation discerned by the individual and by the Jewish people at Sinai.

Baeck's review of Harnack was published in 1901, with an enlarged version appearing in 1902. But the confrontation with Harnack was brought to its climax with the 1905 publication of Leo Baeck's *Das Wesen des Judenthums* [1], which brought him to the attention of the whole Jewish community.

Two years later Baeck accepted a call to a larger community, in Duesseldorf. In his farewell sermon at Oppeln, he reminded the congregation that he always viewed the rabbinic task in its fullest aspects, and never just as a self-fulfillment: "The word 'I' has never been used in this pulpit," he rightly reminded his congregants.[15] His movement from Oppeln to Duesseldorf and, five years later, to Berlin was not so much a "success story" of a professional man moving to the top of his field, as an individual self-realization of a rabbi par excellence. The leaders of the Berliner Gemeinde always retained a certain amount of uneasiness in their relationship to Leo Baeck. He was their employee; and yet he stood above them; their teacher; and yet he always seemed in search of further truth, pressing on into areas where they could not follow. He did not teach the small children [76]; he did not have a large circle of intimate friends; he was not that exciting or dynamic a personality pulling everyone within his reach in those days. But he was—and had to be—their leader. What were the sources of his authority?

Toldot. The interweavings of generations, the Jewish self-awareness of living in the continuum of history—these brought the Berlin community to the realization that they were here confronted by the rabbi who had all of the authority of the past. The liberal elements in the city acknowledged the scholar who was honored by their neighbors but who was the Jewish scholar, the rabbi, at all times. And the traditional Jews, although

---

[14] The same material, surveyed from the Jewish position, leads Klausner [142] to speak of the "anti-Jewish liberal Germany at the beginning of the twentieth century."

[15] Described in the unpublished notes of Dr. Alfred Jospe, a pupil of Baeck who was present at that time. Rabbi Jospe has been of great help to me in sharing his insights on the life and thought of Baeck.

they were somewhat suspicious of him, could not find any flaws in his conduct. Baeck's personal qualities: utter fearlessness, integrity, a devotion to Jewish scholarship—perhaps even a certain aloofness of a man who ever lived in the Pharisaic world of the holy—all this made it inevitable that Baeck would lead his people.

Baeck came to Berlin in 1912 in a twofold role. He was to serve the Jewish community as one of their rabbis; and he was asked to teach midrash and homiletics at the Lehranstalt where he had been ordained. The Jewish community in Berlin at that time numbered approximately 150,000.[16] It had never had a "chief rabbi," but was served by many outstanding rabbis. The only difference between Leo Baeck and his colleagues was that the board had given him freedom from some of the routine tasks within the community so that he could devote more time to his scholarly work and, later, to his national tasks and responsibilities. From the time that Baeck returned to Berlin, in 1912, until the death of the community in the 1940s, he ministered to its needs. There was only one hiatus: With the outbreak of World War I, Baeck volunteered his services as an army chaplain. Baeck saw action on both the Western and the Eastern fronts. His reports, published in the congregational periodical in Berlin,[17] give us an insight into the life of a courageous and dedicated chaplain who was fully appreciated by the soldiers whom he served. They tell us more than that. Baeck always saw his field of service extending to all men. In the heat of war, he was not swayed by chauvinism, but tried to teach the ideals of universal justice. More than a chaplain to the German soldiers, he acted as rabbi to the large number of Jewish civilians who suffered countless hardships in Russia. His knowledge of the pathos of Jewish existence here gained new depth. And the inadequacy of nineteenth-century theology must have become clear to Baeck in the absolute anguish of the battlefront. A careful sifting of Baeck's reports from the front, much of which has only now been located, may yet uncover a personal reaction to the anguish of those days that can be compared with the reactions of Franz Rosenzweig, who wrote his *Stern der Erloesung* as postcards from the battlefront, and with those of Paul Tillich. When Tillich, who was also a German chaplain, lived through

[16] German national census of 1910; quoted by Walter Breslauer, "Die Juedische Gemeinde Berlin," in [160, p. 43].

[17] Leo Baeck, "Berichte des Feldgeistlichen Rabbiner Dr. Baeck an den Vorstand der juedischen Gemeinde," *Gemeindeblatt* (Berlin), 1914–1918.

one battle in which many of his friends around him were maimed and killed, he went through a personal crisis which he has described in this fashion: "All that horrible long night I walked along the rows of dying men, and much of my German classical philosophy broke down that night —the belief in the identity of essence and existence . . . the traditional concept of God was dead."[18] Baeck was not changed in as radical a manner as Rosenzweig and Tillich. Essence and existence were intermeshed for him, but not identical; and he had already reached out from the realm of intellect to the area of human experience as the place of validation. He never had to reconstruct a shattered system; the tension of polarity permitted the constant enlargement and re-evaluation of his approach to a Jewish theology which he saw as self-reflective and ever developing. But Baeck's openness to the *Zeitgeist*, to the breakdown of liberalism and idealist philosophy within post-World War I European thought, left him fully aware that the formulations of the past century were no longer adequate. And, alongside the commandment which is the core of the first edition of *The Essence of Judaism*, there came into being the awareness of the mystery which made the 1922 edition of this work a new statement of Judaism. Baeck's last report from the front to the Berlin congregation was published in June of 1918. He returned to Berlin, sick in body and soul. But he recovered; and a great and productive period opened for him.

VII

When Baeck returned to his pulpit and to his teaching post, he was at the fullness of his power. Soft-spoken, but of enormous vitality and strength, the forty-five-year-old rabbi plunged into a series of activities. He served the Weimar Republic as adviser on Jewish affairs; represented Jewish thought at the meetings of the "School of Wisdom" founded by Count Hermann Keyserling in Darmstadt, and proved the most popular of the outstanding scholars assembled there; participated in the writing of the second edition of a classic reference work *Religion in Geschichte und Gegenwart*;[19] continued his Jewish research—more than twenty

18 Paul Tillich, *Time*, March 16, 1959, p. 47, quoted in [138, p. 262].
19 This edition appeared in five volumes, between 1927 and 1931. Baeck's contributions are listed in [192, item 97].

items are listed in his bibliography dealing with writings from 1918 through 1924; taught at the Lehranstalt; and lectured from the pulpit.

A post-World War II analysis of Baeck claimed that "the Jewish bourgeoisie before 1933 misunderstood Baeck and never really felt itself reached by him." [121, p. 12] But this was a superficial judgment. Fritz Bamberger has noted that there were those who, before 1933, claimed that "Baeck was not a successful rabbi." [76] Bamberger rightly shows that these critics confused popularity with success. Baeck did not court the masses through a large number of public appearances, popular speeches, sensational sermons. His sermons made heavy intellectual demands upon the congregation. Dr. Bamberger recalls that a member of the board of trustees of the Berlin community once labeled Baeck's sermons as "Baeck's private conversations with God." Examining this statement, Bamberger judges that

> The bon mot was intended as a devastating critique, yet no well-meaning description could have fitted better. When Leo Baeck preached he did not talk down to an audience. Choosing each word carefully, building each sentence for measure and rhythm, speaking somewhat monotonously in a strangely vibrating high-pitched voice, now and then underlining a phrase with a movement of his sensitive hands, more often revealing the importance of a thought by an increased sharpness of his eyes, it appeared that he expected the response to his words not from his listeners but from somewhere beyond. [76]

Baeck, in the pulpit and in life, always reached beyond that which was known and ascertained. He was in search; and the congregation was drawn into this search as it listened to the softly voiced statements of revolutionary truths.

In 1912, when Baeck had entered upon his task at the Lehranstalt, he had indicated that he saw his field of midrash and homiletics in the largest possible terms; the teaching of homiletics and the history of religion would be taught as one. His inaugural lecture had been a careful comparison of Greek and Jewish preaching. [20] Baeck's deep involvement with these early centuries evidenced itself here. He stressed the new awareness of the Greek citizen of the *polis* ("city") as he became a citizen of the world, an awareness that saw philosophy and religion as useful guides into the new world. The pulpit had come to assume a new importance in those days. And the Jewish pulpit confronted Greek thought with a unique advantage: The strong chain of tradition had a firmly established position which it could present against the diversities and clashes of the Greek pulpit. Within the fluidity of contemporary Greek thought, Judaism stood out as a solid rock. And yet it was not just something enduring from the past that had no element of change within it. The Oral Tradition permitted the rabbis to take present-day experiences into the ancient framework and make Judaism truly a living religion.

Baeck made this insight the core of his teachings. It seemed to him that this ancient situation had once again come to life for the Jew: Immersed in the crosscurrents of European intellectual thought, he had to be aware of them and had to respond to their challenge; but this had to be founded on the knowledge of the permanent core of Judaism, of the "essence of Judaism." And the sermon had to mirror this creative conflict. It had to speak to the present. But it must speak out of the past, must "remain true to what is unique and best within Judaism. To preach means to teach and to learn." [20, p. 156]

When Baeck returned to his students with an ever deeper awareness of the crisis of the present which had to be related to the past, one of his first addresses to them (in 1919) showed itself rooted in that awareness:

> We have come together here for an hour of memorial meditation. . . . But in this uprooted time of flux and change, who can confine himself only to the hour? How can we keep our question and thinking from that which now streams through our days, that which has taken hold of each of us and touches our most personal aspect? [23, p. 382]

Baeck looked back into the past; the eulogy for those who had fallen during the war also became a eulogy for the Prussian state and its idea which had fallen. His opposition to the thoughts of Luther is given its fullest expression here, as he views the two forces at work within that state: the old conservative forces of Lutheranism with its church-state and its state-church; the other, newer, driving force of the Enlightenment, of national law and Kantian philosophy. "The police state which is everyone's guardian has its descent straight out of Lutheranism" [23, p. 386] was Baeck's charge. And, within Christianity, against Lutheranism, Baeck exalted that Calvinism in which the messianic strivings of Judaism had found a home.

Baeck concluded his talk with a curious charge to the students:

> A new time wants to commence, a time which once more desires to relate itself to the old Prussian idealism in which there are also ideas, born out of

the Jewish spirit, which strive to achieve themselves. The world wants to be different. An individual task, a question of fate, confronts the German Jew in all of this. [23, p. 399]

And suddenly we heard Hermann Cohen speaking out of Baeck. It is not proper to link up these utterances of Leo Baeck's with Hermann Cohen's *Deutschtum und Judentum*. [97][20] But one aspect of Baeck's personality which has been totally obscured or ignored by the scholars in the field is that Baeck was not only a German Jew. He was also a German. Always self-aware, always within the framework of the rabbinate, Baeck yet shared with Hermann Cohen the fervent patriotism for the Prussian German state. He was at home in it, and never relinquished his ties to the German community. His own statements confirm a postwar German statement on this: "Baeck was the man, perhaps the only one among the Jews of Germany, who maintained contact throughout the darkest days with the men of the resistance, particularly with the nobility." [121, p. 11][21]

What was true in the darkest times was also true in the beginning. Loyalty to the young Jewish generation and to his country sent him to both battlefronts of the war. Loyalty to the heritage of what he called "Prussian Idealism" and what he viewed within the framework of the University of Berlin kept him solidly within the stream of German culture. Even in the concentration camp Baeck wrote of the loyalty to the lands in which the Jewish people sojourned:

To interweave themselves with the lands into which the road of fate had led, to adopt the new land inwardly as a homeland, to breathe its air, to think in its language, to win new expression and new form for it and therefore for itself—this the men of this people attempted and achieved wherever . . . a land truly accepted them. More faithful, more grateful beings have scarcely been born by a soil . . . wherever and whenever there was a readiness to understand and to grant justice to that genius with which God had formed them. For peoples and cultures this could turn into a gift, indeed into a blessing. [8, p. 118]

[20] But as we see from Baeck's article, Baeck sought to find Judaism within Germanism, and rejected those elements in German culture which clashed with Judaism.

[21] See *Leo Baeck Yearbook III*, 1958, pp. 351–363, where Baeck is quoted extensively (by Hans Reichmann) on his contacts with the German resistance people in the 1940s.

This is autobiographical. It describes Leo Baeck, the rabbi who asserted the tradition of Goethe and Kant as part of his own heritage and placed it alongside Hillel and Akiba, Halevi and Maimonides.

There is one more facet to the 1919 lecture. It shows us Leo Baeck as the teacher of rabbis, as someone who is not separated from life by his books but who reaches out toward his fellow men. This is one of the few places in Baeck's published writings where the personal pronoun is used. Baeck speaks to the students, who have returned to the Lehranstalt, of those who died in the war. He recalls one of these students who walked with Baeck through the park and shared his hopes and dreams; he speaks of another one who wrote him long letters from the battlefront. And gradually the sermon joins preacher and congregation into one mourning family, where the personal pronoun is no longer an intrusion but an expression of unity in which the rabbi and the students become one more link in the chain of generations which is Jewish history. The final word of this lecture becomes an assertion of *toldot,* this history of the generations in which the ethical imperatives define human existence. Following an ancient rabbinic saying which reverses the words of Ecclesiastes, Baeck concludes:

> An earth goes, and an earth comes, and the generation of humans endures eternally. Times change, and many have their new earths; but man, the same man, always stands upon that earth. Man endures; and therefore duty endures. To labor and to look toward the future is therefore the command for us. An earth goes, and an earth comes, but man endures—man and his duty. With these words we think of what is past; with them, we greet the future. [23, p. 400]

VIII

Communal leadership came to Leo Baeck; he did not seek it out. He was elected the head of the Allgemeine Deutscher Rabbiner Verband in 1922. This association embraced rabbis of all convictions—traditional and progressive. The fact that Baeck could be their leader speaks of his universality, but is also indicative of the ability of the German-Jewish community to unite in a common cause while respecting differences. An aspect of the German-Jewish community here mirrors itself in Baeck's personality: differences of opinion were tolerated within the community. The *Aus-*

trittsgemeinde, in which strict Orthodoxy practiced an exclusivistic pattern, was considered necessary by that group which felt itself swamped by an over-all communal organization in which nontraditional thought seemed to predominate. At both extremes of the religious spectrum some fanaticism and lack of understanding for the opposition existed. Baeck, who stood in the middle, really did express the attitude and thinking of the majority; and he was respected by those who did disagree with him.

Baeck was recognized, from the beginning, as more than a religious thinker or leader of rabbis. Communal organizations turned to him. In 1924, Baeck was elected the president of Germany's B'nai B'rith, the most active fraternal order among Jewry. It had an extensive program of cultural, social, and charitable activities. Under Leo Baeck's leadership, it enlarged the scope of its adult education work. One B'nai B'rith motto had been "to achieve, along with wisdom of mind, wisdom of heart in order to gain a new height and intensity of life." And Baeck added to this what he called the motto of the Jewish man: "The way to our humanity does not lead away from our Judaism; it leads through our Judaism." [122, p. 59] It is well to recall, in this secular framework, the theological position of Leo Baeck. Some critics continue to stress the "humanism" which they feel to be dominant. Baeck does draw his concepts out of human experience; man is at the center of his theology. But at the center of man is faith in God, faith in revelation as evidenced in Jewish history, and a commanding mystery which stresses the ethical task. It is this which led Baeck to the implanting of a new emphasis on the religious traditions within the largest Jewish fraternal organization in existence. And, until the Nazis dissolved the B'nai B'rith Order in 1937, he exercised a strong influence upon all the lodges who sensed that in their president the highest aspirations and insights of their order were not only a symbol but a reality.

Many factions existed in the German-Jewish community of the twentieth century. Baeck stood above all, and all turned to him. The Central Verein (Central Association of Jews in Germany) was not a Zionist organization. Its vast program in some ways resembled the work of such American Jewish organizations as the American Jewish Committee or the American Jewish Congress. Started as a defense organization, it soon became a spokesman for the emancipated members of the Jewish community, particularly through its newspaper, which regularly printed more than 60,000 copies per issue. Baeck soon became a member of the executive committee, and his advice and counsel were trusted and accepted. Nor did anyone accuse Baeck of inconsistency when he became one of the leaders of the Jewish Agency for Palestine, and president of the Keren Ha-yesod, which supported the building and pioneering efforts of the settlers in Palestine. Baeck could work with Jewish groups of diverse convictions; he found, in the program of all groups, aspects of that essence of Jewish life to which assent had to be given. Some of the ideas of the "Jewish war veterans" banded together in the Reichsbund juedischer Frontsoldaten were repugnant to him; he was always critical of those who "wanted to turn German patriotism into a kind of surrogate religion." But Baeck could and did give full support to the work of this organization when it applied itself to charitable tasks, to the care of war victims. His concern with charitable works evidenced itself throughout his life in numerous ways; as chairman of the Jewish central charity association; and in the Liga combining the national charitable organizations within Germany. As indicated, he came to speak for the Jewish community to its Christian neighbours, representing Judaism at the Darmstadt "School of Wisdom"; and employed by the government as an expert on Judaism. With so many tasks filling his days, it is remarkable that his own writings continued to appear at regular intervals. He did not write much; many lesser writers published much more during that time span. But everything which Baeck published had been worked over and reworked. In his later writings, Baeck did not employ footnotes, which he considered "unfinished thoughts"—anything which he was ready to publish was in a finished state.

Taking his writings of one year—1922—we see Baeck immersed in the *Zeitgeist* and in the Jewish tradition. The first selection listed by the Wiener bibliography [192] is Baeck's famous essay on mystery and commandment. [25] Part of this essay is then listed by Wiener as republished in a book on the Jewish holy days, and, again, in the Zionist *Juedische Rundschau*.[22] There is an essay on Jewish culture in Germany, written for a B'nai B'rith publication.[23] Next, we find Baeck's magnificent tribute to Nehemia Anton Nobel, in which the liberal thinker manifested his closeness and friendship to a rabbi representing the best of the Ger-

[22] Listed in [192] as item 58c.
[23] Leo Baeck, "Juedische Kultur in Deutschland," *Vortrag Bne Briss*, 1922, pp. 34–36; listed in [192] as item 59.

man Orthodox Jewish tradition.[24] Baeck shared much with Nobel. Theirs was a kindred spirit, and both of them gave a contemporary meaning to the word "rabbi" which built on the past but added new dimensions to it.

Baeck's other works in that year, containing a record of the convention of the association of liberal rabbis in Berlin,[25] included speeches by Baeck, which once again emphasize Baeck's relationship to liberal Judaism. His scholarship aids the important project of the Verband der deutschen Juden then in progress: the "Teachings of Judaism Out of Its Sources." [24][26] But the most significant writing done by Baeck during the year was undoubtedly his work on romantic religion, which appeared in the *Festschrift* of his school in 1922. [27][27] All aspects of Baeck: his polemics against Christianity, his distrust of emotion, the classic Jewish strain of rabbinic moral activism, and the impact of contemporary thought all join together here. Out of his German tradition, Baeck drew upon men like Fritz Strich, who applied Woelfflin's aesthetic categories of the classic and the romantic to current intellectual structures. [182] At the same time, the new statements by Carl Schmitt on political romanticism helped Baeck direct his criticism against a religion which he felt had joined together with the state to the detriment of both state and religion. [166][28]

These were the days when Buber, Rosenzweig, and Baeck came to be the spokesmen of Jewish religious thought. Buber, in whom the new nationalism found a statement which entered new areas of thought, had his great controversies with Cohen. Rosenzweig, by his interpretation of Cohen's theory of correlation, found Hermann Cohen's writings a bridge between the old and new thinking.[29] Baeck stayed closer to Cohen, and shared some of Rosenzweig's thought. Some of this inner develop-

[24] Leo Baeck, "Nehemia Anton Nobel zum Gedaechtnis," *Korrespondenzblatt des Vereins zur Gruendung . . . einer Akademie fuer die Wissenschaft des,* III, pp. 1–3; listed in [192] as item 60. Anecdotes deepen biography; and I would here add a story from Ernst Simon (told to me December 27, 1965, interview, New York City): An Orthodox Jew in Frankfurt, Mr. E., an adherent of the extremely Orthodox Rabbi Breuer and opposed to Nobel, once invited Baeck to lunch. Baeck accepted, but added: "I can only eat *milchig* in your house." "Do you question my *kashrut?*" E. asked hotly. Baeck replied: "At the home of a man who questions the *kashrut* of my friend Nobel, I can only eat *milchig.*" There is both a sharpness and a loyalty in this word, which deserves mention.

[25] Leo Baeck, "Records . . ." in *Liberales Judentum,* vol. XIV; in [192], item 62.

[26] Listed in [192] as item 56.

[27] Listed in [192] as item 61. The proposed work was not completed by Baeck.

[28] It should be noted that Schmitt welcomed the Nazis in 1933.

[29] Cf. Rosenzweig [165]. But see Altmann [70, pp. 377 ff.].

ment of Jewish thought in Germany can be found in Baeck's article "Theology and History." [45]

These men shared something else: the dream of the Frankfort *Lehrhaus*, an approach to Jewish education which placed the adult in the center of a process of learning in which Jewish existence underscored the religious heritage within the warp and fabric of life. Each of them went his own way (the tragic death of Rosenzweig deprived the community of perhaps the greatest in this trio). But Baeck must also be understood as the educator who wanted to link the people with the essence of their faith, as one who would never be satisfied to be a theoretician, with no direct relationship to his people. Berlin was not Frankfort. But, from the time Baeck came to the city, he initiated a program of public evening lectures which introduced the Jewish community to the comparative study of religion. He had a deep concern for all aspects of Jewish education. In some ways, he felt that contemporary Jewish life could regain the vision of Pharisaic Judaism he celebrated in his "The Pharisees" [39],[30] a holiness that would touch all areas of life and make the Jewish people a true witness executing a divine mission. It is hard to judge the extent of the achievements which might have arisen out of the German-Jewish community then coming to terms with itself and its heritage. What did happen, in 1933, was Hitler's coming to power. And the thousand-year history of German Jewry came to its end.

IX

The Nuremberg Laws of 1933 reinstituted a second-class citizenship for the Jews of Germany; they were the first step toward genocide and mass extermination. From 1933 on, Germany was, in fact, a concentration camp. Its deadliness was still *in potentia* at that time. The jailers were careless, could be bribed to let the inmates escape, permitted themselves the luxuries of feelings on occasion, and concealed some of the evils of their establishment even from themselves. But the outer ring grew ever tighter; and, inside, places of death came into being.

German Jewry did not know this—could not know it. From their knowledge of Jewish history through the centuries, they saw another

[30] The most recent edition, in English [40], has a perceptive introduction by Krister Stendahl.

period of darkness approaching them, similar to times of persecution experienced throughout the centuries. As always before, they withdrew into themselves. If the outer world was to be hostile, they had inner resources which would serve their needs. And so, in 1933, the Jews of Germany united under the Reichsvertretung der Juden in Deutschland (the Representative Body of Jews in Germany). Second-class citizens, they now needed a government of their own, someone who could enter into diplomatic negotiations for them with their jailers, who could run the enormously complex machinery of self-government within the invisible ghetto that was now their livingplace. The history of the Reichsvertretung's founding has been recorded in a number of places;[31] the diplomatic history must still be written. Someday, the achievements of Leo Baeck, chosen by the Jews of Germany to be the president of the association, of his colleague Otto Hirsch, of women like Cora Berliner and Hannah Karminski must be evaluated properly. But we must note that all German-Jewish organizations shared in the structure of this association: the Zionists, and the non-Zionist Central Verein; the large and small congregations and their congregational associations; the rabbis; the war veterans; and all Jewish organizations still permitted to function by the German government.

In a community rich with former statesmen, able lawyers, business executives, and outstanding organizers, many leaders were available. Why was Baeck chosen? One of his colleagues, Bruno Italiener, explains the reasons for this:

> They chose their greatest rabbi . . . for with that sense for the future which long suffering seems to have bred within us Jews, they felt that this time of need required a man who would not only strive to meet the archenemy with the weapons of worldly wisdom. It had to be a man wearing the armor the prophets wore when, in the name of the just and holy God, they called the rulers of their time to battle within the lists; a man who drew his full strength out of his living belief in God, out of his impassioned love for the Jewish people. [138a, pp. 41–42]

Baeck was a man of God, and he represented God's people.

Baeck accepted the leadership of a community that had been isolated and imprisoned. If there ever had been a Jewish-German dialogue, that

[31] Cf. [132, pp. 97–106]. Also [74, pp. 76–85]. A variety of articles dealing with the various aspects of the work done by the Reichsvertretung can be found in the Leo Baeck Institute yearbooks. [187]

dialogue had ceased. [171, pp. 278–280] The Jews now lived in a hostile environment in which all intellectual and cultural contributions made by Jews were declared obscene. And every day, in newspapers, on the radio, at every public meeting, all of the vast resources of the state hammered away at the contention that the Jewish people were an abomination, inferior, less than human; that the Jewish religion was a fraud and a deceit, teaching hatred, theft, and immorality.

There was no way for the Jewish community to win its battle against the Nazis. They had been part of the democratic opposition to National Socialism; but that had been destroyed in 1933. There was no help from the outside. Any resistance had to come from the Jewish group, from within itself. The "new midrash" of that time, as described by Ernst Simon [177], grew strong and gave expression to words which comforted the prisoners and challenged the enemy in numerous, hidden ways. But the main work of the Reichsvertretung which Baeck headed was the task of slowing down the inevitable; of fighting for time, fighting for the rights of children to leave their parents and settle in foreign lands, fighting to keep brutality at bay as long as possible. Baeck could not address himself to the decent elements of the German community; they were given little voice in the government. He could not argue his case in public; it had been decided to burn the Jew. Instead, time and again, he had to enter the mouth of the lion, going to Gestapo headquarters and arguing tenaciously for an extension of time, for a milder form of anti-Jewish legislation than what was being promulgated. The Reichsvertretung thus placed itself between the Jewish people and its persecutors. It tried to slow down the ferocity of the attack. There have been historians who have questioned this,[32] who wondered whether this might not be viewed as an act of collaboration with the enemy. Such questions fail to deal with the existential reality of that moment in history by turning the anguish of the experience into a textbook exercise in black and white. Was there really a free choice for Jews? An illusion of freedom did exist; but the one choice given was that between death and death—death now, or death very soon. Most of the outside world had closed its doors. And Jewish communal leaders, who thought they had a choice between escaping and entering a prison-ghetto which would eventually break through its walls in conformity with the old drama, often considered their decision to stay not only the moral choice but also the better one.

---

[32] See [111, pp. 47–55], where this matter is discussed in more detail.

The Jewish community did sit down at the conference table with the captors. It is true that contact with evil tends to corrupt, and that these meetings could have become collaborations: The atmosphere of Gestapo headquarters tested every moral fiber of the individual who was touched by it. That is why the Jewish community instinctively turned to Leo Baeck. They knew that he could not be corrupted. Perhaps, in assessing his stature as a religious leader, even more than recognizing his greatness in bringing a trainload of children abroad and returning to enter the concentration camp with his people, we should stress the fact that he *could* sit down with the Nazis, gain time for his people, and leave the room intact as a moral being.

What did the Jewish community do with the time gained? First of all, it had to reorganize itself completely. The organizational structure of German Jewry had often been acclaimed by historians. But with the 1933 laws, an impossible load was placed upon it. Jews were barred from the professions, taxed heavily, and their property was gradually expropriated through a number of legal devices. The income of the Jewish community was thus decreasing at an alarming rate; but the expenses were constantly going up. With less money coming in, more people, old and young, needed help. The old-age homes and orphanages had to be expanded; Jewish children who had gone to the public schools now had to be incorporated into the Jewish school system; those who could emigrate had to be taught new skills in training schools; and more funds had to be raised continually to get out at least some of the children. All of this was part of the task undertaken by Baeck and his "government."

Some of these tasks were made possible by the diplomatic work done at the conference table. A certain inner autonomy had been achieved. Concessions for transferring goods to Palestine[33] enabled a sizable group to emigrate; other concessions made it possible to send children abroad and to support them from Germany. Thus, under the presidency of Baeck, approximately four million marks (much of the money coming from abroad) were annually spent in clearly defined fields: emigration, economic help, charity, education, and culture. An autonomous government had been established for an invisible ghetto where the Jews hoped to wait for the end of the storm. At least, there were some who clung to that hope. Leo Baeck, more clear-sighted than most, had opened the first

---

[33] [111], where I touch on the moral problem of a transferral of goods to Palestine which helped not only the Jewish community but also the Nazis by lessening the effect of the boycott against Germany.

meeting of the Reichsvertretung with the somber words: "The thousand years' history of German Jewry is at an end." He did what he felt had to be done, regardless of the darkness ahead. He had resolved to stay with his people, to be the rabbi, teacher, and pastor, "as long as there is one Jew left in Germany."[34]

It is worth noting here how much emphasis was placed upon the continuance of Jewish culture and Jewish education.[35] Martin Buber did important work in that connection. Musicians, denied their place in the outer world, found a new stage for their talents in the synagogue; there was a final outburst of creative achievement in the face of death. There was no large-scale "failure of nerve" here, no acceptance of the Nazi judgment of inferiority. Robert Weltsch's editorial in the 1933 (April 4) issue of *Juedische Rundschau* [186] showed the strength of the Zionist position together with the inner resources of German-Jewish life. Thirty years later, he judged it to lack historical insight; but its moral courage has not been questioned.

Baeck's leadership of the Jewish community from 1933 on often involved him in conflicts. With all groupings of Jewish life included in the "cabinet" of the Reichsvertretung, there had to be basic conflicts that could not be solved easily. Some of Baeck's compromise solutions satisfied no one; but they preserved the union of these groupings, and thus served the welfare of the general Jewish community. Baeck's integrity was a rock upon which the Reichsvertretung could build. An observer of those days has noted:

At the Reichsvertretung in Berlin they sometimes called Baeck "the Cardinal." There did emanate from him a power of representation which reminded one of a prince of the church—benevolently wise and aristocratically worldly, never stooping in speech or manner to the purely political. The authority with which Baeck spoke and acted was not a powerful church, but *das Gebot*, the Commandment about which his thinking had turned for a lifetime. . . . For him, in a pagan world the ethical idea of Judaism has become again what it was in the beginning of Jewish religion—a revolutionary idea, unconditionally new and un-

[34] From a letter written by Baeck to an American congregation, refusing a post in the United States. Dr. Kreutzberger's projected research may well show an openness on Baeck's part to the possibility of emigrating in the 1940s. This would relate more to the changing historical situation, and would not necessarily invalidate Baeck's strong moral stand in the thirties *and* the forties.

[35] Cf. Ernst Simon [177], the basic study for that period.

conditionally in opposition to the present . . . from it stemmed the ethical resistance . . . which characterized his leadership. [76]

Baeck was more than a symbol of German Jewry here; he was its very heart.

X

In 1939, Germany cut itself off from the fellowship of nations. Now, there was no more need to defer to the sensibilities of their fellow men; much earlier, the Nazis had dispensed with the sensibilities of the Germans themselves. In an exchange of letters which took place in 1949, when Leo Baeck had come out of the concentration camp, he analyzed those days in this fashion:

> The misfortune of those fateful years was the widespread action of the individual in resigning his responsibility and letting collectivism fashion his philosophy or presenting it to him ready-made. . . . He was thus relieved of the need to think and simply waited for the "Kommando." God's commandment directs itself to the individual, the "Kommando" goes to the battalion. And the strangeness of this time consisted in the fact that there now also existed the battalion of generals who stood in rank and file, the same generals who were in command. A "collectivity of generals" now existed. The history of that time could be entitled "the war of the 'Kommandos' against the commandment of God."[36]

But if the Germans organized into collectives which overrode the individual conscience, they had to accept the responsibility for what was taking place. The difference between "Nazi" and "German" must be kept in mind when examining this area of history; the shared responsibility between the two cannot be forgotten. And one of the hard questions of that time, popularized by Hannah Arendt, is whether or not there is not even a shared responsibility between the Nazi criminal and his victims.

This question arises when we examine the Jewish community structure after 1939. The Reichsvertretung, founded by the members of the Jewish community themselves, was abolished. In its place, the Germans

---

[36] Dr. Max Kreutzberger, of the Leo Baeck Institute, has graciously given me permission to examine the personal letters of Baeck in the archives. This quotation is from an (as yet unpublished) exchange between Baeck and Dr. Rudolf Jaser of Neustadt (1946–1956) dated September 5, 1949.

set up a successor organization, the "Reichsvereinigung," and insisted that the same men be at its head. A simplistic approach to that history has argued that the Reichsvereinigung was a Nazi organization. Any Jewish person connected with it, therefore, must be branded a collaborator.[37]

This does not deal with the reality of the situation. The definitions of the Nazis, placed upon those whom they imprisoned, do not really describe the prisoners in the internal range of their existence. It is what the prisoners themselves bring to this situation which matters. And since internal resistance, private motives, and inner self-definition do not always come to the surface, particularly when much of the history of those days was written by the oppressors, a full understanding of the way in which the prisoners defined themselves is a prerequisite to any historical judgment.

The unwilling officers of the Reichsvereinigung saw themselves as the equivalent of an "officers' council" in a prisoner-of-war camp, where it is the function of such a council to transmit the orders of the jailers. Such councils—particularly where its members are men of national prominence—can easily become collaborationist organizations, on the pattern established by Quisling in Norway. Or they can become centers of passive resistance, where once again the attempt is made to slow down the timetable of the oppressors. In the case of the Reichsvereinigung, composed of men like Leo Baeck, Otto Hirsch, and Julius Seligsohn, of women like Hannah Karminski, Cora Berliner, and Paula Fuerst, the latter was true. These men and women continued their work in welfare, education, and general maintenance of the Jewish community until all of them had been

---

[37] Recha Freier (see note 1, Chapter 2) is the chief exponent of this view. As indicated, fanaticism here vitiates historical judgment. When she relies on an unsubstantiated hearsay word of a Nazi "But Dr. Baeck collaborates" and sees this not as evidence of Nazi obtuseness but as a fact overriding all the evidence of self-sacrifice and dedication to Jewry by its leaders, the dangers of subjective judgment become self-evident. Rabbi J. Litvin ("The Guilty Men," *Jewish Quarterly*, Summer 1964, pp. 9–13) made the direct charge that "Baeck was alleged to have exploited his position to cause inconvenience to Orthodox Jews, particularly rabbis." The authority quoted for this is "a certain German orthodox rabbi," not otherwise identified. But this charge, which was indeed made, in only evidence that the conflict between Orthodox rabbis and liberals continued even in Terezin. H. G. Adler's *Theresienstadt* [69] shows that factional strife continued between Zionist and non-Zionists; the old grudges did not die. Where this type of allegation is accepted so readily, it is placed within a subjective framework which has inherited all the emotions of an ancient quarrel. Proper history cannot be written where private vendettas intrude.

transported to concentration camps, where most of them died. [cf. 107a, pp. 85–97] And if the dark cloud of the Gestapo hovers over the structure of the Reichsvereinigung, we can nevertheless sense the greatness of the personalities imprisoned within it. We have no complete certainty; the facts that came out of the Holocaust were few and incomplete. But when we look at the total structure which takes in the "new midrash" of the nineteen thirties, the unquestioned achievements of the Reichsvertretung, and the known integrity of the people involved, the image which develops out of this serves as a tribute to the thousand-year-old history of German Jewry which here came to its end.

Baeck had refused to leave Germany. The special Commandment which we find at the core of all his writings was also the center of his life. He stayed, and he continued to work for the welfare of his congregation which encompassed every Jew caught by Hitler in his prison. Constantly harried by the Gestapo, Baeck continued to work for his people, to be their rabbi, their teacher and leader. Finally, in the concentration camp, he became a number—187,894—which was intended to obliterate his personality and to make him one more unknown Jew who would die in the gas chambers.

Terezin was intended as a showplace, a "privileged" concentration camp. Lest we forget what this means, it should be pointed out that 140,000 Jews were sent to Terezin—out of which less than 9,000 survived. And it was not intended that Leo Baeck should survive the camp. Overefficiency betrayed the oppressors at that point. A Rabbi *Beck*, a saintly and aged teacher from Moravia, died in Terezin shortly after Baeck's arrival. And the government was informed that *the* Rabbi Baeck had died. Now he really was just one more number in the grim lottery of death; and, by a miracle, it was one of the few not drawn. Within the camp itself, Baeck was very much alive. Round about him there were those, cracking under torture and persecution, who used their position of leadership, of authority, of contact with the authority, to maintain their own lives for an extra span of time. Baeck stood aloof from this. He did not take an active part in the administration of the camp. But he continued to be a center of moral resistance. In the end, the truest judgment of the concentration camp comes from those who survived and became witnesses of man's inhumanity to man. H. G. Adler, one of the survivors of Terezin, has written about Baeck:

> The most memorable personality in the Council of Elders was Rabbi Leo Baeck . . . who was universally respected among all prisoners and regarded

with ever higher esteem for his readiness to help. He never withdrew from the camp, but it did not seem to exist near him; none of its filth could touch him. Peace emanated from him. He could be gentle . . . but could also speak with zealous anger, for he knew the demand of the hour, knew of the fateful failings to which he and everyone else in the framework of history was subject. This oppressed and saddened him, but could not break him. For he always held himself ready for new tasks; tenaciously, bravely, he never refused them. He knew that he was a witness to the fact that there still had to be a different world from this "ghetto." Incorruptible, he saw weakness and corruption in his surroundings. He exerted his influence against them, particularly through the purity of his own example. . . . He was a shining beacon in the salt tear ocean of despair. [69, pp. 249–250]

In the concentration camp people came to Leo Baeck; and he came to them. From seven to eight hundred persons would press into a small barracks in order to listen to his lectures on—Plato and Kant![38] But there were also the many private encounters in which Baeck reached out to his fellow inmates, serving as rabbi and comforter.

Various accounts help us achieve a picture of Leo Baeck in the concentration camp.[39] If it is not completely clear, we must recognize the turbulence of the situation, the few survivors, and the deadly pressure which never let up. From all that we do know, Baeck's teachings here became his life, and his life became one of the great teachings of our time. But there is one problem which has emerged, dealing not so much with Baeck's integrity as with his judgment: Did Baeck, at any time, have knowledge of the true nature of the death camps which he concealed from his fellow inmates?

Eric Boehm, in an uneven book entitled *We Survived* [81], quotes Baeck to the effect that an engineer (a fellow inmate at Terezin) approached Baeck in August of 1945 and told him, in strictest confidence, that Auschwitz, the "resettlement" camp in the East to which Terezin camp inmates were being sent, was an extermination camp where the inmates were gassed. Boehm's quote of Baeck continues:

---

[38] Cf. Chapter 7, below.

[39] Adler [69] continues as the primary source. Ernst Simon [177] and Hans Erich Fabian [107a] are others. Eric H. Boehm [81] presents an account of those days "as told" by Baeck to Boehm. However, Boehm's reliance upon his own memory, without a written text from Baeck, casts doubts upon the reliability of this account.

I went through a hard struggle debating whether it was my duty to con-
vince Gruenberg that he must repeat what he had heard before the Council
of Elders, of which I was an honorary member. I finally decided that no
one should know it. If the Council of Elders were informed the whole
camp would know it within a few hours. Living in the expectation of
death by gassing would only be the harder. And this death was not certain
for all: there was selection for slave labor; perhaps not all transports went
to Auschwitz. So I came to the grave decision to tell no one. Rumours
of all sorts were constantly spreading through the ghetto, and before long
the rumours of Auschwitz spread too. But at least no one knew for certain. [81, p. 293]

If Baeck did say this, and if his reasons for keeping quiet were as described here (and not doubt of the report and reluctance to spread what
might be a false rumor) we are presented here with a moral problem
which came to many during those dark days: At what point is silence a
kindness, at what point should the truth be given even when it destroys?

Shortly before his death, Paul Tillich discussed his very real admiration
for Leo Baeck with this writer, and addressed himself to the problem of
Baeck's silence:

No one can fully judge the events within the concentration camp. But, in a
way, I would criticize Baeck for not giving the last iota of information
which he possessed. If he did know that Auschwitz meant certain death, he
should have spoken out. The full existential truth should always be made
available, just as the uncurable patient should always be told the full
truth.[40]

Stronger critics of Baeck have added here that had Baeck spoken out,
some sent to Auschwitz might have made a stronger effort to escape,
perhaps successfully. And some who volunteered for labor camps would
have recognized the greater danger and might have avoided the transports
to the East.

The historical question is difficult to judge. The majority of scholars
feel that the Nazis were in complete control at that point, and the possibilities of life and death were not influenced in a substantial way by the
actions of the Jews caught in the Nazi trap. In that case, it is, again, the
motive for the action and not the result that matters. Yet any action by
a leader of his community must take the fullest possible account of what

[40] Interview with Paul Tillich [201], most of it recorded in [112].

results might be produced. Baeck acted in an existential situation, where the pain and anguish of his people would be certain to be enhanced, and where he foresaw very little change in the future were he to share the knowledge that had come to him.[41] With what we know now, it is not unreasonable to feel that Baeck's judgment faltered here.

The moral question is something else again. Paul Tillich's demand for the "full existential truth" on all occasions can encounter difficulties in its application. Certainly, Baeck's decision here to remain silent was a deeply moral act, dictated by concern for his fellow men. To the extent that we have entered historical situations in search of Baeck's personality, we have been confronted by a man who would not and did not falter when a moral choice had to be made. And if we fully realize the anguish of his choice at that moment, it becomes less important to take on the function of the judge and to render a final decision on the rightness or wrongness of Baeck's action.

Another act by Baeck adds to our understanding of an ethical personality that was not crushed by the concentration camp but always able to reach a moral decision and to abide by it. The camp was delivered in May of 1945. Most of the surviving inmates were at the point of death; and a typhus epidemic was raging in the camp. Baeck, who had kept his fellow inmates from killing the camp guards turned over to them by the Russian soldiers who had freed Terezin, remained with those who were sick and needed care and comfort. He was still their rabbi. Only then, his task completed, did Baeck accept transportation to England where the few surviving members of his family waited for him.

He had lived through hell. He had not been broken. The community which he had led had died, but his task had endured. For yet another decade Baeck was to be a leader and teacher of world Jewry and mankind.

XI

There is a photograph, taken in 1953, which shows Baeck in animated conversation with Albert Schweitzer. And, indeed, a comparison with

[41] If the Boehm account is accurate—and no other statement has as yet come to light—it would also indicate that Baeck was unaware of the full truth of the death camps while he was forced to participate in the Reichsvereinigung. Those who would judge those years must take note of this.

Schweitzer readily springs to mind. Both of these men became living legends during their lifetime. Both gave significant impetus to the direction of religious thought within their tradition. Both, as it turned out, had their detractors. (The figure of the saint has always been anathema in intellectual life.) If one were to make a comparison of the pattern of religious thought between the rabbi and a Christian thinker, Paul Tillich would be a more appropriate parallel. Yet something of the rock-ribbed integrity of Albert Schweitzer, tested in experience and not in the classroom, enters into our evaluation of Leo Baeck.

Difficulties persist; it is hard to view the time of the Holocaust objectively. Baeck presents us with the picture of a man of integrity, walking in the midst of utter evil. He is seen as head of an organization established by the Gestapo. And he survived. There have been those, personally touched by the Holocaust, who could not forgive him this, and who cast questions on his role in history. Yet the more we probe, trying to assess Baeck's life and personality from every possible viewpoint, the more we become convinced of a truly outstanding figure whose life and teachings blend together and can only be understood as one.

For the next ten years, Baeck traveled between London, New York and Cincinnati, spending some time in Israel annually, generally during the Passover. He was a spokesman of progressive Judaism, serving as the honorary president of the World Union for Progressive Judaism. In London, Baeck taught and lectured to the remnant of the German-Jewish community whom he also served as president of the Council of Jews from Germany. He became a British citizen. Once again, he immersed himself in lectures for the general public, for B'nai B'rith, for the synagogue. He was intensely interested in all aspects of the reconstruction of European Jewish spiritual life, although he was convinced that Jewry would never again flourish in Germany.

As much as ever, Baeck believed in man. In assessing the past with its evils, he did not so much stress the demonic aspect of man as the weakness of the very proper citizen whose lack of concern can present the state to its criminal elements. He had confidence in a better world of tomorrow. In his private correspondence Baeck wrote:

> It is a decisive protection [against the criminal] that the number of righteous and true human beings grows and that their influence grows stronger. The force of this protection, for example, is England's strength. It was Germany's weakness that this protection was lacking or failed; and it was

the fault of England and France that they were not concerned at the right time with the maintaining of this protection within Germany. The process of recovery depends upon this today. The great comfort is always that a new generation, and with it a new and great possibility, arises.[42]

This hope in man brought Baeck to resume his task of teaching the rabbinical student. At the Hebrew Union College–Jewish Institute of Religion in Cincinnati, Baeck once again taught Midrash and the mystical texts. In private and in public, he trained young men who shared his concern with the mystery and the commandment. He spoke to many groups, ranging from a joint meeting of the houses of Congress in Washington to small Reform congregations scattered throughout the land. Many honors had come to him. A congregation in Los Angeles called itself the Leo Baeck Temple. An important research institute, the Leo Baeck Institute, was established in New York, London, and Jerusalem, starting upon a series of significant publications even during his lifetime. The Leo Baeck School in Haifa is one of the better educational institutions in Israel; and the Leo Baeck College in London trains Reform and Liberal rabbis in Baeck's approach to Jewish thought. His books were reprinted, translated, and became paperbacks which reached into many new areas where he had not been known.

On October 29, 1956, Baeck signed his name to the proof sheets of the second volume of *This People Israel*. He was stricken that afternoon, and died three days later, aged eighty-three. Countless tributes appeared at that time. They can be summarized in one sentence, written by Walter Kaufmann in his introduction to Baeck's essays on Judaism and Christianity: "Baeck needs no eulogy. He only needs to be read."

At this point, having ascertained the outer structure of Baeck's life, having confronted a personality within the dynamics of an existence in which the history of an epoch, a community, and one man blend together, we have to turn to Leo Baeck's writings to gain the deeper understanding which we seek. There is a polarity here: The life testifies to a clear and established system of beliefs; and the beliefs are validated by that life. Both come to instruct us concerning the mystery and the commandment which are the essence of Jewish existence.

[42] Leo Baeck private correspondence (letter to Dr. Rudolf Jaser, May 6, 1947) in archives of Leo Baeck Institute [66].

3

First Encounter:
Baeck's Polemic Against
Harnack

During the winter semester of the academic year 1899–1900, Adolf
Harnack delivered sixteen lectures on the nature of Christianity to a
class of some six hundred students drawn from all the faculties of
the University of Berlin. The stir created in Berlin communicated itself
to the general community when these lectures were published under
the title *Das Wesen des Christenthums* [133] in 1900. Here was
an eloquent statement of the Christian faith with a minimum of theological dogma, ornate rituals, and ecclesiastical claims to power; an
exposition of liberal Protestantism which claimed that the essence of
Christianity was contained in two teachings of Jesus: the fatherhood
of God and the brotherhood of men. The Gospels were taken out
of the flux of time, isolated from the Jewish tradition of earlier times
and the Christian thought of later times. All was to be measured
by the teachings contained in them. Harnack tried to present the
religion *of* Jesus, instead of the one *about* Jesus. Viewed against that
simple, original Gospel, the proliferating institutions of Christianity
with their complex dogma were seen as the product of the essence of

Christianity found in Jesus, subservient to it as historical forms of
expression and not to be worshiped for their own sake. Harnack felt
that the Gospel did not need historical forms—dogma, church polity—
to produce belief. Following Troeltsch's dictum to "overcome history
with history" (i.e., to act with cultural responsibility in the present
in terms of criticizing one's historical heritage), Harnack gave the
assent of his own time to that aspect of the Reformation which abolished
dogma in favor of gospel; and he expressed his conviction that the
historical nature of Christianity made further authoritarian perpetua-
tion of dogma impossible. In a way, Harnack here anticipated later
thinking which separated the Christian principle from its historical
forms of expression. Yet he was very much the product of his time;
his lectures have been viewed as "a baseline from which to measure the
theological trends of the century." [138, p. 256] They represented
the position of nineteenth century liberal Protestantism, of bourgeois
idealist thought, soon to be shattered without hope of repair.

If today's Protestant theologians tend to ignore Harnack (forgetting
the enormous debt owed to the great church historian who trained a
corps of competent disciples and ignited their enthusiasm for the task
of tracing the development of Church dogma through all of its permuta-
tions with a reverent respect for detail), it must be noted that Baeck
challenged a prominent personage then at the peak of his power. Baeck
often judges Harnack too harshly, but Harnack's great book on Marcion
does show Harnack's fundamental opposition to Judaism as an aspect
of Church history. Harnack pointed out that the Church was right
in rejecting Marcion's attempt to be freed of the Old Testament; the
new religion needed the foundation of the Old Testament in the second
century. But then Harnack went on to deplore the fact that the Reformation was still dominated by this fatal heritage and did not make
iself independent of it; and he concluded that as long as the Church
retained the Old Testament it would be paralyzed and unable to make
any progress. Baeck had to challenge this by pointing to the historical
sources which the Christian theologian had ignored. In this challenge,
he joined a number of Catholic and Protestant thinkers;[1] but the answer
within the Jewish community deserves separate attention.

[1] Loisy [147], Baumann [77], Bousset [85], Troeltsch [185], and others.

I I

Baeck's article in the *Monatsschrift* [17, 18] was paralleled by a response written by Felix Perles [154], who adopted an often laudatory tone in assessing Harnack's thoughts, and felt that Judaism could learn a great deal from Harnack's method of discarding historical institutions and pruning mysticism and apocalyptic thought from the religion of Jesus until only the pure essence (completely acceptable to modern liberalism) remained.[2] There is a new tone in Baeck's critique in which fundamental differences of approach are stressed. Baeck is not cautious. He does not praise Harnack. At times, he is not even polite. Since Baeck sees the chief value of Christianity in its Jewish heritage, Harnack is viewed as attacking Judaism not only directly, when he presents false characterizations, but also indirectly, when he presents an "edited" Christianity.

Baeck starts by challenging the veracity of Harnack's work: "A work which is pure apologetics appears before us with the claim that it offers us pure history." [18, p. 5] Everything Harnack found displeasing in the Gospels—asceticism, socialism, etc.,—is dismissed as unimportant until all that is left is "the recognition and acceptance of God as the Father: the certainty of redemption; humility and the rejoicing in God; strength of action and brotherly love" [18, p. 6] which is then all identified with Jesus. But, says Baeck, it is what is important for Harnack which is identified with Jesus; a subjective apologete is speaking here, not an objective historian.[3]

Harnack was viewed by Baeck as continuing Ritschl's thinking. And Baeck applied Theobald Ziegler's criticism of Ritschl to Harnack:

> Since the value which dogmas have for man become determinative as to their validity and are used to prove the existence of that which is their

[2] Bergman [80] discusses the position of nineteenth century Judaism which claimed Jesus as a Jewish thinker and Christianity as a daughter religion, and also tried to present Judaism as the "religion of reason." This negation of Jewish mysticism, and the "falsification of Judaism" by this apologetics, is here seen as responsible for driving thinkers like Husserl, Weil, Stein, and others out of Judaism.

[3] This criticism was also made by Harnack's Christian critics. Cf. Alec R. Vitler, *The Church in an Age of Revolution* (London, 1961): "The point was later made by George Tyrrell when he said that Harnack looked at the Jesus of history down a deep well and saw his own face reflected at the bottom [pp. 123–124]."

foundation, Ritschl's theology approaches the teaching of Fuerbach that the wish is the father of the belief. But just this tendency is fateful for this theology, which commences so critically but ultimately simply declares whatever it desires to be valuable—and therefore true. This is, of course, very comfortable; but it is neither Kantian nor quite honest. [18, pp. 8–9]

In justice to the "value-judgments" of the Ritschlian school, it should be pointed out that its adherents did not consider value-judgments made by religion to be completely subjective. These judgments dealt with something which did exist, but which was not to be judged disinterestedly but in terms of its practical worth in satisfying the highest purpose of human life. That is why, ultimately, Jesus and his thought as Harnack understood it become Harnack's revelation; and Baeck's understanding of the people Israel as a revelation is not too far removed from this.

Baeck felt that Harnack did not have a proper understanding of Jesus and his times. Harnack mixed up such terms as "the kingdom of God" and "the days of the Messiah"; but "the kingdom of God" in the days of Jesus never contained his eudemonistic expectations found in the term "days of the Messiah." Harnack had written:

The message of Jesus embraces . . . two poles; at the one pole . . . a purely future event . . . at the other . . . something inward. Jesus took it from the religious traditions of his nation . . . and added new aspects. Eudemonistic expectations of a mundane and political character were all to be discarded. [134, p. 52]

Yet Baeck felt that the emphasis on the "inner" aspects of the kingdom of God within Jesus's teachings and the exclusion of other elements found in Jesus and his contemporaries all made for something Harnack should call "my Christianity," but not "the essence of Christianity." Harnack replaced the climate of opinion of Jesus's days— the anguish of messianic days, asceticism, and apocalypticism—with the rational climate of Harnack's days; and the teachings of Jesus were selected in terms of the modern climate.

Baeck objected to Harnack's method of explaining away Jesus's teaching of "turning the other cheek." Harnack had written:

But, we are asked, are we in all cases to renounce the pursuit of our rights in the face of our enemies? Are we to use no weapons but those of gentleness? . . . I venture to maintain that, when Jesus spoke the words . . . he was not thinking of such cases. [134, pp. 111–112]

Baeck thought otherwise:

> Others will dare to say the opposite. What appears unthinkable to Herr Harnack, *at that time* can have been considered not only thinkable, but also necessary. What he views as prejudice, *at that time* can have appeared in the eyes of many, perhaps just the best of them, as the precondition of morality. [18, pp. 10–11; Baeck's emphasis]

And Baeck deplored the fact that Harnack was not only an apologete instead of an historian, but also one who watered down his own faith:

> In regard to many moral demands, Harnack claims that they are neither unconditioned nor always valid; that they are not categorical imperatives and do not include all conditions; that they do not have to be obeyed constantly and without exception; that one should only be in the position of being able to fulfill them under certain conditions—and thus is surrendered precisely what is most impressive, the imposing prophetic dignity of the moral commandment which shows itself precisely in the lack of interest in all terrestrial considerations, in the paradox and in the unyieldingness of its postulation. [18, p. 11]

Baeck's basic contribution here is the application of a sound knowledge of Jewish texts to the study of the New Testament. But Christian scholarship, at this stage, did not place much emphasis upon the Jewish sources. Rabbis who entered into this area were viewed as intruders, as not-disinterested polemicists. A dogmatic reliance upon Christian authorities existed. As Baeck cried out despairingly: *"Wellhausen locutus est, causa finita est."* [17, p. 7] The rabbi could not presume to challenge the great historian of Christianity on the teachings of Jesus. Where Baeck challenged the methods of Harnack, rather than the conclusions, he was on a firmer ground.

In Baeck's preface to the second edition of his review, he indicates that "he has received support from Christian theologians of all factions" [18, p. 3] and has incorporated some of their suggestions into his revisions. Nevertheless, this second edition shows a stronger polemic against Christianity. In his initial review, Baeck had attacked Harnack's interchangeable use of the divine attribute of justice with the ethical postulate:

> The religious belief in God's justice and the moral demand of the law are two completely different things. It is not possible to deduce the one from the other. . . . Of course, Church history is rich in examples where

there was great inclination to substitute teachings regarding God for moral law, dogma for commandments of duty. [17, p. 9]

In the second edition, we find a footnote added in which Baeck comes to assert the dependence of Christianity upon Jewish ethics which remained a key statement in his polemics over the years:

> Already this one fact, that the commandment of active justice is at least ignored through silence within the New Testament, shows clearly how little of its religious and ethical nature can be maintained by the New Testament without the Old Testament. Love of one's neighbor without justice is no virtue (cf. Kant, *Definitivartikel zum ewigen Frieden*, Anhang II). —S. Stern, *The Fight of the Rabbis versus the Talmud*, Breslau 1902, p. 146: "The modern social movement is the declaration of the bankruptcy of love of one's neighbor without justice."—And let us also recall how negative a position the New Testament takes in regard to family life. It is impossible to construct an ethics just out of the New Testament; this alone reveals how senseless it is to attempt placing a New Testament morality alongside the morality of the Old Testament. [18, p. 14, n. 1]

And at the same time, Baeck started his defense of the Pharisees who were attacked by Harnack as "thinking about God as the despot who keeps guard over the ceremonials which are his household ordinances," of seeing God "within His law which they had made a labyrinth of dark crevices, false pathways, and secret exits." [134, p. 33]

The Pharisees are a basic issue of contention between Baeck and Harnack. Baeck finds in them a true pattern of positive Judaism. To Harnack and Christian scholarship in general, the term "Pharisees" was still one of opprobrium. For Baeck, the teachings of Hillel and his colleagues were evidence of the love of humanity found within Pharisaism, while Christian scholars dismissed these sayings or found them atypical. It is not surprising that this defense of Pharisaism was attacked by Christian scholars. Baeck found it necessary to add some footnotes in the second edition indicating that the love of God and love of man are indeed joined together in the Torah. [18, p. 13, n. 1][4] Harnack had already dismissed the fact that the Pharisees taught this love of God and man. He had stated:

---

[4] In citing Leviticus 19:18 as the place where the love of man is enjoined through love of God—the commandment ends with "I am the Lord"—Baeck for the first time foreshadows the polarity of mystery and commandment which fills his later teachings.

Pharisaic teachers had proclaimed that everything is contained in the love of God and the love of man; they had spoken glorious words which could have come out of the mouth of Jesus! And what had they achieved? That people, that above all their own students rejected the one who was serious about these words. [133, p. 31][5]

Harnack stressed harsh legalism as the norm of Jewish religious life, and Baeck challenged this introduction of ancient prejudices into modern scholarship. In his polemic he indicated that judgments made by Christians upon the Talmud can equally be made upon the Christian literature of those centuries: "In that literature . . . there is likewise contained a great deal else, not particularly beautiful and uplifting, as one can see especially well if one reads Mr. Harnack's writings." [18, p. 17]

According to Baeck, Harnack simply did not know Judaism. Unaware of the difference between Halacha and Aggadah, Harnack could write about Jesus that

It is highly unlikely that he went through any Rabbinical school; he nowhere speaks like a man who had assimilated any theological culture of a technical kind, or learned the art of scholarly exegesis . . . and hence he caused a stir by appearing in the schools and teaching at all. He lived and has his being in the sacred writings, but not after the manner of a professional teacher. [134, pp. 31–32]

Baeck's criticism of Harnack is excessively severe here; but his major point is a valid one: Harnack was unaware that the rabbinate always contained more than dialecticians and legislators; there were the Haggadists, the preachers, the religious thinkers and poets. The parables and sayings of Jesus are quite typical of the rabbinic literature of his time, fitting one type of rabbi, just as Paul and his work represent a different type of rabbi.[6] The mere fact that Jesus spoke in the synagogue

---

[5] In a note added to the 1908 edition, Harnack took cognizance of Baeck's criticism: "If indeed one or another Jewish teacher did let the moral law take precedence over the ceremonial law, this is not decisive here. Such a teacher did not come to stand out of the total structure of the Jewish teachers of that time." [p. x.] In the same place, he decided to leave in his statement on some actions of Jewish leaders as "horrible," since he had qualified this in his original lecture on page 31: "The Pharisees also had the teachings of Jesus; but *unfortunately they had a great deal else as well.*" [p. x]

[6] Baeck [18, p. 20, n. 1]: "Casuistic hairsplitting belongs to a much later time than Jesus. On the other hand, we find that Jesus also establishes his point of view halachically (Mark 2:25 ff. and parallels) and completely in the manner of the old Pharisaic teachings."

did not create a stir; and there did not exist the type of "professional teacher" in Harnack's sense. The rabbis of that time were farmers, artisans, carpenters, men who were immersed in daily life with the people, drawing their analogies from these experiences, as did Jesus.

One point becomes clear here: Baeck claims Jesus for Judaism. The young rabbi was more daring here than many of his colleagues whose cautious praise of Jesus was often related to their desire to create a better relationship between Jew and Christian. There is a warmth here unmatched by twentieth century Jewish thinkers—until Martin Buber acclaims Jesus as his brother.[7]

It is important to place Baeck's appraisal of Jesus into his polemic against Harnack's Christianity:

> Jesus, in all of his traits, is completely a *genuine Jewish* character. A man such as he could only grow up on the soil of Judaism—there are nowhere else. Jesus is a genuine Jewish personality; all of his striving and acting, his bearing and feeling, his speech and his silence bear the stamp of the Jewish manner, the imprint of Jewish idealism, the best of what Judaism gave and gives, but what only existed, at that time, in Judaism. He was a Jew among Jews; out of no other people could a man such as he have come forth and in no other people could a man such as he have been able to have this effect; in no other people could he have found the apostles who believed in him. [18, p. 28]

And it is the same assent to the Jewish aspects of Christianity which leads the young rabbi to write concerning Jewish hatred of Christianity:

> This [hatred] never existed. A mother never hates her child; but the child often forgot and denied its mother. The Jewish theologian . . . will not deny recognition, let alone injure or denigrate a religion which fulfilled and still fulfills a gigantic, world historical mission. [18, p. 30]

Again, Baeck sees Christianity receive its validation from a Judaism which has a mission in which Christianity shares: the teaching of Jewish ethics to the world.

Harnack and Baeck had to disagree on this point. For Harnack, Jesus achieved a new ethic which was separate from the cult. Harnack

---

[7] Martin Buber *Zwei Glaubensweisen* (Zurich, 1950), p. 11: "From my youth on, I always experienced Jesus as my big brother."

identified Judaism with ritualism; and Baeck had to challenge this premise:

> The ethics contained in the Bible and in the rich moral teachings of that time was *not at all* tied up with the ritual, but completely independent of it, so independent that it was often set up in opposition to the cult. . . . Harnack . . . is misled by the circumstance that the cult is established upon a moral foundation and is to realize moral goals, that the cult has been ethicized, something which is different from a pagan cult. [17, p. 18][8]

As often as not, the polemic turns into apologetics.

Baeck challenged Harnack on two levels: in the field of history and in the theological area. The historical challenge pitted the young rabbi against the great Christian historian who refused to use Jewish sources in his study of Jewish history, who maintained a theological prejudice against the Pharisees and the Jewish community of Jesus's time. Baeck's emphasis on the difference between Halacha and Aggadah was important here. It pointed toward a new evaluation of rabbinic texts, in particular the midrash, as a rich source for the history of religion at the time of Jesus.

Baeck does not only rely on the scholarly work of Geiger and the "scientific study of Judaism." [18, p. 10, n. I] Moving into Harnack's territory, he quotes Renan and other Christian scholars whose views he shares; and he shows full awareness of the Tübingen school and its disagreement with Harnack. In the course of the review, Baeck quotes Theobold Ziegler (a David Strauss disciple), Karl H. Cornill, and Emil Schuerer [18, pp. 7–8; p. 10, n. 1; p. 27, n. 1] And he indicates his willingness to work in the field of "higher criticism" as outlined by Wellhausen and Kuenen, as long as their mistakes are recognized alongside with their merits. Baeck felt comfortable in the field of Biblical history. In time, he was to subjugate history to theology; but the pious devotion to individual facts, the Rankean effort to see things as they really were, the determination of relationships—this remained part of Baeck.

The principal challenge of this review to Harnack was the theological one. Baeck asserted that it had not only been a lack of knowledge of the Jewish sources which had flawed Harnack's presentation. The

---

[8] Baeck's second edition of "Harnack's Vorlesungen" [18] enlarged upon the Talmud's stress on good deeds as ethical actions.

Essence of Christianity contained another, fatal philosophic flaw inherited from Ritschl: The history of New Testament times had been isolated, set apart in time; the history itself was to be the essence of the Christian faith. It was itself unique and absolute. The Jewish history which preceded it could not be taken seriously, lest it challenge that uniqueness. Indeed, even the Christian history which followed it had to be called inferior. And so, writing not history but apologetics, Harnack's work ultimately was not even a work of apologetics for the Christian faith: it presented one isolated aspect of that faith—Harnack's personal beliefs, which he considered the essence of Jesus's preachments.

This was Baeck's first major excursion into polemics; it is best understood as a preparation for his next work. Three years later, Baeck published a work of apologetics which became the classic presentation of Judaism in his time: *The Essence of Judaism.*

4

The Essence of Judaism

In 1905, Leo Baeck published his major exposition of Judaism: *The Essence of Judaism*. [1] Its title is evidence that the confrontation with Harnack continues here, even though no direct reference is made to *The Essence of Christianity* in the text (but there are three footnote references to Harnack[1]). And, in the opening pages, Baeck characterizes Judaism as the religion which does not begin and end with one prophet, be he Gautama Buddha, Zarathustra, or Mohammed (with the notable omission of Jesus from that list). In Judaism,

> The master is followed by the succession of masters, the great man by a chain of equals. No one serves as the totality, no one represents the totality. The fullness of religion is not contained in any individual, nor yet in several. . . . The whole content of Judaism rests first of all in its uncompleted, eternal history. [1, pp. 27–28]

The emphasis on the concept of *toldot*, the chain of generations which is Jewish history, opens the way for Baeck's finding the people Israel itself a continuous revelation which confronts the world as an eternal witness with a constant mission.

[1] [1, p. 5], referring to Harnack's *Wesen des Christenthums;* p. 45, referring to Harnack's *Mission und Ausbreitung des Christenthums;* p. 148, referring to the same work.

The Essence of Judaism is Baeck's statement of the continuous chain of tradition, Judaism, which confronts the Christian who finds the essence of his faith solely at Calvary. Yet this work is more than a challenge to Harnack's *Essence of Christianity*. It can be seen as a parallel development to it. Both works share the language and thought of the turn of the century; both emphasize the ethical act as the center of religious life and draw away from religious metaphysics. It is only when Harnack judges Judaism and the Pharisees in a manner which turns historical writings into apologetics that they clash. This clash is between two revelations: the Christ of redemption who stands beyond and outside of history, and the covenant people who are a continuous revelation and who find their redemption in the human task existing within history. Harnack's book, in the context of his writings, is a popularized continuation of the task he set himself in his *History of Dogma*: that of eliminating the accumulated theological debris of the centuries and of returning Christian thought to the purity of the Gospels. Baeck's writings, particularly this 1905 work, stress Judaism as the ethical task arising out of the categorical Ought, and deny the existence of dogma.[2]

The quest for the essence of religion determined the nature of both works. It was part of the *Zeitgeist;* and this search for the underlying essence of intellectual constructions also came to Baeck through his teacher Wilhelm Dilthey, whose *Essence of Philosophy* was published in 1907. [102] Influenced by Dilthey, Baeck always searched for the Gestalt underlying a literary creation—be it a polemical midrash or a mystic text. Yet Baeck also followed Dilthey in recognizing that there were definite limits to the psychological approach. One begins with personal experience, but moves on beyond it:

> The history of civilization and history of philosophy demonstrate how man's experiences within himself, this picture that the realms of his self seemed to show him, were the first creation, and how only from here a picture of the community and of the cosmos were built up. [60, p. 13]

Beyond the inner life, the outer world of the mind has its own laws. The life of the soul is individual; the life of spirit is the larger world in which the individuals interrelate with one another. Psychology is a tool for the exploration of the inner processes of the individual;

[2] See also Baeck's "Hat das ueberlieferte Judentum Dogmen?" in [5, pp. 12–27].

it cannot view the *Geistesgestalt* of Judaism itself. Dilthey said the same thing in his study of Roman law: "Understanding this spirit is not a matter of psychology. It is the rediscovery of a spiritual form which has its own structure and laws."[3]

Dilthey's concern with presenting a type as corollary to the understanding of civilization is part of Baeck's approach. But where Dilthey writes of many types and compares them with one another, Baeck only deals with one type: the Jew and his faith. And the fact that he is describing himself cannot be left out of our considerations. There is more than Dilthey's method of empathy here; there is self-knowledge. *The Essence of Judaism* has an autobiographical aspect.

The Essence of Judaism is not a philosophic description of a system divorced from the experience of Jewish life. Judaism is presented as a living configuration which is permitted to speak for itself, out of its existence as a covenant people linked with God. And Israel's God is not discovered as the result of a chain of reasoned argument. God was experienced at the genesis of the system. He is accepted on faith from the very outset, as "the One God whose essence is the moral law. He is the guarantee of morality, the certainty for its eternal reality." [1, p. 59] If the method is that of Dilthey, the concept here is that of Hermann Cohen. But Baeck does not rely upon Cohen's system of proving the philosophic necessity of God as an idea which guarantees ethics; he turns to the inner experience of Israel and its testimony of God. The twofoldness of his presentation begins to emerge. Cohen's teachings, his optimism, his exaltation of reason, the insistence that religion must be ethical—these dominate Baeck. He echoes Cohen's concept of the Unique God:

> The God of Israel is the Eternal Unique One not because He does by himself alone what all the pagan gods are and do in concert, but because he is *different* from all of them and does different things than they do. [1, pp. 64–65]

But the teaching is viewed in the framework of an inner experience which is approached by Baeck in the manner of Schleiermacher and Dilthey. There is something of Schleiermacher in Baeck's statement that

[3] Wilhelm Dilthey, *Gesammelte Werke*, Vol. VII, p. 85, quoted by Bollnow [83, p. 189].

Divine love, this all-embracing divine attribute, is paralleled within man by a basic religious feeling which is the inmost source of all faith and all religious sentiment, all receptivity and openness toward God. It is *humility*, which is nothing else than the awareness of the unmeasurable Divine love. . . . It combines apparent opposites . . . the feeling of standing before God as *little* and insignificant, and without merit; but also the firm personal confidence that one is *God's child* in Whom one has the rock and support of existence; that one can always hope for His kindness—to be unutterably insignificant before God and yet also unutterably great through Him. [1, p. 71]

In this, we can sense Schleiermacher's stress upon the essence of religion resting in the profound feeling of dependency upon the Deity. Yet elsewhere Baeck takes direct issue with Schleiermacher's thought by noting that his "conception completely disregards the demanding element of the religious unity: its commandment to freedom." [1, p. 80] In this combining of apparent opposites, one can already note Baeck's "religion of polarity."

II

The 1905 edition of *The Essence of Judaism* contains 167 pages, including four pages of notes. Although there are some drastic revisions in the second edition, of 1922, it is correct to say with Professor Mayer that "Baeck's view of the essence of Judaism is there in its totality from the beginning; it is only the method of searching and finding which is enlarged and deepened." [150, p. 22]

The first section of *The Essence of Judaism* deals with the dynamic relationship between the unity of Judaism and the constant development within it. Baeck notes how Judaism and the Jew have entered the cultural life of every era of Western existence; yet the people and the faith preserved their individuality. And Baeck comes to describe a paradox of life, a polarity:[4] Israel, and the nations of the world. Israel, as a minority, is constantly challenged, constantly pushed into a re-evaluation of its religion:

By its fate, every minority is forced into thinking. It constantly has to regain for itself the conscious awareness that it possesses the truth, while

[4] The 1905 edition uses the word "paradox," and not "polarity." But the preconditions for the system of polarity are established here.

for the ruling groups . . . their power is a sufficient guarantee. That is why the Jewish *philosophy of religion,* engaged in this struggle, entered all layers of those professing Judaism . . . and almost the whole community participated in this intellectual struggle for the right of existence. Nothing is as characteristic for the Judaism of the Diaspora as this philosophic trait. [1, p. 2]

We are here made aware of Baeck's preference for the experience which is to validate the philosophy. The essence of Judaism is placed in the dynamic experience of Jewish existence. It does not begin in that experience. Faith in God precedes the life of the people of God: "Basic religious teachings are contained in a positive religion . . . but only become dogmas when cast into *firm unbreakable forms* the acceptance of which is the condition of the true believer." [1, p. 34] While Baeck asserts basic teachings, he will not place them out of reach of inquiry and the test of experience. A belief which has been sanctified into dogma becomes weakened; it is taken out of human life. Baeck warns that institutions tend to grow around systems of thought, tend to isolate them. Truth that has become redeeming gnosis is lost to man. The sanctified mystery can become overpowering to the mind of man reaching out toward the mystery. That is why, according to Baeck, the commandments which demand religious and moral action must precede the dogma which tells of God's mystery: "The *duties* toward God precede the *knowledge* of God." [1, p. 3] In the place of the ended, complete formula, Baeck saw the demand of the unending activity of thought; a people, acting ethically in accordance with the commandment, found their way toward the mystery through these acts of life. Religious thinking was part of life, was not isolated from it. It was the constant—that which was always created within the Jewish people—transmitted through the chain of generations. The character of Judaism remained unchanged here, and its unity abided in the midst of its development:

> Foreign ways of thought were permitted to enter; but no concessions were made to them. At the same time that they were assimilated they were also conquered . . . only that remained which could become Jewish. [1, p. 5]

Was this process of assimilating outside cultures identical with a Christian development like the Greek-Catholic Church? Baeck disagreed. Christianity is viewed as accepting the Greek faith and cloaking it with a Christian garment, instead of coming to terms with it. Baeck denied that this also happened to Judaism. Unity moved through diversity in Judaism; it was always open to different customs and ideas, but transformed them: "The ability to shape new material in an original manner—quite apart from the prophetic religious discoveries—is one of the essential traits of Israel's independence." [1, p. 6] With the *Babel und Bibel* controversy then at its high point, Baeck could not deny that a great deal of foreign material had entered into the life of Israel. His answer, alongside that of other Jewish scholars, was that Judaism transformed that material. But, without being aware of it, he is also here following the method he challenged in Harnack: The Jewish people is set outside other peoples as something special, as a revelation. Baeck's historical presentation at least tends to become an apologetics for his people and his faith. Nevertheless, Baeck's data are taken from experience and are thus accessible to others; he is prepared to subject his presentation to the critique of the historical discipline.

Israel is a special type of religious personality among the nations, gifted with religious creativity; this is at the core of Baeck's thought. Its inner development is that of a continuity of epochs, the *shalshelet ha-kabbalah*, the chain of tradition which is its very life. Baeck stresses that "every *system* of the Jewish religion is of necessity a *history* of it." [1, p. 9]

Baeck constantly returns to the tension between the polarities of this developing faith. Static and dynamic factors abound: the stasis of authority, the dynamism of freedom. The Bible is, in one way, a static authority. *All* of the Bible—the Law cannot be separated from the Prophets—is the promulgated law of the covenant and the way of life practiced by all of Israel. And not only the canon of the Bible, but also the authority of its interpretation, the Oral Law, the Talmud, gives full assurance for a center of gravity, a static and abiding foundation of Jewish life.

At the same time, the Bible also became the dynamic factor of Jewish existence: "It contains the *word of God* which has to be the word for all time; each age must be able to find itself within it. . . . 'Thou art the man' is the motto of Scripture." [1, p. 11] Baeck here joins his colleagues, the "new thought" of German Jewry, in their evaluation of the Bible as a living text (but with a liberalism of his own in which part of the revelation is the contemporary response). Buber and Rosenzweig felt the same need to confront modern man with the Biblical word from which he was estranged:

Unlike earlier generations, he [the contemporary Jew] no longer presents himself to the Biblical word in order to listen to it or to be angered by it. He no longer confronts his life by the Word. . . . Thus does he cripple the one force, among all those existing, which is most likely to save him. [91a, pp. 17–18]

The Bible as the static force undergirding life; the response of each generation as the dynamic force linking Jewish existence—this is how Baeck views the tension between the people and the Word. According to Baeck, each age acquired its own Bible: a Bible of Philo, of Akiba, of Maimonides, of Mendelssohn. Moses, in the rabbinic tradition, does not recognize the Bible of Akiba—each generation creates its own. And so the Bible lives within Jewish existence. In the end, the interpreters fade into the background; it is the ideas which matter, never the authors (Baeck did not employ the personal pronoun in his writings). And the work itself is never completed:

Religion is never that which has achieved fulfillment. Its ideal is not that which has been completed, which is already given: it is a goal, a task, to be achieved through constant striving for the truth. Bible, Oral Law, philosophy of religion, mysticism, the pious poetry and the moral teachings of the Middle Ages, the stirrings of the new era—these are the links of the continuous chain in the intellectual work which was constantly renewed and taken up again. [1, p. 16]

Optimism here includes the pessimistic view, but dominates it. Baeck's style tends to incorporate and thus to answer the challenges to his system. We see this in another passage which in addition mirrors the evolutionary thinking current at the turn of the century:

Pauses have existed in this development, tired times when it stood still for a long time; there were also times of lassitude and regression. . . . Nothing is easier than to discover in any epoch of Judaism . . . that which runs counter to the ascent toward the ideal. This is no valid criticism of Judaism and its development, as long as the straight path continued, as long as that which was lowly was overtaken, as long as that which had little worth was conquered. Judaism always *rediscovered* itself and found its way. [1, pp. 16–17]

In the evolutionary process, the fit survive. And the prophets always lived on for Baeck. In the long-range view of history, the flaws of Israel are subjugated to the total structure; they are the finite flaws of the revelation which entered into history and now makes its way through history.

Having established, as the first ingredient of the character of Judaism, this unity and development, the static and dynamic poles of the faith, Baeck now presents another polarity contained in the essence of Judaism: the prophetic religion and the community of faith. Constantly, we see in this tension between polarities the faith as it confronts the existence of Israel.

The prophets are the special character of the faith, more easily defined by what they are not than by what they are. They are not scholars; not theologians. They follow no set pattern of thought; they do not speculate:

> A moral force makes them think, a stab of conscience bids them speak; irresistible truth overwhelms them. . . . They speak because they must. . . . God gave them their message; theirs is a spontaneous, inner receptivity, the deepest religious experience. [1, pp. 18–19]

The mystery and the commandment are contained together in the prophetic experience. And the prophet transmits both aspects. He does not generalize; the message stays real, personal, and definite. He is not influenced by past traditions to the point of passivity. Indeed, he often attacks the past in places where he finds tradition idolized and blindly worshiped.

The prophet starts with God. He is not concerned with proving Divine existence. He knows. He has encountered God. And Baeck saw the prophetic function in its practical ethical nature as the prophet proclaims God's will, the moral law. Once again, Baeck emphasized the life experience, dominated by what his time viewed as the "religion of duty":

> The ways of God are the ways that man should go. On these alone are we led unto God; only in the right deed does the essence of God reveal itself. Do your duty; then you will know Who God is. . . . To seek God is to strive for good; to find God is to do good. [1, p. 22]

In this seeking and finding God and the good Baeck sees the proper union between religion and life, in which the certainty of the moral task banishes mysticism:

> Religion is thus removed from all mysticism and all magic. The *thoughts* of God cannot be plumbed; they are lofty beyond the thoughts of man, as heaven is high above the earth. But the *commandments* of God are not distant and not hidden. . . . The pious man knows what he should do. . . . He knows his duty which the coming day will bring him. [1, pp. 22–23]

Again, Hermann Cohen can be seen here. But behind him there stands all of the moral rigorism of the rabbinic tradition with its emphasis upon the *mitzvot* ("the commandments") and the ethical tasks of life.

Baeck stresses the religious foundation of the Bible. The tasks are not presented to man because metaphysical speculation has arrived at them, but because the encounter with God has presented Israel with a covenanted commanded duty. No conflict between faith and knowledge exists here: "On the one hand, the conflict does not exist between man and religion as represented by life; on the other hand, it does not take place because knowledge can never prove religion." [1, p. 25] By not abstracting the ethical contents of the human experience touched by revelation into a system, the prophets were not forced into the position of having to prove doctrines. They were living witnesses of religious experience which moves from man to man—the Bible is a continuous great confession of the human spirit. Its personalities become human history, a chain of transmission in which the personalities themselves are stressed as part of the revelation.

In an age which knew the great philosophic systems—and opponents like Kierkegaard who attacked the system—we find Leo Baeck stressing the prophetic word and expressing his fears of any system:

> Every system of thought is intolerant and breeds intolerance, because it fosters self-righteousness and self-satisfaction—it is significant that the most ruthless of inquisitors have come from the ranks of the systematizers. Fixing its focus of vision at a certain definite range, a system cuts itself off from all who are outside the focus of that vision. It thus prevents the living development of truth. On the other hand, the prophetic word is a living and personal confession of faith which cannot be circumscribed by rigid boundaries; it possesses a breadth and a freedom carrying within itself the possibilities of revival and development. [1, p. 27]

Dynamic development and revival of life, as we shall see, come to be key concepts in the framework of Baeck's theology.

The prophetic word goes out to all; and Baeck sees the Jewish community organized without inner divisions. No one group is granted the exclusive truth of the revelation:

> It is part of the essence of religion that it has an ideal applicable to all, and that its demands reach out to all. Religious personality is demanded, and from everyone—but not a special religious existence. [1, p. 30]

Where God and the world are separated, according to Baeck, one must leave the world in order to reach God. And Baeck sees Judaism grounded in this world. He recognized the exceptions to the rule, the many Jewish mystics, individually and in groupings, who tried to escape from a dark and anguished existence into mystic contemplation. But normative Jewish thought viewed the daily existence within the community as the place where God was encountered. The rabbis were artisans and workers, part of the community. The basic division in religious life was between those who taught and those who learned. This, too, was a shared enterprise. Returning to his quarrel with Harnack, Baeck once again presented a corrected picture of the Pharisees:

> Many called themselves "separated ones—Pharisees." But, as the classical explanation stated, this only meant: "Separated from the sins and . . . abominations [in Mechilta to Deut. 19:6, ed. Weiss, p. 71b]." There were pious circles who designated themselves *chaverim* [fellows]. But where the essential areas of religion began, they too accepted only one basic rule "All Israel are chaverim." The unity of the religious community was not breached. [1, p. 30]
> [Baeck here attacked those scholars who interpreted the name Pharisees (separated ones) in terms of an aristocratic group who had separated themselves from a community which they despised. He showed that the Pharisee was part of the people.]

The Pharisaic task, as Baeck saw it, promulgated moral commandments which by their nature drew all into their sphere, making Israel a "kingdom of priests and a holy people."

Baeck's fear of dogma—based on what he considered the failure of the Christian experience—breaks through in many places. Placing religion so much into the experience of the people, and into every man through the inward experience and commitment, Baeck does not want to see religion burdened with dogma. The people experiences the revelation; need that revelation be concretized? It should not be carved into stone or wood; should it be carved into well-polished words? Looking at the Christian experience with its dangerous use of words which replace acts, he sees that "Protestantism places importance in the so-called witnessing. . . . It is assumed that the word and particularly its profession can be fully possessed." [1, pp. 34–35] Baeck makes the distinction that "in Judaism, religion is not *experienced* but *lived* ['nicht *erlebt,* sondern *gelebt*']" [1, p. 35] It does not present itself from outside of life; it *is* life. The universal teaching embraces all; the right deed is demanded from all. And it is the right deed for Baeck which brings man to belief: "We can only believe that which we do; faith, too, is rooted in will. One who does not become aware of God through good work . . . will also not become aware of God through an inner experience." [1, p. 36] Cohen's teaching of Kant's categorical imperative can be found here; but it is not so much discovered by the inquiring mind as it is encountered by the life of commitment, by the action which precedes all else for Baeck.

Baeck realizes that the Jewish community was also affected adversely by this stress upon action. Ritual actions assumed too great an importance —Baeck's liberalism comes to the foreground here—but even the ritual actions were based on the ethical content of the tradition. And the tradition rose out of a history of Jewish existence in which optimism asserted itself over all tragedies. The messianic hopes, for Baeck, are no more than the declaration that the time will come when all men will act ethically:

> History, with all its anguish . . . practically demanded that Israel should pray and hope. Certainty of God's nearness . . . was an integral part of the faith. Without the strength of this belief, the history of Israel would have ended quickly. The right deed gave the content for *life;* faith gave the *strength to live.* [1, pp. 37–38]

A later lecture elaborates this point of the content and the foundation of Jewish existence. [31]

The tension between the static and dynamic elements within Judaism and the people is now to be extended to the rest of the world. The polarity between Israel and the nations has to be the heart of his apologetics. Baeck outlines Judaism as a special revelation which—as any true revelation—has to speak to the whole world.

Judaism's special revelation, the unique contribution to the world, is seen in its ethical contents. Ethics "are Judaism's essence, its fundamental principle" [1, p. 39]; and

> Monotheism is the result of a realization of the absolute character of the moral law; moral consciousness teaches about God . . . and this definite ethical character thus indicates the creation of Israel's religion, the new way which was found. And it is *completely new,* not merely the changed continuation of the old. [1, p. 40]

Ethical monotheism was something new in religion. Nature religions can make an alliance with ethics to protect the community; but they cannot develop into ethical religions in which morality is the essential content of the faith. This change can only take place through a revolution; and Baeck sees Judaism as such a revolution. It is not the last word in an old way of thinking, but the first word in a new way of thought. It is—a revelation.

Baeck recognizes only two basic approaches in religious thought: Judaism and Buddhism:

> The first signifies the affirmation of the relationship between man and the world in an ethical manner through the will and through the deed; the latter demands the rejection of this relationship through the contemplation which has no will and sinks into itself. One is the religion of altruism, the other is the religion of egoism. . . . [1, p. 40]

In the revised edition, Baeck softens this judgment which, indeed, is a superficial one and does not take into consideration basic aspects of Mahayana and Hinayana Buddhism. Yet Baeck insists on the primacy of a Judaism

> which is a revelation . . . the *classic* appearance of religion, despite its every possible and necessary development not only a beginning, but also an ideal. For every true idea is a totality, it represents a goal pursued by every era. [1, p. 41]

Even where Baeck does not spell out the details of the revelation, he has to see it as complete: the Written and the Oral Law were the traditional way of saying this. The liberal rabbi cannot do so; he will not have the revelation spelled out by the Talmud and the rabbis. Instead, he places it into the inner consciousness of the people, whose existence is the revelation, whose history are the details of that revelation, whose ethical actions are the future of that revelation. That is why the *election* of Israel stands at the center of Baeck's thought.

A people which carries within itself the revelation is, of necessity, different. But Baeck does not see this difference in the manner of Franz Rosenzweig who placed Israel outside of history, fulfilling by its election a unique function which Christianity complements by its work within history. For Baeck, election is a quality found in a people who have encountered the revelation and are one with it. It is a self-realization, a deep personal feeling of man created in God's image becoming aware of what he is. The clearer the revelation, the more certain man is that he has been chosen, i.e., the prophetic stress in Israel's chosenness is due to the deep impact the revelation has made upon it. Election, for Baeck, is a *character trait* of God's people. It is a surrender to the absoluteness of the revelation; and Baeck's assent to it is a statement of faith and not really a historical judgment.

A problem arises here. Baeck has denied that a group of the "elect" exists within Israel. Is he now stating that Israel is the "elected one" among the nations? The answer is twofold: On the one hand, religious "election" describes a Diltheyan "type" found everywhere. It is a character trait of any religious community which has encountered a truth, has opened itself to it, has lived in accordance with that truth: "Side by side with religion, there is given the feeling of certainty which is essential for the process by which that religion comes to fulfill itself as truth for its adherents." [1] But Baeck is also describing one special type: his people Israel. He is committed to them, he accepts the revelation. Even Israel's stubbornness and occasional excesses are accepted in Baeck's affirmation of his people. Its existence through three millenniums and more becomes the proof for the truth of the revelation. And if Baeck states the psychological truth of the true believer who is elected by the truth which shapes his life, he is also affirming Israel as the projection of the transcendental revelation which has its constant witness in the existence of Israel. Baeck does believe in the "chosen people"; but he also believes that any people may be chosen; man is the *individuum ineffabile*.

The concept of the election has to lead to the polarity between particularism and universalism. Baeck saw Israel's particularism as a necessary character trait of a people and a faith anxious to avoid syncretism and the assimilation of lesser values:

> Judaism always had to begin with the particularism of emphasizing its unique approach; the prophetic teaching had to demand the separation from the neighboring peoples. . . . Exclusiveness is the "negative side of the duty to confess one's faith." [1, p. 45]

But the people of ethical monotheism could not but make this an *ethical exclusivism*:

> National exclusiveness became the demand for *ethical exclusiveness*, and the uniqueness of Israel's historical situation was understood as a uniqueness of religious duties. Israel is chosen when it choses itself. "Ye shall be holy . . ."; "This is My covenant. . . ." [1, p. 47]

Ethical particularism has to culminate in the *mission*. Israel becomes the messenger of God, the light to the nations; Israel is a messiah figure. The tension between particularism and universalism is resolved in the mission which fulfills the election:

> The idea of the election here received its unconditional correlative: the *idea of humanity* . . . When one group has the mission to proclaim the One God . . . to all the world . . . the fact that all belong to God is clearly enunciated. . . . The religious idea of humanity, religious universalism, here comes to be a basic, essential aspect of religion; it becomes the *principle of the historical religious task*. The religion of Israel developed through this into a world religion . . . *the* world religion. [1, pp. 47–48]

Baeck is also writing an apologetics for Judaism. Ultimately, it becomes an *apologia pro vita sua*: testimony, election, mission, and responsibility for fellow man runs through all his teachings and life. For Baeck, the universalism in Judaism is at its very heart, as he stated on another occasion: "One can only be a Jew if one sees the totality, if one thinks in a universal manner." [48, p. 370] Particularism and universalism both belong to the typology of religious groups. But when one polarity is infused with an ethical awareness, the other polarity is also ethicized. And the ethical act has to make the particular the universal faith. When that faith is Judaism, the affirmation of ethical monotheism, the polarity of the one religion and the one humanity creates the one way of ethical action:

> The *One* God can only mean *one religion* to which all men are called and which can only find its complete historical fulfillment when all profess it. As long as this has not yet taken place, it has to indicate the days which are yet to come; its history remains incomplete; and the goal set for it is only viewed by the vision which looks into the boundless future. [1, p. 48]

One final bridge exists between Israel and mankind: Judaism, as the religion of ethics, is a pathway for all mankind. The revelation is to be shared. In the last pages of the book, Baeck has to commit himself to a mission for his people which affirms a missionary task.

Was there anything new in the position of Baeck? The revelation of Israel as the unique entrance of ethical monotheism into the world had certainly had its earlier proponents. Abram Geiger, in particular, had placed this revelation into the life experience of a people expressing its strong individuality, unwilling to let its particularity be dissolved into the universality of mankind.[5] Leo Baeck, it must be noted, is Geiger's pupil at this point. But there is a difference between them: the difference between the nineteenth and the twentieth century.

Abraham Geiger's "science of Judaism" applied the insight of historical scholarship to the data af Jewish existence. The child of his era, he looked for the underlying *idea* of Judaism as it comes to achieve full reality through the millenniums:

> The idea enters into the world of appearances with all of the fullness and freshness of youth, yet still pressed into the frame of space and time which are its place and hour of birth; overlooks . . . the limitations clinging to it . . . looks up to the ideal heights . . . but has to live in the fenced-in valley. . . . Once it has gained a firm footing, it wants to change the surrounding environment, and does have an influence upon it, but is also conditioned, modified; the more it stretches out, the more it loses its identity. It becomes one-sided, splintered . . . gains a sometimes worthless wealth. Finally, it arrives at the third stage, pulls itself together into inner contemplation, filled with rich experiences. . . . This inner development which is also its historical formulation even though moving through many changes, is the *threefold* area of the *Science of Judaism.* [118, pp. 9–10]

That is Geiger's understanding of Jewish history, which he divided into four epochs:

> The free creativity of the *Revelation,* covering Biblical times . . . the treatment of that material . . . within the *Tradition* until after the completion of the Talmud . . . followed by the *crystallized legalism* of casuistry until the middle of the 18th century . . . and the new freedom of our time of *criticism.* [118, pp. 31–33]

[5] Geiger [118]: "A new thought will only develop within a strong individual. . . . Even more than applying to a single man does this hold true in regard to a single folk-individuality. Science, art, and religion appear in their purest form only within a people to whom special talents are granted. . . . It is precisely the strength of Judaism . . . that it can express itself as healthy folk-individuality *which, on the one hand, sees humanity completely realized within itself and, on the other hand, nevertheless seeks to embrace the whole world of humanity existing outside of it.*" [pp. 4–6; italics supplied.] As a source for Baeck, Geiger attracts our attention as well when he writes: "Christianity is the genuine mother of mysticism and romanticism; Judaism, on the other hand, is clear, concrete, filled with fresh life . . . does not deny the world here below . . . a definite people . . . which yet embraces all of humanity." [p. 7]

This pattern seems to be drawn upon by Baeck in his own outline of Jewish history, written in 1938, and which was the framework of his last book:

> Three great times encompass the intellectual history of Judaism: the time of the Bible; following that, the time of penetration, the "midrash" which constantly takes hold of the Bible and ever anew emanates from it . . . and finally this new time seen so far only in its beginnings, extending the ways of a newly awakened strength of faith. [6, p. 9]

Geiger is not denied here. But an idea that has lost itself and must be reclaimed is no longer part of Baeck's approach to Jewish history. A more positive note is sounded. It is no more the idea alone which is stressed, but the carriers of that idea and their existence through the ages: the people Israel. Baeck never lost his link with Geiger and the "science of Judaism"; but the scientific exploration of the essence of Judaism had been enlarged to include the psychological inner depths of Israel. If the idea shaped the people in its process of attaining reality, a prophetic people had its own contribution to make within this process.

In his preface to the second edition of *Essence of Judaism,* Baeck has a clearer recognition of his own method:

> To recognize the essence, one must attempt to see the totality. One must look together upon the revealing and upon the determining, upon the organic and upon that from which all growth and development come, as well as what unfolds within all growth and development. One would seek to comprehend the driving, basic power which operates in the individual phenomena of a great historic life. . . . The historical and the systematical, the knowledge of the facts and the recognition of the ideas here interconnect and guide one another. It is the psychology of history which would prove itself in this task. [2, p. x]

Baeck's final work, *This People Israel,* stresses the nonrational aspect of man together with his reason. [8, p. 7] But already in 1905 there is an insistence upon man's inner development in which the categorical demand of ethics is *met* by an awareness for the *Mitmensch* and a readiness for the universal task which is contained in the essence of the individual, a readiness which is part of Israel's prophetic nature.

In outlining the essence of Judaism, Baeck comes to write a psychological study of the Jewish people. A people which responds to the moral law and lets itself be possessed by God *is* a special type, a chosen people. Within it, a strong particularism continues. But since it is tied to a universal task, it could not cause the character of this people to draw into itself, to reject the rest of mankind and to become hermits concerned with personal salvation alone. The personality of the prophets here testifies to the personality of this people which reached out to its neighbors in accordance with the prophetic word.

What is the tone, what is the feeling toward the rest of mankind within Israel? Baeck sees a spirit which has pride in itself, but also an openness toward the neighbor:

> Softly but clearly there sounds through the Bible the clear word that all men seek God: "From the rising of the sun unto the going down thereof the Lord's name is praised"; the heathen also seek to be pious. More and more, the only contrast which matters is the one between those who revere God and those who are godless . . . Terms like "Zaddik," identifying *the best among Jews,* now begin to be applied to the *heathens* . . . until we arrive at a statement which has become canonical: "The pious who are not Israelites also attain eternal bliss." [1, p. 48]

Something reaches out of the *soul* of Israel and touches the neighbor; and once again the polarity becomes operative. Into the polarity of Israel and the nations there is introduced the same tension of ethical imperatives existing in the tension of particularity and universality. But where the latter tension is logically derived out of ethics, Baeck now turns to Jewish existence in order to demonstrate that it is part of the nature of the (particular) people Israel to reach out in ethical action toward (general) mankind.

Israel's very flaws are adduced as proofs:

> Only in the kingdom of angels might there exist the separate, pure idea. Among human beings . . . where every soul has its body and its individuality, religious faith can exist only in some concrete form. It must unite with the specific character of a people or a community. . . . The so-called national particularism, a favorite reproach against Judaism, is nothing but the intense individuality which is the guarantor of permanence. In the area of religion there is no individuality which is not nationally determined and to that extent limited. [1, p. 50]

Israel's stubbornness is a necessary quality of life for a prophetic nation. A people must be self-confident, must express its individuality. The vital spark of its existence must accompany its message to the world. "The prophets speak *of the world* and its salvation, but they speak *to Israel;* only the colorless epigones always call to all humanity that it might listen and admire." [1, p. 52] Israel's harshness against the world, as often as not, is the hatred against sin so strongly ingrained in the prophetic character that an Abraham or a Job will battle God to see the better world established. Passion, *personal suffering,* and the experience of martyrdom gave Judaism that deeper individuality of a people who know the pathos of historical existence and write of it in their psalms and prayers. And because that religion is bound to the flux of human experience, there exists within it the love for man which is also the confidence in God Who is the foundation of all human existence.

Within this sketch of what can be called a psychological history of Israel, Baeck never forgets to stress the universal teachings of Judaism which keep Israel from being a closed church and makes it a world religion with a mission. That mission was not an expansionist policy of a nation, but an inner need of a people to share the truth revealed to them. The convert was welcomed; Israel only ceased mission work because of outside pressures. Israel needed mankind. Existence without the other nations is not possible for it: the revelation, the covenant, and the mission would have no meaning. And the history of the world, of humanity, would be just as impossible if there were no Jews. Baeck has the profound faith that is his own way of life: Israel is God's revelation. Through Israel, all the world will in the end come to God.

Baeck is presenting the essence of Judaism here. But underneath, not yet fully articulated, we come to see the character and essence of the Jewish people. The essence is to be known through the existence, the faith through the people. Judaism makes its way into the world in the polarity of a people and its faith.

III

The central section of the book is entitled "The Ideas of Judaism." It is divided into two parts: "Faith in God" and "Faith in Man." The latter section, in turn, is subdivided into three parts: "Faith in Ourselves," ". . . in our Fellow man," and ". . . in Mankind." It is significant that the section on man was enlarged to twice its size when Baeck rewrote *The Essence of Judaism* sixteen years later.

Baeck's opening statement in the 1905 edition presents religion in a manner not dissimilar to Harnack's and Ritschl's approach:

It is the task of science to observe and to explore the world; it is the task of religion to judge the world and to determine our personal relationship to it. Religion does not seek to know and to explain our experiences—*Weltanschauung* is the task of philosophy—but it tries to assess their intrinsic value. . . . Every religion goes back to the fundamental problem of optimism and pessimism, and to the fundamental question of whether or not there is a world order which makes for the good. The belief in the one or the other makes the essential difference, the unbridgeable opposites between religions. [1, p. 59]

Judaism, for Baeck, is the religion of optimism, the closed optimism of ethics which is not founded in finite man but in the one God whose essence is the moral law. With Cohen, Baeck sees God as securing morality, as the certainty for its eternal reality. [1]

In the second edition, these sentences are expanded into two pages; and, for the first time, the terms "mystery" and "commandment" enter the text. Where Baeck's religion of optimism had no problems in recognizing God's will in the moral commandment, the revised text places the mystery alongside the commandment and explores an area the earlier, more optimistic philosopher had tended to ignore. Yet Baeck was aware of anguish from the very beginning, and felt that the purest optimism was that which arose out of tragedy which in the end reconciles man with fate by pointing to the future. Optimism, for the 1905 edition, is central to all Jewish tradition:

The optimism of Judaism is *faith in the good,* i.e., *faith in God* and the therefore consequent *faith in man:* faith in God, who is the security for the true good; and faith in man, for whose sake the true good exists. . . . The faith in man has its threefold relatedness. First of all, it is *faith in ourselves* . . . ; then, it is *faith in one's neighbor* . . . ; finally, it is the *faith in humanity:* all men proceed towards the same holy goal. . . . Moral assertion of self, the full awareness of equality, the messianic certainty of God's kingdom; these are the expressions of this optimism, depending on whether it reaches toward us, our neighbors, or humanity. [1, p. 60]

Man—individually or as the community—is here seen in the context of a faith which affirms God as the good and has to approach the world with an absolute optimism in which the attitude of the nineteenth century is summarized. In this religion of ethical optimism there is no room for shadows, and there is a fundamental dislike of any mythology. Baeck did not deny the existence of mythological material in the Bible; but he found it controlled by Biblical ethics. Mythic imagination helped man express the Divine in life; but Judaism was not preoccupied with defining God. The prophets only show what God is to man:

> What they know of God is that He has proclaimed to man what is good . . . the one true good. . . . Morality is the content of the idea of God, is the essence of God. Where this insight rules, there is no room for . . . mythology. [1, p. 63]

The mystery is here rejected. It is the moral law, the ethical imperatives which are the essence of God and are available to man. The definition of the one God calls for the one loyalty, the total commitment of one's heart and soul and might to the set task; and the seeking out of the mysteries is seen as an evasion of that task. Behind this thought, there is the knowledge of the Jewish religious community and its encounter with God in all aspects of existence. Israel is to be holy through its obedience to the moral imperatives which are the will of God. And this will of God is clearly known by Judaism. Nevertheless, religion is more than a philosophic discussion:

> Religion does not consist of our *recognition* that there is a God. Only that is religion: that we can *love* God and should love Him; that our confidence, our courage and our humility turn to him; that we can think of Him and pray to Him, that we can hear His commandment and revelation. God is the God of religion only when He is *our God* and we can speak to Him: Thou, O God, art our Father. [1, p. 64]

The personal God enters a structure of idealistic thinking; and we are here reminded that the faith in God always preceded thoughts about God for Baeck. And Baeck's Judaism is more than the religion of duty; it stresses the warm and intimate relationship between man and God; the God to Whom one speaks, the God Who loves man.

Baeck presents Israel as the first to teach a love emanating from God, embracing all humanity:

> God loves us. This means: always and everywhere, He is close to us, so that we are protected in all places and at all times and can trust in Him. . . . Love is therefore the basic revelation of the Divine essence. [1, p. 68]

He indicates many of the Biblical references to God's love in which we see Israel come to full awareness of this aspect of God's essence.

But love has to lead to the concept of grace, since Israel cannot possibly have earned all of the blessings granted it. In this, too, Baeck finds evidence for the personal God as a necessary concept:

> The deeper God's love was felt, the more human was its form of expression. You can only proclaim love in the manner of human love. That which we experience as the most personal . . . we can only apprehend in personal words. One cannot pray in concepts; one cannot hope in definitions and in the abstract. The God toward Whom our devotions and our confidence strive can only be the *personal* God, Who loves us, Who is our Father. [1, p. 70]

Next to the *Sh'ma*, the affirmation of God as One and Unique, there comes the Biblical theophany of the merciful and loving God.

Man's response to Divine love is humility; "the inmost font of all faith and all religious mood, of all receptivity and openness to God: *humility*, which is nothing but awareness of the immeasurable Divine love." [1, p. 71] Within man, the sense of humility is matched by his awareness that he is God's child, and he always turns with confidence to the rock of his being. Baeck sees the great contradictions of human existence in the paradoxes of religion:

> Here, in the humility, the *first of these paradoxes of religion* reveals itself: the conscious, definite rejection of all conflict between the finite human life aware of its finitude and also its unending hopes and longings; between the limited life on earth which knows of its boundaries and between its searching and confidence which span the world and look up to God. [1, p. 72]

The tension between these contradictions of human existence, according to Baeck, does not result in a reasoned, logical act. The ability to *surrender* to God is not the end product of logical thinking. It is that wisdom of experience and life which gave confidence to martyrs like Chanania ben Teradion who could praise God's justice on the way to the funeral pyre, to the great Rabbi Akiba, a man of anguish and sorrows who suffered so much that it might have seemed a mockery for a lesser man to say what Akiba did say: Whatever God does, is done for the good.

Baeck's description of suffering as a way of learning, of the nobility of suffering which has marked Israel, might have seemed an unnecessary excursus for his readers at the turn of the century. Was it really necessary to exalt such strange statements as Simon ben Jochai's "The best which was given to Israel was given to it through sorrow"? Could Baeck really say:

> Human sufferings are a religious possession to the extent and in so far as they can become a duty. We are not only to *suffer* pains—it would turn them into the saddest misfortunes if we only knew to bear suffering—but we must actively *carry* them, we must meet their tests with all of our strength. We should not deny pain and persecutions by sinking ourselves in God and explaining all suffering as deceitful appearances; we must affirm suffering with secure certainty; by turning it into an ethical imperative. Do your duty, and the worst will have to become good for you; all the masters and teachers of Israel are agreed upon this. The question of theodicy is answered—or eliminated—for them since life is viewed as a body. It is not a present that it should be or is given to us, but a task to be fulfilled; and therefore, it is worthwhile to be lived. [1, p. 75]

Baeck placed his emphasis upon the fact that the masters and teachers of Israel had not argued their way to this position; it had come to them out of the experiences of their own existence. Baeck took this point of view into his system as a necessary balance to an optimism which was not perfect until it had come to terms will all aspects of life including the tragic one. True optimism is not conditional, is not self-deceiving; it must know the dark side as well. In Baeck's life we come to recognize the same teaching in its concreteness: In the concentration camp, suffering became an ethical imperative in which God was present.

Baeck did not teach humility as an independent religious sentiment; faith that is only faith, humility that is only humility, are sharply rejected. If humility is a sentiment, it can result in abject humility before God and the worst kind of arrogance unto fellow men. Baeck compares humility with modesty: Something must have been achieved first. Faith and good action endure only as one religious unity. It is man's responsibility to act, and, in this way, to resolve what Baeck here calls the second great paradox of religion:

> For Judaism, the independent ethical personality of man is the integrating factor of religion. Faith in the just God necessarily contains faith in oneself. Only thus do we solve the *second great paradox* of religious awareness: that man is completely dependent upon God and is yet free, that his whole life endures only through God and that man yet has his own independence. [1, p. 75]

Again, twofoldness: the feeling of humility and the joy of action, dependent man who can act independently as God's partner and thus enter the "kingdom of God." There is no mythical kingdom—it is the simple classical word for the free service of God, for joyful, ethical obedience.

Baeck's faith is grounded in this world, in the ethical action, in the reality of the good. It unites religion and ethics in an unbreakable union, strengthening ethics by guarding against relativism and ethical opportunism. It is the unconditional call: Thou shalt, thou shalt not. It gives commandments, not suggestions; prohibitions, not just warnings.

God's justice becomes the elevation of morality, becomes God's holiness: "The Holy God shows His holiness through justice." Baeck's teaching here is in full accord with traditional Judaism. Nevertheless, his liberalism breaks through: When God's holiness comes to shine clearly in the acts of social justice and their imperatives, ritual takes on less importance; the holiness of God needs less of a traditional framework if it penetrates all life as ethics. For Baeck in this work, the holy is the ethical, and the ethical is the holy. And it is in the nature of this polarity to move outward toward the universal, rather than inward toward the traditional particularity. Its existential reality differs for a Baeck, who lives in both Jewish and Western culture, and for the traditional Jew to whom Halacha and liturgy speak in far less flexible terms. Baeck's polarities embrace all Jews; but in the construction of *The Essence of Judaism* there is more room for the liberal than for the traditional observer of Judaism.

Baeck also takes note of Divine anger. He sees it directed against evil rather than evildoers—all ideas of God become part of his structure of ethical imperatives which demand specific action from the individual and the community. Out of this idea of God's nature, a third paradox is constructed:

> Before the one God we cannot be humble without doing good, and we cannot do good without being humble. To have one and to lack the other would mean cutting God in half. And yet, and this is the *third great paradox of religion,* God, Who is filled with eternal love, also has a definite expression of His essence in His angry and zealous justice. To relate this to man: Our life has its *eternal worth through God*; and yet it is *worthless and godless without human virtue.* God gives the true life, and God demands the true life. The idea of *atonement* gives the answer here. [1, p. 86]

Man stands between devotion and duty; and all of existence becomes his duty. Both aspects are brought home to him by his religion which, fundamentally, is *the religion of life*; it is not that which is brought to life—it is life itself. And Baeck here picks up the mood of twentieth century man in his estrangement and loneliness which is both man's anguish and his greatness: "In the inmost soul, everyone is ultimately alone; for every personality is unique upon earth." [1, p. 87] The way to fellow men here leads through God, whom man finds is an inwardness which in the end links him with his neighbor whose life is established upon the same foundation. Baeck sees this inner loneliness as a place of realizing oneself—in the context of an ethics which is built upon the awareness that all men are unique, and that it is in the world, among our fellow men, in the ethical action, that self-realization takes place. Man's alienation from the world is shattered by the response to the ethical imperatives which rise out of this world, enter man's ethical awareness, and bridge the gap between man and man, man and the world, man and God through acts of justice in which man achieves himself and becomes a co-creator of the better world, a partner of the Divine. In Baeck's ethical idealism loneliness becomes a strength, not a weakness. It is an aspect of man's nature linking him with an ethical task in which it is not the Divine grace which heals man's split from the world but the redemptive action which is found within the ethical powers of man. Baeck does not place this outside of religion: Prayer, the Sabbath, the richness of Jewish existence are all part of the sanctification of existence in which man encounters the Divine; but the encounter, throughout this work, is the ethical act. Yet Judaism is instructed by God as to what the ethical act must be; there is no ethics in Baeck's faith without the concept of God.

Baeck closes the section on God by once again stressing the principle of dynamic development: The Jewish concept of God has grown through the ages. In Baeck's methodology, the idea has its own reality which language very often does not begin to grasp; the words lag behind the concept. Attacking current (1950) Biblical scholarship and its use of *Jahwe* which ignores the spirit behind the Psalmist's words, Baeck here shows a relationship to the traditional thinking of men like S. R. Hirsch and David Hoffman. The heart of Judaism is the faith in God:

> The martyrs died for the One God, the God of love and of justice. . . .
> Faith in God gives our history its world meaning, its heroic purpose.

Only he whose existence is determined and established within the One Unique God is a Jew. . . . Hear O Israel, the Eternal is our God, the Eternal is unique. [1, pp. 91–92]

IV

"Faith in Man," the next section, was completely rewritten and enlarged to twice its size in the 1922 edition. The basic approach remains the same: Religion is grounded in human experience which, fully explored, is a statement of the Divine revelation which is the foundation of man. Its opening sentences are a defense against the charge of humanism or pantheism:

The consequences of faith in God is faith in man. We live through God and in God, but as free, independent beings. This is the difference between the teachings of Judaism and *pantheism* which sees God only in us and us only in God. We are free and independent, but not completely isolated and set apart from God; that is the difference between Judaism and the so-called *deism* which has only intimations of an indefinite God of the "far away" who is not accessible to the searching heart. [1, p. 96]

Deism also has to be rejected since it limits the quest of the religious personality. And the strong assertion of the human area as the place for the revelation is given its theological foundation through the given faith in God. The tension of polarity which is man's existence before God makes pantheism impossible for Baeck; this same split between the human and the Divine, seen in its more tragic dimensions, is made the basis of an attack against pantheism in "Individuum Ineffabile," one of Baeck's final writings. [54]

Judaism's definition of man begins in the Bible for Baeck. Man formed in the "image of God" is more than a poetic statement; it is the affirmation of the *oneness of humanity* demanded by the One God. Baeck affirms the field of ethics as the one area where the human being can be a genius, can be holy. Yet the holy is out of reach; man is man and not God.

Developing the concept of man as it exists in the Biblical tradition, Baeck stresses the worth of man which is not so much derived from an as yet unredeemed world as from the imprint of God upon man's features. Yet once again, the paradox of human life arises: Formed in God's image, man has a task given to him which he cannot fulfill in its totality. How, then, shall he justify himself before God?

The revised edition clarifies the pattern; but in this 1905 statement we already find the interpenetration of the three paradoxes which is at the heart of Baeck's system of polarity. Man's knowledge of his own finiteness and his infinite hopes; his recognition of his utter dependency upon God and his independence of ethical action—these blend together in the paradox of a life of inestimable worth which is yet found wanting before the Throne of Judgment. For man comes to know both the God Who is far away and the God Who is near, as man asserts his independence in righteous action. The work itself hallows the world and brings the immediacy of God with it; and the goals for which man strives are with the distant God Whose unutterable greatness is then linked with striving man. And at that point the third paradox is resolved. Man is redeemed, and so is the world. It is only a momentary redemption, for man cannot remain holy. But each righteous act justifies his existence, and makes him aware that there is worthwhileness in his life which can and does make him, at the point of ethical action, little lower than the angels. He can never feel adequate to the task; he will always live in tension; but the knowledge of the near and the far God, of man's limitations and man's potential as a free agent—these bring him to that task with the hope that God's justice will be balanced by God's mercy.

Baeck comes to resolve the stated paradox through the liturgy of the Day of Atonement, where individual man must appear before God to be judged. The idea of original sin cannot be maintained in the face of the concept of individual man. And if man is responsible, his life continues to have meaning, even through failures:

> Man nevertheless remains the image of God, the child of God. He remains thus *by strength of his essence,* however little he may have done to prove himself as such *by strength of his actions* . . . since it is established in the essence of God that the God of justice is also the God of love. [1, p. 99]

Justice and love are reconciled in Judaism, the religion of redemption and reconciliation.

In Baeck's concept of man, the redemptive act of the ethical deed takes precedence over all else. Baeck here found himself at odds with conditional doctrines and practices concerning the sacrificial service—

and he did not hesitate to attack. The idea of the sacrificial service, according to him, obscured the great teaching of reconciliation. The sacrifice as atonement pushed itself between God and man and acted as mediator. While it was to be a bridge, it acted as a wall. And Baeck applauds the daring words of Rabbi Elieser: "On the day the Temple fell, an iron wall fell which had erected itself between Israel and the Father in heaven." Baeck granted the educational value of the pageantry. He rejected the theological idea behind the institution of the Temple, and felt that Israel had, in effect, rejected that idea as soon as the full concept of atonement and expiation had been clearly understood by the people.

The task to be holy does not permit man to come to rest in Judaism; it drives him onward to its ultimate logical development of *kiddush ha-Shem,* "the sanctification of the Holy Name." As every immoral act is a profanation of God's name, so does every ethical step move man closer to the Holy, to the sanctification of the Divine. God's existence is established by the reality of the ethical road which leads to Him.

Kiddush ha-Shem is viewed as more than a category of Jewish understanding; it is also a category of Jewish existence labeled "martyrdom." It rises out of Jewish life and Jewish faith:

> Martyrdom is the truest sanctification of the Holy Name, the clearest testimony of God, the most certain proof of God's existence. It is the final word, the ultimate consequence of moral responsibility. Where there is the unconditional duty to testify of God through faith in Him and obedience to His imperatives, the boundary of our existence is not the boundary of the duty. Our life is little and poor against the exaltedness and fullness of the task. The finest life means nothing compared to the moral demand. And thus we must be ready to sacrifice our life for the good. The ethical will finds its sole goal in its agreeing with God. And to agree with God, man must be able *to surrender his will for life.* [1, p. 105]

Against the acknowledged multitudes of those who died for *kiddush ha-Shem* without knowing why, Baeck would have us remember men like Akiba who "served God with all his soul—with his death as with his life." In the revised text, Baeck comes back to the martyr's death and sees it as overcoming the mythology of death as the final proof of creation and of life itself.

Even martyrdom has a twofoldness for Leo Baeck. Alongside the death which is the final word of the ethical imperative, there stands the sometimes far more difficult martyr's life. At times the martyrdom of life precedes the death; it too is a culmination of the ethical imperatives in human existence. It speaks of the unyieldingness of the ethical drive, of Israel's stubborn faith characterized by Tacitus as *fides obstinata*. Israel always had the will and the capacity to suffer for its faith. In its suffering, Baeck saw another twofoldness:

> In the area of martyrdom there is fulfilled the commandment that our intention must unconditionally become our action and must find its clear and constant expression in our life. That is one commandment of ethical truth, one side of it. The other side is the injunction that our action must be, always and only, the consequence of our thought and feeling. The two together are the truth which Judaism demands from all its adherents: *the truth of life and the truth of the heart.* They belong together: "Speak truth in the heart" and testify of it through life itself. [1, pp. 106–107]

Baeck here applies his method of "twofoldness" (in the terminology of this 1905 edition) to *hypocrisy*. There is the hypocrisy of action, devoid of meaning because it is not infused with inner conviction and is thus a simulation, an act performed for the benefit of those round about. There is the hypocrisy of thought, which cannot pass the basic test of Judaism: Its realization as an ethical act. It too is a simulation, the self-deception of one who would like to entertain noble thoughts without responding to the challenge. The inner and outer world must waken to each other and must meet in the field of ethical action. Baeck's emphasis upon Jewish thought stresses the necessary existence of moral law, of the Ten Commandments, behind ethical action; and his awareness of the depth of man's nature extends the realm of moral law into the thoughts and desires of man. The twofoldness of thought and action may not be separated; only together do they bring man into the true realm of the moral life. And both Spinoza and the Talmud are quoted to show that thought and action must be one, and that they are built upon a *selfless* motive: "Happiness is not the reward of virtue, but is virtue itself" and "the reward of fulfillment of duty is the fulfillment of duty itself; and the punishment of sin is sin itself."

According to Baeck, the dynamic development of Jewish thought is bound up with this principle of selflessness. If it also includes, as do other religions, the concept of rewards for righteous actions, Baeck would remind us that there is more in the hope for reward than selfishness. Man wants to complete and to fulfill himself, and his striving for happiness merges with his striving for perfection. Out of the tensions of his life of paradoxes, there emerges man's hope of immortality, for

> as an ethical personality man belongs to another world than just the world of the senses; he is "a son of the coming world." That which is divine within him carries the seed of perfection in it and is therefore above death and defeat. Faith in immortality has its deepest foundation in the eternity of our task and our purpose, in the contrast between the ethical ideal and the terrestrial fact. This abyss, as we have seen, is closed through the concept of atonement. And therefore the essential place of immortality resides in the concept of atonement. Eternity is the great atonement of finiteness. [1, p. 109]

For Baeck, this notion of immortality is essential in presenting man as a creature of infinite worth whose life has meaning and purpose. It is a view which rises out of man's nature; in the end, the pureness of man in this world reflects the vision of the world to come.

Where does this faith in man lead Baeck? Primarily, to the assertion of the religion of duty which lifts him beyond his boundaries: "Two things are united in man: the sure relationship to the reality of this world, and the clear experiencing of the insufficiency of this reality. . . . Without the one or without the other there would be no Judaism." [1, p. 112]

Some would say that the Jew clings too much to this world. But if there is no value in this life—can there be value in the life to come? Both worlds are emphasized in Judaism: *There is no teaching of doctrine in Judaism without the teaching of ethics.* Faith in God and in redemption is empty without sure faith in ourselves as ethical beings who live and act freely in this world. And sometimes, a "Hellenic" *Weltanschauung* has accused the Jew of looking too much beyond this world, of giving too little assent to the gifts of life. Baeck would remind those critics *that there is* NO TEACHING OF ETHICS *in Judaism without the teachings of doctrine.* We can only believe in man because man is divine, fashioned in God's image. Judaism is faith in God, in His redemption; it is the noblest optimism in which eternal life is part of the Divine gift of life, is part of the eternal task. And man's moral powers, his ability to do the ethical act, is in the end grounded upon the great vision of Judaism and its faith in man.

V

The section on "Faith in Man" in *The Essence of Judaism* is divided into three parts. From the assertion of faith in himself, man must of necessity move outward, first to his neighbor, his fellow man, and from there to all of humanity. Baeck and also Buber are very much dependent upon Hermann Cohen at this point.

Cohen's pioneer study of 1888, "The Love of Neighbor in the Talmud" [96, I, 145–175], had defended the Jewish community and its literature against a virulent anti-Semitic attack. Basing himself upon Biblical critics like Rudolf Kittel and Franz Delitsch, Professor Paul de Lagarde had claimed that love of neighbor was absent in Judaism; even the Biblical injunctions to love one's neighbor (*rea*) only referred to fellow Jews. Cohen correctly denied this and established that *rea* referred to the *Nebenmensch*, i.e., the other one who exists alongside of us, who in the end is one with us. Hermann Cohen wrote, in 1888:

> The love of the stranger is therefore a creative moment in the development of the concept of man as the one next to us. And for the history of moral ideas one fact must be firmly established by me: love of neighbor, more accurately love of one who by nationality and faith is a stranger—this love is a commandment of Judaism. [96, I, 150]

Baeck refers to Cohen in his footnotes, and clearly shows his indebtedness to his teacher. [1, p. 165] But Baeck does not only follow Cohen in establishing that love of neighbor is part of Jewish ethics; he makes it a fundamental aspect of Judaism, a necessary consequence rising out of faith in God:

> Just as faith in God necessarily results in faith in ourselves, so does it lead to faith in our neighbor. The prophet derives it in this fashion: "Have we not all one father, has not one God created us? How could we be faithless one against the other?" And thus, too, we have one of the sages of the Talmud, Rabbi Tanchuma, stating: "Say not: because I am despised, may my neighbor also be despised as I am; because I am cursed, I will also curse my neighbor. When you think and act thusly, know whom you despise and whom you curse: Him Who has created man in His image."
> [1, p. 113]

The idea is clear, and the text accurately reflects the approach of Judaism in the Biblical and Talmudic tradition. We can note Baeck's constant struggle with the language of his faith. Earlier, Baeck had expressed his conviction that one cannot follow the text slavishly and expect a full understanding of the idea which is trying to break into speech. Baeck always reached for the idea behind the text. Many Biblical verses express the idea of the neighbor as equal, as brother, to be loved, to be recognized as oneself. In probing these verses, Baeck exhibited a certain daring in his translations which often departed from the norm. The text above is a good example of this (Malachi 2:10b):

מדוע נבער איש באהיו ?

The standard translation reads: "Why do we deal treacherously every man against his brother . . . ?" Biblical scholarship has accepted "faith-lessly" as a better version.[6] Baeck uses "brother" and "the other" inter-changeably here. It is a prophetic word which rises above the historical framework of the utterance (Ibn Ezra relates it to the divorce of the Samaritan wives); a word in which the criticism ("Why do we deal faithlessly") becomes a positive assertion ("How could we be faith-less"); a word in which it is so clear that all are God's children that the term "brother" and the term "other one" are identical. In the end, it becomes an illuminated translation.

Baeck's translation of the rabbinic text also has its own literary quality. The Hebrew text (Bereshit Rabba, Parasha 24:8) reads:

בן אזאי אומר זה ספר תולדות אדם זה כלל גדול בתורה ר' עקיבא אומר
ואהבת לרעך כמוך זה כלל גדול בתורה שלא תאמר הואיל ונתכליתי יתבזה
חבירי עמי הואיל ונתכללתי יתקלל חבירי עמי אמר רבי תנחומה עם עשית
כן רע למי אתה מבזה בדמות אלהים עשה אותו.

Our translation, as literally as possible, would be as follows:

Ben Azzai said: " 'This is the book of the generations of man [when God created man, he made him in His image].' That is the key principle of the Torah." Rabbi Akiba said: " 'Thou shalt love thy neighbor as thyself' is the key principle of the Torah. Thou shalt not say: because I have been despised, let my neighbor [*chaver*, 'comrade'] be despised with me. Because I have been cursed, let my neighbor be cursed with me." Rabbi Tanchuma said: "Know against whom [*l'mi*] you direct this despising. In the image of God made He him."

[6] Julius Bewer, *The Prophets* (New York, 1949), p. 595, suggests "faithless" for "treacherous." Bewer is considered one of the sounder older critics.

Differences in Baeck's translation can be noted here. Possibly, Baeck was quoting without having the text in front of him. Nevertheless, the slight change from "let my neighbor be cursed" to "let me curse my neighbor" is significant. For Baeck, the imperatives of ethical action see passivity which results in harming one's fellow man as a direct act of evil; and, in the context of the verse, his translation is quite accurate. This also applies to the ending. The Hebrew text can only indicate elliptically that man, in despising man, despises God. And Baeck is absolutely faithful to the idea behind the text when he translates that the man who curses his fellow man curses God. In the revised edition, Baeck turned to the first part of this midrashic text for an even stronger example of the principle that God's image unites all men. Baeck here was the exegete, the *baal ha-midrash,* who felt the need to wrestle with the text and to extract the fullest meaning from the tradition.

The Biblical injunction of loving one's neighbor as oneself is a statement containing Baeck's stress on faith in self and faith in fellow man, in the *Mitmensch*:

> There is an absolute law which can never cease: the law of the right of men. Because of it, every human being can demand that we recognize him as our fellow, as our *Mitmensch*; and our sense of justice should already turn us into good and loving men.
>
> Through the emphasis on this right which we are to grant our fellow, man is taken out of the uncertainty of mere feeling and is placed upon the firm soil of clear duty, the sober action. [1, pp. 115–116]

We are back to the religion of duty here; and, indeed, Baeck quotes Kant's *Zum Ewigen Frieden*: "Both, love of man and respect for the right of man, are duty. One is conditional, the other one unconditional, an absolutely commanding duty." [1, p. 116][7]

Baeck sees the rights of man dominating Judaism in a number of ways, including the redefinition of slavery in ancient times. In the Greek and Roman world, the slave was an object treated in the corpus juris under the section on property. In Jewish law, he was a person with rights, and his master was not his owner. The Jewish society was not founded upon the institution of slavery; and its social legislation included everyone:

[7] Baeck is here quoting Kant's *Definitivart: zum ewigen Frieden* Anhang III.

All who are encompassed by the area of a state belong to one another morally, are members of a moral community of duty. . . . *The ideal concept of society* is hereby created. Every individual is honored as a member of the human community. Not only political and economic interests but also human tasks and human achievements are the bond which unites all the inhabitants of the land. They are a community of human beings. And therefore all duties relate to *man*, i.e., also to the stranger. . . . Social understanding awoke here and became action. [1, p. 122]

The social legislation of the community thus became a duty for the individual: to recognize in the right of the *Mitmensch* the Divine right. "Give God what is God's; for you and what is yours are God's."

Baeck notes that there is the just act, and the feeling of benevolence; and the latter cannot be a substitute for the former. Both are duties of life. Love for fellow men—"Love thy neighbor as thyself"—turns acts of duty into encounters between soul and soul. And the enemy is included. The apologetics of the book come to defend Hillel's negative formulation of the Golden Rule: The negative decision to hurt no one results in the positive love for all. This whole section was rewritten and improved by Baeck when he published the second edition. What remained was his insistence upon *the moral courage of love* with its quality of justice. It is love for one's neighbor which leads us to reprove him for his sins, which makes it an obligation to show him the right way. Yet sensitivity for the unique worth of the individual must dominate our relationship, according to the Talmudic word: "He who shames his neighbor, who causes him to blush in public—has shed blood."

The mission of Israel is contained in duties we have toward our fellow man. Israel's testimony to the One God Who is approached through the ethical deed stands in the center of community life which turns this testimony into a covenant where everyone must be helped by his neighbor. The wrong committed by one man in the community becomes the burden of all:

The community is not only responsible to God if someone dies of hunger or freezes to death in its midst, but is also responsible for the man in its midst whose soul rigidifies and whose conscience dies. The totality is to be responsible for all its souls . . . as . . . redemption enters into it. It is a community of justice and of love, a *community of atonement*. [1, p. 131]

Love of neighbor is here seen as the essence of Judaism; and the polemic against Christianity is resumed with the repetition of Baeck's position, outlined in the last chapter, that Christianity has to go back to its Jewish origins for this ethical emphasis. Even so, according to Baeck, Christianity denies salvation to some, limiting its concept of man. Buddhism's "moral lassitude," by the same token, lacks the full reverence for fellow men; only Judaism contains this to the fullest degree possible. In Judaism, zedakah links love of neighbor to self-fulfillment; and "if our life has its never-ceasing moral strength in the faith in ourselves, the unmeasurable wealth of its contents is gained through the faith in our fellowman." [1, p. 133]

The progression of Baeck's presentation is from faith in self to faith in fellow man, and from there to faith in mankind. But its foundation had to be an abiding faith in God Who has set the good into mankind and Who guarantees that it will be realized in the days ahead. Faith in God brings with it faith in the future.

The tension of the paradox finds one resolution in mankind's unlimited future:

> Man is called to the upward path of ethics, and the unmeasurable task is set before him. Yet here on earth, the strivings of individual man are confronted by the boundaries of his short existence in which he cannot achieve perfection. Only humanity continues. The endless way stretches before it, the possibility of endless striving is open to it. . . . In it, the good is to be realized. [1, p. 134]

The paradox of finite man and his infinite task are solved for Baeck in the affirmation of mankind which joins together finite moments of individuals and reaches out toward fulfillment. The infinite task needs infinite time. For man, this means immortality as a postulate of faith. For mankind, here affirmed as the area in which the good realizes itself through ethical action, it means a world which will endure as the place where the task will be performed, a world in which the future of mankind itself will be secured. The infinite here touches the finite and leaves its imprint: an optimism, a messianism which was also the vital spark of Hermann Cohen's Judaism.

Faith in man thus culminates in faith in mankind which will fulfill the task of redemption; and it is affirmed in Biblical and Talmudic thought by the joyful affirmation of "the days which are to come." The twofoldness of the promise together with the commandment enters Jewish life here. The future itself becomes the task, a salvation which has to be earned by man. This gives the ultimate meaning to history, which is a universal history of mankind responding to the ethical challenge [1, pp. 134–135] (a hopeful evolutionism here gives evidence of the unclouded optimism of the world in which Baeck still found himself in 1905). Yet this faith in man was grounded upon Baeck's faith in God: "It is not the human element but the Divine which makes history. . . . It is not the plans and designs of man which shape what endures . . . the proudest nations are only a tool of God." [1, pp. 135–136] The ancient Biblical words here come to affirm the universality of history. Ethical monotheism needs the dimension of history; and history thus becomes a category of religion. Baeck notes at this point that "the prophets did not understand God through history; they understood history through God." That is why all injustice can be viewed with the optimism which sees injustice ultimately conquered, why evil and evildoers must fall: The theodicy of history will not permit anything else.

In Baeck's presentation, the messianic future, in the framework of an optimistic faith in mankind, is based on one humanity which has achieved reconciliation with God and man; universal peace is the attainment of ethical action which was the prophetic imperative of the end of days. And because the prophets had this faith in man and mankind, they spoke less of the time to come and more of the man to come. There arose the concept of the ideal man of the future, of Israel's anointed one: the messiah. And, as Baeck seeks the concept behind Biblical language, so does he strive to go beyond the poetic imagery and the allegory which finds its way into Jewish theology. The poetry is not rejected. Instead, it is placed in the realm of ethics. Baeck sees the vision of perfect man fusing with that aspect of Jewish life in which the task for the future becomes the test for the present: The Jewish New Year, in which man's actions of the past year are reviewed, is also the *messianic festival* in which the dream of the future must meet the test of the moral law. It is ethical messianism which is presented by these festivals. The most intense and particularistic Jewish Holy Days—when Israel is as the high priest appearing before God—asserts the universality of a faith which sends Israel out of the sanctuary in search of its fellow men.

As Israel gained in tolerance, it also emphasized its *messianic task* which did not limit the worth of its neighbors. Its own history was understood as world history. And, since it was often tragic history, the concept of *its suffering for the sake of the world* came to contain both faith in man and faith in the future. Its own fate became a messianic sermon in which an answer was given to the paradox between the sufferings of its existence and the fullness of its expectation. Baeck saw his people Israel crowned by this self-assured concept of ethical messianism. Against Buddhist resignation and a Christian messianism which Baeck considered particularistic, Baeck asserts this Jewish ethical messianism as one of the great contributions made by Judaism to the world. In it, history becomes a moral process: Generations who cannot repay the debt of the past must bestow blessings upon the future.

> So it is in the life of the individual. We pay our children that which we have received from our parents. And so it shall be the history of humanity. Every era must work for the coming days and build a new step which will lead up to God's kingdom of the future. That is the meaning of world history. Through this faith in humanity, existence gains its eternal goal for life. [1, p. 146]

Once more, the exploration of an aspect of Jewish thought has led Baeck to the point from which he had originated: The call for ethical action is paramount throughout the Jewish faith.

Yet one question remained: If the messianic mission is essential to Judaism, why are the Jews not engaged in missionary work? And why does particularism express itself so strongly in this people of the universal faith? What progress has this people Israel made in its last two thousand years of existence in terms of the goals presented to it by the classic Judaism of its first thousand years? In the final section of this work, Baeck attempts to cope with these questions.

A close comparison between Harnack's *Essence of Christianity* and Baeck's *The Essence of Judaism,* up to this point of our presentation, shows more likenesses than differences. But one basic difference endures. Harnack concentrates upon that unique moment in time when divine revelation cut into history and separated Calvary from ordinary life. Baeck concentrates upon a millennium of Jewish development, from Moses to the Talmudic sages, in which classic Judaism was forged. Had Baeck also lifted that millennium out of history, no major difference would exist between him and Harnack. One moment of eternity is as another before God. But Baeck extended the process of revelation to all of time. Every moment of existence is holy, God's revelation is in the creation as in the redemption, and it comes to everyone. Judaism does not go back to Sinai to relive the moment of revelation. The life of the people Israel, from then until now and until the end of time, is part of the continuous revelation which enters the world with every moral act.

The counterpart to Harnack's Calvary is Baeck's people, Israel. For Baeck saw the Jewish people as a continuous revelation to mankind, as a unique people. Israel had brought ethical monotheism to the world; and every generation of Israel moves through the chain of its tradition and encounters God in its past—which is also its present—and in the world of man. The essence of Judaism and of Israel is the openness to the revelation, the continuous receptivity to the will of God which is then to be communicated to the world. Israel is the priest-people which is to be a light to the nations—but it is not lifted to a different plateau from the rest of humanity. It acts within the world; it is elected because it is *part* of mankind, and mankind contains within itself the knowledge of God which can never be made an exclusive knowledge, reached only through special rituals. The essence of Judaism is the twofoldness of the faith and the people: The ethical monotheism unfolds in the moral action of a people which would realize the messianic vision by fulfilling itself—together with the rest of mankind—through the creation of God's kingdom on earth. But why—Baeck has to ask—did Judaism and its people appear to falter in its task? Why did it not bring all men to the knowledge of the creative task which is fulfillment and redemption?

Baeck notes that Judaism did start out as a missionary movement. As the Diaspora expanded, so did the Jewish mission reach out to the world. Much of the success of Christianity was due to the preparatory work of the Jewish missionaries. But the Jews were and are a people of history; and history now rose up to overwhelm them:

A promising Jewish dissemination was ready to bear fruit, when a far-reaching catastrophe destroyed the harvest. With the violence of an earthquake, the foundations of Jewish life were destroyed by two fruitless risings. The first was against Trajan, by the Jewish Diaspora; the second, against Hadrian, by the homeland. Hundreds of thousands died. The victors knew no mercy. It was an unending blood-letting. [1, p. 147]

Fateful consequences ensued. Israel's life as a people was maimed; it became a living martyrdom. Whatever strength remained to it had to be used for self-preservation. And so the cultivated field was given over to Christianity which had obtained more favorable political conditions for itself. Israel turned away from the Graeco-Roman world, appalled by the cruelty and viciousness of its triumph over Israel. A gap opened between Israel and the nations. When time had healed the wounds, the Church stood between Israel and the world. Inner necessity made the Church an enemy of a faith in which it had to acknowledge truth despite its claim to the one truth. And, as the power of the Church grew, Israel saw itself threatened by death if it pursued its missionary activities. Israel then drew into itself.

Now, Israel came to realize that the paradox of its life was also its preservation: By preserving itself as a particular people, Israel could remain true to its universal task. It served mankind by guarding the treasure entrusted to itself:

> Israel understood that *existence, too, can be a mission;* the mere perpetuation of self became a sermon preached to the world. More and more, it appeared to be the plan of providence that the nations of the world should first enter the environments of other confessions in order to be led by them into the world of religion; but that Judaism through all this time was to preserve the pure faith in the One God as the definite goal of the religious development of humanity. This was the exalted mission in whose service Israel labored. [1, p. 149]

But can a religious community isolate itself? Baeck tried to show that the Church, as its temporal power waned, used *doctrine* to build a protecting fence around itself and its adherents. In Judaism, on the other hand,

> definite actions were demanded in which concern for the preservation of the totality found expression. The tasks established by faith in God and faith in man were joined by the obligations rising out of membership in the community; and both had to be fulfilled by action. These obligations . . . are the *ceremonial legislations.* [1, pp. 150–151][8]

Ceremonial legislations were not to be confused with the Torah, were not considered "good deeds," and were to fade away in messianic times. Yet Baeck recognized their usefulness in preserving the community (although the traditional Jew was naturally upset at this liberal treatment of the ritual). He saw in ceremonials an expansion of the religious dimension of Jewish life. Time becomes hallowed by prayer; home and sanctuary are enriched by the symbols which lead to deeper contempla-

---

[8] His position here recapitulates his statement of 1895, covered earlier.

tion and sentiment. Ceremonies form a link between the people and the past with its great traditions. The outside world might strive to turn the Jew into a peddler; the structure of his faith, instead, turned him into a religious thinker. Ceremony did not separate man from God; it led to Him. Each holyday held built-in imperatives which led Israel to love of neighbor and thus to God: Sabbath and Passover brought the stranger into the home; the task for the dead united everyone in the hallowing of life; and family life took on a dignity and beauty in which the basic worth of life was ever celebrated. The "fence around the Torah" did preserve Israel—one need not inquire, therefore, as to its necessity.

Baeck here enjoins the mission of Judaism as a contemporary task.

Every Jew has been called to testify through his conduct of life, to show the meaning of his religion. He must so live and act that all will see what he is and what his faith is, what it can do to educate and to elevate man. That is the *commandment of the mission which is set for all*. And no one has done his duty unto the community until he has acquitted himself of this. [1, p. 156]

In 1949, almost half a century later, after the concentration camp, Baeck was just as adamant about the mission of Israel:

Mankind is hungry and thirsts for that which Judaism can say. Many an example can be remembered. . . . Should we not begin anew? Should we not send our missionaries to Asia, to East Asia and to other places to the people there waiting for us? We are in need of expansion for our own sakes.[9]

A new reason is adduced for the mission in 1949. With the rise of the state of Israel, a new particularism exists in Jewish life which must be balanced: "Now one center is a national center, the State of Israel, and the other should be . . . for the sake of equilibrium, a missionary center . . . a center of internationalism."[10] In 1905, Baeck's stress was more upon the Jew as witness to the world. Israel's very existence was to express the *moral principle of the minority* through which the world is reminded that "without minorities, there is no world historical goal." [1, p. 158] The very existence of Israel is, for Baeck, a positive act lead-

[9] "The Mission of Judaism," *World Union of Progressive Judaism Report*, Sixth International Conference, London, 1949, p. 74.
[10] *Ibid.*, p. 80.

ing to the redemption of the world. Even Israel's suffering comes to remind the world of justice. Those who abandoned Israel's faith did so to better their lot—even their desertion was a positive testimony for Israel, which clung to its faith against all outside pressure. Baeck ends *The Essence of Judaism* with a magnificent self-confidence: he applies Ranke's words to Jewish existence: "Is it not the greatest thing which can happen to man that he can defend, in his own affair, the universal?" But his final word came from the Talmud, as the rabbis take a Biblical word and apply it to the fullness of Jewish existence: "The beginning witnesses for the end, and the end will ultimately bear witness to the beginning" (Kiddushin 31a).

From the date of its publication, *The Essence of Judaism* was recognized as a major statement by the Jewish community. Its core was the solid tradition of Bible and Talmud—as Geiger and the science of Judaism has presented this tradition to the modern Jew. Its philosophy was the unimpeachable neo-Kantianism of Hermann Cohen, in which the ancient ethical rigorism and messianism joined together in a strong appeal to the rational man of the end of the century. Where the Jewish community had felt itself faltering in a world which seemed disinclined to keep the promises made by the age of reason, it gained new confidence in Baeck's proud statement which confronted *The Essence of Christianity* with an *Essence of Judaism* which did not claim equality but superiority.

Much of Baeck's position was a summation of nineteenth century Judaism, including his challenge of Christianity. But a new language was employed here; and the dimensions of Jewish existence supplied a warmness to the essence of Judaism which had not been present before. The next edition, in 1921, has come to terms with two decades of Jewish thought, with Buber and Rosenzweig, has doubled in size, belongs completely to the twentieth century. But underneath it we still find this "lost" 1905 edition in which so much of the New Thinking found its first expression. And there is an excitement—sometimes leading to excessive polemics—which is peculiar to the 1905 edition. The revised edition is a calmer, undoubtedly superior exposition in which the original structure has been strengthened at its weak points; and much which had only been suggested in 1905 was carried to its logical conclusion. Yet the heart of Baeck's theology is found in his first major work; it is remark-

able how little change takes place in Baeck between 1905 and 1955—
although the changing emphases make us see his system in a completely
new way.

What *is* present in the 1905 edition, and what is absent from it? In
its simplest terms, what is present is Hermann Cohen's system and the
emphasis on the commandment; and what is absent is the *emphasis* upon
the mystery. (But the mystery itself is already indicated here. It exists
within the methodology of Dilthey and the awareness of the nonrational
aspect of human nature.) Also, the word "polarity" has not yet made its
appearance here. But the dynamic, rhythmic development of Judaism,
partially captured in the nineteenth century understanding of the emergence of the spirit as it achieves itself in the world, is already noted.

Buber's *Reden* in 1911 had brought a fuller awareness of Zionism to
the German-Jewish community. Baeck's 1905 book is deeply aware of
Jewish peoplehood; and its emphasis opens up Cohen's system to the
twentieth century in a way which differed from Cohen's—but also from
the approaches used by Buber and Rosenzweig. Baeck always remained
a rabbi, a theologian rather than a philosopher. As a rabbi, he defends
his faith and his people. He is not dispassionate and objective. There
are intemperate passages in this work, and subjective attacks on Christianity. He is first of all an apologete; and his prototype is not Maimonides
but Jehudah Halevi. Since his book is centered in the people, in human
experience, he finds the essence of his faith much more *in* the world, not
in a one-time revelation coming from the beyond. Israel is the revelation; but the humanistic aspects are held in check by the fundamental
faith in God which Baeck finds on every level of Jewish existence.

Jewish existence lives in the revelation of the categorical commandment which comes from God. The prophets are here seen as over-
whelmed by a moral force which bids them speak. Confronting the near
and the far God, they find the one link between finite man and the infinite to be the moral act which is God's will revealed to man. The
prophet does not develop the God concept for his people. His is the
voice of "practical reason" which tells Israel of the right things to do.
And it must always be man's ethical action which reconciles the paradoxes
of man's existence. The paradox is not resolved for Baeck in an Hegelian
dialectic. In this work, it is the precursor of the polarity in which two
opposites live on within one another. Israel and the nations are clearly
established here as one such polarity; the concept of election and mis-

sion is a theological statement of the particularity which must become the universal. The dynamic quality of this process makes it mandatory for Baeck to view the people Israel as the revelation, to shift, in effect, from the essence of Judaism to the existence of Israel, from the moral imperative to the moral act of life. Israel has a moral responsibility to the nations; revelation, election, and mission are all part of this moral task of moving from the particular to the universal which is the redemption of the world and of man. For Rosenzweig, the separateness of Israel and the nations will be resolved at the *end* of time. Baeck, far more conscious of Cohen's ethical messianism, would have the revelation taken to all mankind so that all are joined in the moral task and so that the split between Israel and the nations can be resolved *in* time. For that reason, Rosenzweig arrives at the concept of Israel as the meta-historical people—and Baeck arrives at a theology of history.

Summarizing the structure of the paradoxes which lie underneath the idealistic presentation of the basic concepts of Judaism, the traditional teachings of God, man, and Israel, we see that they are woven together and that they do interpenetrate. Finiteness and the sense of infinity as a religious mood of Judaism; the feeling of dependency countered by the knowledge of man's worth as a creator of ethical action; the task and the promise; and limited man and infinite God reconciled in atonement—a paradigm both for the individual and for Israel as related to fellow man—these present us with a Judaism in which the ethical rigorism of the rabbis and Hermann Cohen's ethical messianism with all of its optimism can reach out toward the tragedy of existence which Baeck emphasizes (with what today must be called prophetic insight). Baeck used the method of Dilthey to find his way into the religious typology of man; but it was his own faith and his own people which he described with passion and commitment.

The Essence of Judaism is a worthy answer to Harnack's *Essence of Christianity*; it does not contradict—it gives an alternative. The exposition of that alternative is the heart of Baeck's polemic against Christianity which now becomes our concern.

5

Baeck and Christianity

Baeck's first encounter with Christianity had resulted in a statement of the essence of Judaism with which he confronted Harnack's construction of Christianity. Essence met essence here, still touched by the climate of the nineteenth century. Apologetics, the confrontation with Christianity, continues to shape Baeck's concerns over the decades. As we examine his writings, we constantly find "romantic" Christianity tested against "classic" Judaism and found wanting. But as the twentieth century takes hold of Baeck, the tone changes. The move from essence to existence necessarily leads to a reconsideration of such topics as Paul— Pauline teachings are still challenged, but the figure of Paul, the person, is judged more sympathetically. But, in another way, the judgment is sharpened. The Jewish scholar who delights in the Gospels is also the leader of the German-Jewish community surrounded by nominal Christians who torture his people, who kill. As Baeck now learns of the essence of Judaism through the anguish of Jewish existence, he comes to look at the Christian community, finds it flawed, and seeks for the explanation of these flaws within the Christian faith.

In darkest times, Baeck reached out to his neighbors. Jew addressed non-Jew. Gershom Scholem, for one, has questioned whether there ever was a "German-Jewish dialogue":

I oppose the notion that such a German-Jewish dialogue in any genuine sense ever existed as a historical phenomenon. . . . The attempt on the part of Jews to explain themselves to the Germans and to present them with Jewish productivity, an attempt carried to the stage of complete self-surrender, is a significant phenomenon . . . but I cannot hear anything of a dialogue within it. . . . The supposedly indestructible spiritual community of the German essence combined with the Jewish essence . . . was never more than a fiction in the field of historical reality. [171, pp. 278–280][1]

Scholem's bitterness is an expression of Jewish community life which has consistently felt itself rejected whenever it strove for "dialogue." The current Jewish disenchantment with the Christian community's position during the Six Day War in June of 1967 is another example of this. Yet Scholem's judgment is overly sharp, a part of a total rejection of that configuration of Jewish life which desires "dialogue" with the neighbor. It also makes him a bitter opponent of the earlier "science of Judaism." Baeck, Buber, and Rosenzweig, by contrast, had all reached out to their neighbor—and at least scattered answers had come to them. They were the disciples of Hermann Cohen, whose essay on Germanism and Judaism now seems to Scholem characteristic of an unrequited love of German Jewry to their neighbors which took "the step from the sublime to the ridiculous." [171, p. 280]

Baeck follows Cohen; and the dialogue between Jew and German is carried out in his life. But he also notes the rejection; and he cannot examine a culture turned inimical without noting aspects of the Christian faith which seemed to him contributive of Germany's shortcomings, which supported the irrational aspects leading to National Socialism. In 1925, at a time when there was some optimism in Germany that the irrational aspects of political life were on the wane, Baeck wrote to a friend:

It is the spiritual and moral misfortune of Germany . . . that Germanism has been made into a religion. Instead of believing in God, they believe—and the Lutheran pastors have taken the lead here—in Germanism. This is the fundamental nationalism that knows only peoplehood and not the world of God. . . .[2]

[1] A later issue of the bulletin carries challenge and reply, but does not really enlarge on Scholem's point, which was made clearly and succinctly (Bulletin of Leo Baeck Institute, 1965, p. 30; and Scholem's answer).

[2] From correspondence of Leo Baeck quoted in [75, p. 21].

Noting the climate of the times in which Baeck wrote his studies of Christian thought, his sympathetic approach is to be admired all the more—and his critique should be taken ever more seriously. Christianity is always seen as a totality, is credited with a living unity in which contemporary shortcomings must be related to flaws in the historic structure and dogma.

The rabbinic confrontation with Christianity, found in the midrash, is continued in Baeck, the master of midrash. The right of the neighbor to exist is stressed out of the context of those days, when Judaism underscored its position as a world religion fully aware that the particular had to maintain itself but not at the expense of the universal. In Baeck's theology, all have the right to exist; there is an underlying unity which will prevail in the end—the one God is worshiped in diverse ways.

Baeck's approach is clearly seen in his essay on "Neutrality" (1929):

> Neutrality is the ability to understand . . . a particularity, whether it be a personal or an historical form, as different and as much opposed it may be, which must now be recognized as existing together with its right to life and an enduring right for its task. Even if it cannot always be accepted fundamentally, it must yet be accepted in reality [*wenn auch nicht immer grundsaetzlich, so doch tatsaechlich*]: if not in its theory, at least in its daily practice. This is especially true of the relationship between the great religions. . . . In principle they are opposed . . . and really have to deny one another because of this principle. But alongside the theoretic rejection there enters here the conscious practical recognition; alongside the fundamental conflict the desired actual neutrality. In all modern states there exist totalities . . . which negate one another in principle . . . who are yet drawn together in a common community of fate and of history. [42, pp. 217–218]

In part, we are here dealing with the then current discussion of *Gesellschaft* and *Gemeinschaft*. But the validity of Baeck's presentation finds its ultimate text in the discussion of theological conflicts, particularly when he states:

> Positive neutrality demands that the ultimate and innermost questions be raised honestly. Open and not concealed, complete and unqualified, they must gain room for themselves with all their opposition and ungivingness . . . the understanding for that which unifies and binds together does not come in spite of opposites but through them. . . . [42, p. 221]

Recognition of others, giving freely of self to community, leads to self-knowledge in which the particularity is also aware of the totality; and that, says Baeck, is "the positive neutrality which not only takes but also gives." [42, p. 222] The complex aspect of Leo Baeck which we have called humility is involved here. But in that humility there are the sharp barbs of the polemicist who grants everything to the Christian, but nothing to Christianity.

Hans Joachim Schoeps [169] fails to do justice to Baeck's contribution to the Jewish-Christian argument in modern times—perhaps they differ too much. For Schoeps (somewhat similar to Buber and Rosenzweig) places Christianity on the same level with Judaism. For Baeck, Christianity is "the other": to be tolerated, appreciated—and challenged. Its virtues are its Jewish contents; and Jesus is still in the frame of Jewish existence, but not Paul. Krister Stendahl, a recent critic, in his introduction to the English edition of Die Pharisaer [40], has suggested that Baeck's "critique of romantic Christianity is actually a critique of a peculiar interpretation of Jewish eschatology." [40, p. xvii] But the point to be kept in mind is that the same element, brought into a new structure and given a far different emphasis, produces a different result. The ethical rigorism of the rabbis controlled Jewish eschatology, in Baeck's judgment; and he did not see similar controls in Paulinism.

One study dealing with Baeck's views on Christianity, by Rheinhold Mayer, sees the contrast between Baeck and Rosenzweig's view on Christianity as based on a different ideology and methodology:

> Franz Rosenzweig and Martin Buber take serious notice of the Church in its historical form. Laws and historical forms are recognized in terms of the concrete individual aspects taken out of the lived reality. Everything is concretized. And what has been found in history is tranferred into the theological field, thus leading to the possibility of recognizing the Christian approach as a legitimate way to God. Preconditions are also created which can lead to a personal encounter, to Jewish-Christian partnership.
>
> In Leo Baeck, by contrast, it seems to be the construction which is given preference. History is deduced and interpreted from general historical processes and laws. And these unchanging laws are the object of all new meditation. In this construction and meditation there is no room for a theological recognition of another faith. While there is practical toleration in the human domain for the man representing a cause which must be theoretically rejected, that person in conjunction with his cause simply

finds no place in this system which only allows for Baeck's own cause. The other matter stands alongside, a foreign phenomena; it cannot be examined for motives, it can only be rejected. The other way, the "purely Christian," is not one before God; it is only a way for humans. In Baeck, everything is to be consciously abstracted and to be led back to ultimate formulae. It might even appear that universal laws are given preference over concrete relationships, that everything is reduced to an impersonal thing and removed out of life. [150, pp. 101–102]

There is some validity in this judgment, particularly as it applies to the first encounter with Harnack, where essence met essence. The idealist construction tends to ignore the human encounter as an avenue of understanding between faiths. But the later Baeck participates in the new thinking far more than his critics have realized—his idealistic language does more than report on contrasts between general processes. Underneath the calm surface, the existential encounter has taken place; and critics like Mayer must come to terms with the full scope of Baeck's critique: not only Christianity, but also the Christian has been weighed and found wanting. Baeck's middle way unites the judgments of the field of theology and of the existential encounter; and his "neutrality" gives full recognition to the universal element which unites every Christion with every Jew and flows out of the human situation into the realm of a theology which is never cut off from the existential encounter.

Baeck judges Christianity with more sharpness than do Buber and Rosenzweig. But Mayer also overstates Buber's relationship to Christianity. While leaving the sharpest polemics to Baeck, Buber can also say, "We are not able to define God under any aspect of this [Christian] revelation." [89, p. 20][3] And, as we examine the documents of Baeck's polemic against Christianity, we come to see him as a representative of the Jewish community in its two thousand year old confrontation with its daughter faith.

II

The Essence of Judaism of 1905 incorporates the approach toward Jesus and Christianity which the 1901 review of Harnack's book had already enunciated. In 1901, Baeck had affirmed Christianity as the daughter

[3] See Note at end of this chapter.

which the mother could never hate [17, p. 30]; Jesus was recognized as "a Jew among Jews" [17, p. 28]; and Christian ethics were seen as derived from Judaism. [17, p. 14] The Pharisees were defended and Jesus was firmly placed in their ranks as a "genuine Jewish personality." [17, p. 28] And the opposition and misinterpretation of Pharisaism on the part of the Church came to be seen as a great weakness of Christianity from its beginnings to the present. The dynamic Jewish core was displaced from the center of Christian thought: "Church history is rich in examples where there was great inclination to substitute teachings regarding God for moral law, dogma for commandments of duty. . . ." [17, p. 9] Christianity's "individual historical" claim to absolute validity is thus questioned; its accreditation, moral fervor and inner dynamism are derived from a Judaism which new elements of the Christian faith tend to negate.

The polemical aspects of *The Essence of Judaism* are a necessary hidden dimension of what is, after all, a work of apologetics. Jewish polemics, historically and psychologically determined, is often a hidden substratum of Jewish texts. Here, as the picture of Judaism begins to emerge, we find it defined against a Christianity which is often mentioned only indirectly. An early example of the "silent" confrontation can be found in the definition of Israel as a prophetic religious community:

> No single prophet began the structure of Jewish religion and none completed it; it is significant that Israel lays claim not to "*the* prophet" but to "the prophets." That is where it differs from most other religions which are based on the one Gautama Buddha, the one Zoroaster, the one Muhammad. In Israel the master is followed by a train of masters, the great one by a line of his peers. None . . . offer the total revelation and none embrace the entirety of the religion . . . a system may lay claim to completeness and perfection; a human being cannot. The whole content of Judaism truly lies in its unended and unending history. [3, p. 43]

Baeck here confronts the Christian thinker who places his revelation totally into Jesus, outside of history. But Jesus is not mentioned alongside Buddha and the others—he is still to be claimed for Judaism.

Another example of the "silent" polemic occurs in a passage claiming Jesus in the context of that Jewish particularism which knows that self-realization is the bridge to universalism:

The power of Jesus's words, rather than narrowness of vision, can be witnessed when he wants his word to go out solely unto Israel (and indicates this road only to his disciples). . . . The prophets speak *of the world* and its salvation, but they speak *to Israel.* It is only the colorless epigones who ever summon all mankind to be the admiring audience. [3, p. 73][4]

The hidden attack here is against Paul and his followers (all "epigones" to the rabbis) who separate the message from Jewish particularity and who create a rootless universalism. Baeck is not concerned here with the fact that Christianity's teaching of the new covenant, the Church, and the new Israel do in fact build a new particularism underneath Christian universalism. The parent still mourns the wayward child and indicates that Jesus, still in the Jewish tradition, would not have wanted the break.

The very schema of Judaism and its role in the world places Christianity into a subordinate position:

There are but two fundamental and determining forms of religion, that of Israel and that of Buddha. . . . The one is the expression of the command to work and create, the other of the need to rest. . . . Judaism seeks to reconcile the world with God, while Buddhism tries to escape from the world. . . . Judaism is the religion of altruism . . . Buddhism is the religion of egotism. . . .

Between these two religious polarities the choice must be made; one or the other is the religious revelation. All other religions tend toward one or the other of the two . . . Judaism is the classical manifestation of religion. [3, pp. 60–61]

Buddhism lives in the openness of universality; but it is Judaism which makes universalism its task and its mission and moves through its subordinates—Christianity and Islam in self-fulfillment:

Judaism [views all embracing universality as its chosen task] expecting historical fulfillment in the universal kingdom of God which is to embrace all humanity. The same is true also of Christianity and Mohammedanism which are world religions insofar as they are derived from Judaism. When they see the religious future in light of their religion and thus see in it *the* religion, they are espousing an essentially Jewish belief. [3, pp. 76–77]

Baeck discovers the influence of Jewish universalism on the great spiritual movements of Western life, ranging from the religious revival

---

[4] This passage, however, was retranslated from the original, particularly since the Schocken edition omitted the reference to the disciples.

within the Renaissance to the socialist movement; and he stresses the persistence of Jewish ideas within Judaism and Islam which tend to discard later acquired ideas in order to return to older Jewish ways; "here one need mention only the Reformation, the Anabaptists and the Unitarian tendency in modern Protestantism." [3, p. 80][5]

The 1901 work on Harnack had already stressed Baeck's contention that New Testament ethics draws heavily upon the Hebrew Scriptures, that love of neighbor is dependent upon Hebrew texts. Here, Baeck presses on to show that

> love is limited and confined in the New Testament by the fact that salvation and bliss are made dependent upon right faith and thereby ultimately upon dogma and creed. This means that salvation and bliss are denied . . . to the nonbelievers. . . . In Christianity the determining factor is to experience the miracle of grace and thereby be redeemed; thus the "I" of the individual man stands alone at the center of religion, apart from his fellow man. [3, p. 222]

Arnold Wolf's perceptive essay [194] equates this with the quasi-Buddhistic egotism which is the opposing religion of Baeck's schema. In that schema, the derivative role of Christianity is clear. Within Christianity, there are opposing forces which stress faith over against work; the individual in place of humanity; grace more than justice; and Paul's teachings dominate this structure.

Baeck accused Paul of fostering the Christian misunderstanding of Torah as *nomos*, with the implication that *nomos* could become bondage and could indicate despotism. The polemic of Paul's Epistles stressed the new covenant of faith over the inferior, temporary covenant of law. Within that polemic, Baeck also saw the value of human action negated by the miracle which now had to be accepted. [3, p. 264] Paul confused the law of Judaism, which Baeck affirmed, with the "fence around the Law"; and this confusion is seen as a basic weakness of Christianity. Polemics joins apologetics here.

Since Christianity is generally brought into *The Essence of Judaism* for the sake of comparing it with Judaism [3, p. 262] it is not surprising

---

[5] Mayer [150 p. 71, n. 135] here notes some interesting changes in the second edition of *Essence of Judaism*. *Glaubenswegen* ("ways of faith") is a concretizing of the *Glaubensgedanken* ("thoughts of faith"); *machtvolle Bewegungen* ("powerful movements") is changed to *grosse, entscheidende Bewegungen* ("great, decisive movements") —Baeck's rejection of mere might grew over the years.

that the judgment rendered is a negative one. A Judaism without dogma
notes how Christianity is overdependent on it, using dogma to shore up
its tottering institutions. [3] Secular power is wooed so that Christianity
might be forced upon unbelievers. [3, p. 54] Extolling the Jewish concept of *emunah,* the living consciousness of the Omnipresent which man
may have, awareness of life founded on God, Baeck once again moves
into the silent polemic against Christianity.

> In Jewish literature trust in God is also called faith (Emunah), but the
> word "faith" has here nothing of the dogmatic and denominational sig-
> nificance which it has elsewhere acquired. It does not refer to outlooks
> in which a knowledge of the beyond is offered by a gift of grace; it is not
> steeped in scholasticism. In Judaism there is no rigid confession of faith,
> no dogmatic system with an elaborate structure of thought seeking to reach
> to the heavens. . . . [3, pp. 118–119]

Alongside the indirect critique of Christianity, there are direct stric-
tures dealing with the Christian concept of man, of community, the function of the Church, the structure of Christian thought and life set
alongside the synagogue.[6] Taken out of context, summarized in this
fashion, this appears a bitter diatribe. But the same paragraph containing
strong condemnation also affirms, in the spirit of "positive neutrality,"
that the moral future of mankind rests on the belief in the One God:
"This does not mean that the belief of all men will be uniform . . . yet
all will have *one* belief . . . 'do justly.' This belief in the One God can
unite all men." [3, p. 86]

Paradoxical as it sounds, Baeck loves Christianity. The figure of
Jesus is prominent in Baeck's writings. With the possible exception of
C. G. Montefiore, there are few Jewish scholars who have read and reread
the Gospels with such warmth. And the mode of thought which is the
opponent of Judaism is Buddhism, not Christianity. Christianity is still
seen within the Jewish framework; the child is not denied. And Judaism
responds to what it sees of itself within Christianity.

Then why so bitter an attack, granted that it is not destructive but kept
within the framework of positive tolerance? The key may be found in
Baeck's favorite Latin adage: *corruptio optimi pessima.* It is precisely
because Baeck sees so much of the Jewish heritage within Christianity

---

[6] Wolf [194] summarizes much of this, although any such summary must become
an overstatement. Also worth noting is Walter Jacob [138b].

that he feels the need to attack those aspects which have moved it outside the Jewish framework. Even the technique of confronting the opposing tendencies of the faiths contains the assertion of kinship: It is done in the framework of the theology of polarity. Baeck's quarrel with Christianity is not that it believes—but that it believes blindly; not that it carries within itself the feeling of dependence—but that this becomes surrender, abdication of personal action; not that it has a vision of the future—but that this vision is taken out of the realm of realization and placed into a beyond which cannot be attained by works but only by grace. Christianity contains truth: it was once Jewish. Now, entangled in allegiances with secular power, frozen into rigid dogma, it is corrupted. Speaking and writing in a Christian world, Baeck dared to present Judaism as the norm; Christianity was set against this standard and was found wanting.

The Essence of Judaism speaks to Israel ("the prophets speak to Israel"); but apologetics always addresses itself to the opposition as well. And in the stress upon Israel's mission and the Christian share in that task we can see a reconciliation between Christianity and Judaism. The particular meets in the universal. And the sharpness of Baeck's critique is part of his concern for the Christian who must join in the common task which is in the realm of human experience, directed by his ethics which rise out of his Jewish heritage. The language of idealism, the whole enterprise of searching for the essence, the need of self-definition against a faith which in Harnack's Essence of Christianity denied its parentage—bring Baeck to the sharpest possible statement of the flaws of the Christian structure. But the bridge of reconciliation has been built in the human task, in the realm of experience, and in the vision of the mission of Judaism. The Christian who reads The Essence of Judaism with close attention comes to hear himself addressed: confrontation becomes dialogue.

III

When Baeck turns from the totality of Christianity to an examination of its particulars, he is no longer writing polemics. A student of comparative religion, he assesses particular facts in the framework of objective scholarship. Reverence and respect for the detail, and the need to be fair to the particular are evident. Baeck turns to the Gospels. He is dealing with material he considers part of the Jewish tradition, for which he has empathy and understanding; defining aspects of Christianity, he also defines Judaism and areas of his own life.

"The Gospels As a Document of the History of the Jewish Faith" [50, 51] places these texts within Jewish existence: "The Gospels must be understood, not in terms of textual sources out of which they might have been composed, but in terms of the tradition out of which they originated." [51, p. 41] Baeck was here speaking of the Oral Tradition, that special method of transmission known by all Jewish scholars as a key to the understanding of the Jewish life into which he placed the Gospels. In the past thirty years, New Testament study has caught up with Baeck's insights. Modern form criticism and the study of transmission now take full cognizance of the Oral Tradition, and Baeck's study has been judged a contribution to this field.[7]

Baeck's presentation established the oral transmission within Christianity out of the Gospels, the Church Fathers, and from Jewish sources. In addition, he asserted that "even if we did not possess these ancient testimonies in which the primitive Church itself reports on its oral tradition, the spirit of the people among whom the Gospels originated would still point to the same direction." [51, p. 45] In this, we can discern the later Baeck: It is the living reality of Jewish existence which supplies us with our insights. There is no differentiation between Jewish and Christian types in this continuum: They rise out of the one people, out of the one tradition. There, the Bible speaks to every generation, to its students and teachers who place the tradition into their own lives and thus hand it on. *Toldot*—the interpenetration of people and faith—transmits revelation. And a pious imagination (*fromme Phantasie*) honors the past by embellishing it, links it to the present. This is the nature of Jewish life: it is also the nature of the Bible:

> Scripture . . . was read in a peculiar manner. . . . There was the wish to place everything in a particular time and situation . . . on the other hand, there was the tendency to raise the words of Scripture above the particular incident . . . and specific time to which they might belong: they were lifted into the realm of timeless being, even into the sphere of the pre-existent and

[7] Krister Stendahl, in his introduction [40, p. xx, n. 18], judges Baeck's contribution impressive. He refers to the development of this field of Biblical study, a survey of which may be found in B. Gerhardsson, *Memory and Manuscript: Oral Tradition and Written Transmission in Rabbinic Judaism and Early Christianity* (Uppsala, 1961).

ideal. . . . All Biblical history did not only tell something, it also meant
something. . . . [51, pp. 49–50][8]

The Bible was Revelation, applied to all of life. Israel was the people to
whom Revelation had been given. Between them, they created the tradition. Once more, the inner thought moves toward Baeck's identification
of Israel, Revelation, and Bible as one and the same—all living, dynamic,
continuous in development. The Oral Law is contained in the Written
Law of Sinai, and lives in the chain of tradition, the links of which are
the generations of Israel.

Baeck shows this living process within the Bible, showing, for example,
how the Book of Chronicles fills in the details of David's story told in the
Book of Samuel. [51, p. 54][9] Thus, too, we see the process in the Oral
Law, by comparing *Pirke Avoth* with the *Avoth of Rabbi Nathan*. [51,
p. 55][10] The creativity of every generation takes the ancient revelation
and gives it new life. And the Gospel with its oral transmission belongs
in this stream of Jewish life. In the Gospel, as in Jewish life, can be
found the following:

> The beginning is that pupils have heard the words of their teachers . . .
> It is their pious obligation to hand on what they had seen and heard . . .
> The tradition comprehended words and events . . .
> Everything was placed into the traditional words and frame . . .
> The tradition was handed down by individuals and invariably reflected their
>   individuality . . .
> The imagination saw, and creation and the will to give form explained
>   and supplemented . . .
> The words of Scripture directed, commanded, and exerted an inner com-
>   pulsion . . .
> A fixed content, a fixed religious doctrine, was there to begin with and was
>   most vividly real and the whole truth . . .
> Their master's lot and fate had been long revealed and always pre-
>   ordained . . .
> Every great event was nothing but an answer given long ago and the ful-
>   fillment of a prophecy . . . [51, p. 63]

The Jewish tradition and its conscious assertion is thus located within
the group around Jesus. Baeck does not make it clear here that the identifi-

---

[8] The contemporary quest for the *kerygma* is related to this.

[9] Baeck here compares II Samuel 7:8–14 with I Chronicles 22:8–10.

[10] Baeck here compares Avoth 1.1 with Avoth of Rabbi Nathan 1:2–3.

cation here is with Aggadic rather than Halachic Judaism, although that point, and the inner conflicts of Jewish life, are noted by him elsewhere.[11] Since Baeck's writing, the Dead Sea Scrolls and new scholarship have brought to light other traits within the Jewish community at the time of Jesus. These underscore the Jewish aspects of early Christianity, but also place into Jewish thought aspects of what Baeck called "romantic religion," apocalyptic modes as well as ascetic actions, ways of thinking found in the Gospels which Baeck tended to place outside of Judaism.

Baeck then showed the process of transmission within the Gospels, comparing the versions of the Lord's Prayer in the Synoptic Gospels. [51, p. 64][12] But what took these texts outside of Judaism? The disciples believed, and the teacher followed them in this belief, that the teacher was really the messiah. And in these texts, certain ideas found within Judaism receive a special coloration: Satan and the Second Coming; expectations basic to Jesus's followers which take on individual characteristics which are part of an oral tradition passing through different disciples. Peter, John, James, and the others: each had his own version, his own listeners. And then there was Paul.

Baeck deals with Paul in a number of essays. [29, 31a, 59] From *The Essence of Judaism* [2, pp. 264–265],[13] still dominated by nineteenth century scholarship and its stress upon the split between the teaching of Jesus and the theology of Paul, there comes a basic picture of Paul within Baeck's writings which only changes in Baeck's final writings. Baeck polarizes Christianity into that which is Jewish and that which is Hellenized, romanticized faith which is personified by Paul. Once more, it must be stressed that in polemics a position becomes overstated. For Baeck, Paul became the "other one," the enemy who betrayed his own community to the pagan world, who chopped at the roots, the spokesman of the mystery which abrogates the commandment. Baeck was reluctant to admit the romantic elements of Paul's faith into the Jewish framework,

[11] Hermann Strack [180] quotes Baeck ("The Old Opposition to the Aggadah," in *Maybaum Festschrift*, pp. 164–172) on "Christianity whose Biblical interpretation had close affinity to the aggadic style. . . ."

[12] Baeck uses Marcion (Harnack's edition) to indicate a still later treatment of the Lord's Prayer in Christian thought.

[13] The first edition [1, p. 152] is much less critical of Christianity in this passage than the 1922 edition [2], where what has been called "Christian polemic" becomes the "Paulinian polemic" and receives much more extensive and harsher treatment from Baeck.

to recognize in Paul's actions, personality, and theology a position still part of Jewish life. Only in Baeck's last essay on Paul, when the polemic had shifted from the discussion of essence to the existential encounter between the faiths, when the emphasis was more upon the man and less upon the faith, does Baeck come to affirm the Jewish Paul who shared in the mission and task of Judaism.

In this work on the Gospels, Paul is seen primarily as "a man out of the Graeco-Oriental world of Asia Minor" [51, p. 70] who never forgot the mysteries and sacraments of the non-Jewish world. Baeck saw Paul as the gate through which the pagan mysteries of the dying and resurrected god streamed into the messiah concept, through which the followers of Jesus found their way to the outside world. There were other avenues, of course: the Jewish world was open to its environment; and there existed a network of Jewish missionary activities which was eventually taken over by Christianity. But as Christians entered that world, the Jewish messiah was taken over by the Soter of Hellenistic thought. Romantic longings were reciprocated and strengthened; and Christianity moved away from its ancient heritage.

These were almost apocalyptic times. Religious types emerged. Baeck, trained by Dilthey, stresses these:

> The years of Jesus's life . . . were now oppressive and now exciting. . . . Some were overcome with a feeling of helplessness; resistance, . . . any activity at all, seemed senseless. . . . Others wanted to be defiant and fight. But both experienced the present as a time of transition. Things simply could not remain as they were: clearly, one era had to come to an end . . . another, promised era must be about to commence: the vacillating sense of the merely provisional took hold of many minds. [50, p. 77]

Baeck saw flaws both in the passive refusal to resist as well as in the blind defiance which substituted action for its own sake. He grappled with the idea of a "time of transition." Messianic hopes are basic to Judaism. But they are built into the world of concrete human existence and depend on human action as much as on Divine grace (Baeck here underplays the strength of Jewish apocalypticism in those days). The crown of human achievement, the Messianic Age, is set at the end of time —time, the continuum in which the ethical is realized. The dream is also part of the continuum, is its poetry. But when the poetry overwhelms the real world of the commandment, when the messiah appears to be at hand, the sense and purpose of human existence, the ethical act, becomes blunted. A "time of transition" is bereft of purpose; and the "vacillating sense of the merely provisional" brings the romantic who dreams of tomorrow instead of working for the end of days.

This romantic type, who wants less to live than to experience (he prefers *erleben* to *leben*) was delineated in Baeck's "Romantic Religion": "Therefore the romantic 'personality' is also something totally different from say, the Kantian personality who confronts us as the bearer of the moral law and who finds himself, and thus his freedom, in being faithful to the commandment." [28, p. 193] Baeck was not just discussing Kant. Both in terms of the times and his own orientation, he uses Kant for a philosophical expression of rabbinic ethical rigorism. And rabbinical rationalism and ethical rigorism of those days combined to control the messianic speculations of those first two centuries.[14]

Baeck represented the rabbis of the past who sought to control mysticism and messianic speculations. We misunderstand him if we see him only as a post-Kantian figure of modern times who tries to apply modern philology and philosophy to the texts of the first century. He is a rabbinic figure; more than analyzing these texts, he really listens to them. They are words addressed to him, transmitted through the chain of tradition which creates a specialized dialogue all its own. The Hebrew Scriptures stand at the center of that dialogue and move through every generation of the rabbinic tradition. And Baeck is part of the Jewish reply which comes to both Hadrian and Hitler. The Gospels are part of that reply, even if the differing interpretation of the Jewish suffering makes the

[14] The Midrash in which Baeck specialized is packed with details of the nature of the messiah, his rule, the time span of his kingdom (40 years, 2,000 years, etc.), of his suffering (it is significant that Rabba and others cry: "May he come—but I don't want to see him!"), his pre-existence, etc. But the text is filled with the moral and rational challenge against apocalypticism: Rabbi Yochanan cursed those who attempted to calculate the time of the messiah (Sanhedrin 95b) and Ulla taught that Jerusalem would only be redeemed by righteous action (*ibid.*) In the third century, Rab challenged Samuel, stating that "redemption is dependent upon our self-betterment" (*ibid.*); in fourth century, Rabbi Pappa teaches "when the arrogant cease to be, the oppressing might of the Magi will also vanish; the end of false judges is the end of their soldiers" (*ibid.*). More than a reaction against Christianity, more than a challenge to messianic ideas, rabbinic opposition centered on the fear that messianic hopes would blunt man's concern with everyday existence. If Baeck underestimated apocalyptic thinking within Judaism, he was still correct in stressing the strongly antiromantic feelings of leading rabbis who taught in those days.

fall of the Temple an intensification of the community for most, but a breaking of this bond for the Gospel writers.

The details of Baeck's analysis of the Gospels lie outside our scope. But it is worth noting that in this small book Baeck presented the Jewish community of Germany—in a time when not only their neighbor but also their neighbor's Church seemed to have abandoned them to destruction—with a warmly sympathetic introduction into Christian texts bridging two thousand years. He seeks to reclaim the Jewish core of these texts by applying the following standards:

> All of the following are indicative of later strata: first of all, whatever accords only with the experiences, hopes, wishes, ideas, and the faith and images of the faith of a later generation; then, events which were clearly begotten in the image of either biblical verses or gradually developing dogma and its symbolism; also, whatever is related or spoken with an eye on the Graeco-Roman world or the Roman authorities . . . currying favor . . . attempting not to be confounded with Jews . . . whatever is in the Hellenistic style, modeled after the Hellenistic prophets and miracle workers; . . . finally, all that reflects the age of the catastrophe [after 70 A.D. when the temple was destroyed]. . . . [51, p. 87]

Yet there are difficulties in applying these standards. Hopes, wishes, and ideas can be dormant for centuries, can be part of a hidden tradition finding expression in later days but belonging to earlier times. Baeck had accused Harnack of reading his own religion into the community of those who followed Jesus. The same danger resides in any attempt to separate the strata of a text on the basis of ideas contained in them, where repugnant ideas are excluded by definition. Mysticism and apocalypticism are not the exclusive property of Hellenistic prophets and miracle workers. And while Baeck comes to determine, with great sensitivity and understanding, the Jewish aspects of Jesus's teachings, his criteria tend to exclude Hellenisms which are not necessarily derived from the outer community but have been transmitted through the Jewish tradition. The basic standards for Baeck's synoptic reconstruction of what he considers the Jewish urtext of the Gospels are clear and consistent:

> Whatever is completely different from the tendencies and purposes of the generations which came after the first generation of disciples; whatever contradicts the tenets which later became part of the faith; whatever is different from, or even opposed to, the intellectual, psychic, and political

climate in which these later generations gradually found themselves; whatever, in other words, exemplifies the way of life and the social structure, the climate of thought and feeling, the way of speaking and the style of Jesus's own environment and time. In all this we are confronted with the words and deeds of Jesus. [51, pp. 99–100]

It is subjective; but his profound knowledge of that time brings with it illuminating insights and contributions to scholarship which the objective critic must acknowledge. And this very subjectivity aids us in coming to a clearer understanding of Baeck's dialogue with Christianity.

Baeck saw the early Christian community and its teachings as fully Jewish. Brilliantly, he depicted the essence of Jewish thought of that time: the Biblical teaching enters the world and illumines it, while contemporary thought enters into that Biblical world and transforms it while judging itself at the same moment. The commentary is added to the text and becomes part of it, enlarging and illuminating. And the Gospels are part of that tradition. Contemporary scholarship may differ with Baeck on the degree of emphasis to be placed on the interior environment of Christianity and on the outside influence. It cannot ignore the deep understanding of the Christian beginnings which rise out of the full familiarity with the Jewish patterns of thought evident on each page of the Synoptic Gospels. Details of Baeck's reconstruction of the urtext are open to question. But, reading it, one gains a new understanding both of the Jewish element in Jesus and of the love which unites Leo Baeck with that early Jewish teacher whom he now claims:

In the old Gospel which is thus opened before us, we encounter a man with noble features who lived in the land of the Jews in tense and excited times and helped and labored and suffered and died: a man out of the Jewish people who walked on Jewish paths with Jewish faith and hopes. His spirit was at home in the Holy Scriptures, and his imagination and thought were anchored there; and he proclaimed and taught the word of God because God had given it to him to hear and to preach. . . . We behold a man who is Jewish in every feature and trait of his character, manifesting in every particular what is good and pure in Judaism. This man could have developed as he came to be only on the soil of Judaism; and only on this soil, too, could he find his disciples and followers. Here alone, in this Jewish sphere . . . could this man live his life and meet his death—a Jew among Jews. Jewish history and Jewish reflection may not pass him by nor ignore him. [51, pp. 100–101]

Baeck always approached a text of revelation not as a passage that had to be understood, but as the living expression of personalities that enter actively into our lives as we interpret them. The "old Gospel that opens before us" is a living expression of a Jewish teacher, Jesus, and is a document of Jewish faith. That is why Christianity is not assigned the position of ultimate opponent. To the extent that Christianity shares in the Jewish tradition and experience, it shares the Revelation and the Mission. Christianity's task here is the propagation of the ethical insights of Judaism's ethical monotheism. Its link with Judaism is a continuous aspect of Christian history. And in this work by Baeck, which his fellow Jewish scholars appreciated for its scholarship without really entering its theological dimensions [27, 28], the shared revelation is expressed in strong terms.

Revelation . . . mission . . . Israel: the Jewish people moving through history: These are one for Baeck. Christianity broke away and tore the chain of transmission. The methods were still at hand: Students listened to teachers and applied traditional exegesis to the master's words; but a pagan spirit had entered into their deliberations. Mystery became mystification, and the sober sense of ethics, applied to concrete situations and enforced by religious observances sanctifying life, became transformed by a romantic longing for the better world which would come into being through supernatural intervention. It was Baeck's love for the Jewish elements which now led him into his sharpest polemic against what he considered the corrupting elements contained in Christianity. Summarizing his statements over more than three decades, Baeck published his essay on "Romantic Religion." [27, 28]

IV

At one point, Baeck had planned to write a major work to be entitled "Classic and Romantic Religion." This never appeared. Instead, a first form of the essay on romantic religion was published in 1922. [27] This essay, changed and greatly enlarged, appeared in the same 1938 collection in which Baeck affirmed his love for the Gospels. It was the sharpest polemic possible.

Baeck's self-identification with the Pharisees espoused that holiness which rose out of ethical actions and centered in the sanctification of the concrete situation of life, which opposed the holiness which arose out of withdrawal, out of dreams and longing. The rabbis of the first four centuries could not deny the messianic dreams of a suffering people; but they could contain those dreams, could see them as the poetry of existence which was necessary—but dangerous.[15] Baeck was one of the ancient exegetes, a *baal ha-midrash*.[16] The same Biblical word and its exegesis, the same hermeneutical rules and inner logic, and the same Jewish community in search of holiness surrounded him. He lived in a continuum where unreason had always been the enemy—both from within and from without. The romantic element was never excluded from his thoughts; but he remained firmly identified with the rationalist tradition of Judaism.

As there are lines of influence between Baeck and Hermann Cohen, so, to a lesser extent, Baeck learned from Heinrich Graetz. Baeck did not let the feelings he shared with Graetz include Graetz's prejudices against Eastern Judaism and Chassidism. But Baeck's total view of Jewish history made much of the living progress of ethical action and rational thought, of a voluntarism which was also part of Graetz's system.[17] And Baeck was also the spokesman of liberal Jewish thought, of the science of Judaism, which is perhaps best summed up by the name Abraham Geiger.[18] It is these Jewish foundations of Baeck's thinking, from the ethical rigorism of the ancient rabbis to the theories of liberal Judaism, which must be understood before we turn to the outside influences which shaped the language of Baeck's polemic against romantic religion.

Dilthey's typological approach is clear. But there were many influences

[15] Fritz Strich [182] shows that both love and caution are necessary approaches to romanticism in our times: "In 1929 I saw it my task to defend the right of romanticism against classicism. Historical developments have now brought me to the recognition of German romanticism as one of the great dangers . . . which brought disaster to the world. Its aesthetic magic remained. But I have learned that one cannot accede to it too much, and that it can seduce and lead astray within the realm of existence." [p. 9]

[16] *Baal ha-midrash* is not a common technical term, but is rather employed, in this study, in order to define Baeck alongside the recognized *baal ha-Halacha* from whom Baeck is separated by the hermeneutics of midrash, the poetry of his life.

[17] An earlier rationalist historian was I. M. Jost. But it is precisely because Graetz's system also enclosed within itself romanticism that it becomes related to Leo Baeck. Jost was too one-sided. Baeck's system of polarities could never exclude the romantic mode: it had to use it, had to control it.

[18] Thus, Abraham Geiger's *Urschrift* (1857) breaks ground for the modern appraisal of Pharisaism so important to Baeck.

at work upon Baeck ever open to the *Zeitgeist*. Shortly before the essay had appeared, Woelfflin had applied the typological method to art. Fritz Strich had drawn upon Woelfflin in his book on classicism and romanticism which not only identified Christianity with romanticism but also delineated a theory of polarity reflected in Baeck. Strich stated that

> No aesthetics could establish a fundamental concept which cannot and must not be countered immediately and necessarily with the polar contraconcept. Every time and every art must decide for itself, of course, and each has the inalienable right to consider itself the final and only truth; for only out of such a conviction does it gain its creative and achieving power. But the science of history sees its task precisely in this: in maintaining the awareness of the oneness of the spirit throughout all changing appearances and to arch the rainbow of peace over the battle by comprehending the battle only as the mystery of life, the twofoldness as the mystery of the unity. [182, p. 23]

He set up the polarities of the classic against the romantic, the fulfilled against that which is unending, eternal rest against eternal movement in the framework of eternity—polarities again encountered in Baeck. Strich identified a restless sense of time which is alienated from life and experience as the inner core of romanticism, of the baroque, of the Gothic, and of Christianity; and he saw two streams in romantic thought—the Christian and the Dionysian type. [182, p. 25] But behind the whole framework—Strich, Woelfflin, Dilthey, and Baeck as well—we still have the inheritance of Hegel shaping the dialectics of the age.

In this postwar time, the romanticism which was alienated from life and experience was not only defined in the arts and in religion. It was also understood as a pattern of political thought. Carl Schmitt noted the failure of the romantic mode when it entered politics. In an essay written in 1919, Schmitt defined political romanticism as "subjectivated occasionalism" in which everything can become romanticized and nothing matters:

> The core of political romanticism is that the romantic, within the organic passivity which belongs to his occasional structure, wants to be productive without becoming active. As subjectivated occasionalism, political romanticism—despite countless psychological niceties and confessional subtleties —did not have the strength to confront itself and to objectify its intellectual essence in a theoretical or practical coherent structure. Its subjectiv-

ism led it away from concepts and philosophical structures, to a type of lyrical circumlocution of the experience which could be combined with that organic passivity . . . always without its own decision, its own responsibility, or its own risk. [166, pp. 223–224]

Baeck's ethical rigorism could not but take note of a political romanticism and its dangers. And not only Schmitt's writings indicated the dangers of political romanticism; his own life showed his impatience with the democratic process. Caught up in the dangers he described, Schmitt was in the vanguard of those who welcomed Hitler.[19]

Baeck thus came to the critique of a faith which seemed to him weakened by unholy political alliances in the world around him. The church seemed a victim of the romanticism of the present; but Baeck saw the seeds of the weakness introduced into Christianity at the very beginning, through Paul. It was a romantic faith. And Baeck began his polemic with his definition of romanticism which, one-sided as it is, does give us an insight into a certain mood and mode of religion. Applying Schlegel's statement about the romantic book as one "which treats sentimental material in a phantastic form" to religion, Baeck notes an exact parallel:

Tense feelings supply its content, and it seeks its goals in the now mythical, now mystical visions of the imagination. Its world is the realm in which all rules are suspended; it is the world of the irregular, the extraordinary and the miraculous, that world which lies beyond all reality, the remote which transcends all things. . . . [28, pp. 189–190]

The romantic person caught in this mood luxuriates in a longing that does not reach out toward the infinite and does not culminate in action: it is longing for the sake of longing, in the manner of Novalis, who praises his Christianity for being truly "the religion of voluptuousness."[20] The

---

[19] Carl Schmitt [167, p. 49]: "The salvation of Germany could not come out of the system of [civil constitutional] legality. It came out of the German people itself, out of the National Socialist movement . . . with a German soldier, but precisely a *political* soldier, Adolf Hitler. . . . Now, the way was open to reach clear internal political decisions." Schmitt opened a 1936 scientific congress with the charge: "We must free the German spirit of all Jewish falsifications of the concept of spirit [*Geist*] which have made it possible for Jewish emigrants to label the wonderful work of Gauleiter Julius Streicher something nonspiritual." [quoted by Juergen Habermas, "Der deutsche Idealismus der juedischen Philosophen" in *Portraets zur deutsch-juedischen Geistesgeschichte,* Thilo Koch, ed. (Cologne, 1961), p. 123]

[20] Reinhold Mayer [150, p. 95], misses the point when he defines Novalis as a sober, rational person. Life and teaching are not always identical.

romantic mood is seen by Baeck as an ecstatic abandonment, as that aspect of religion turning piety into something passive and weary, into dependent feeling. Romantic religion, with its surrender to the mood of helplessness, destroyed ethics—this was Baeck's chief charge against it. The romantic personality withdrew from the world and journeyed into the past. And a religious type of romantic personality developed—the type Baeck found dominant in the Christian faith.

Baeck realized that there are certain romantic elements in every religion, that there is an interweaving of types in life. His last writings celebrate the totality of Jewish existence in which the romantic expression finds its proper place. But he did not retreat from the position taken here, which sees that the romantic aspect of one religion is a quiet side excursion, while it becomes the main road traveled for another faith. That is the distinction Baeck sees between the classical religion Judaism, where the romantic is a controlled minor note, and the romantic religion, Christianity, where the romantic aspect dominates the faith.

What made Christianity a romantic religion? According to Baeck, Paul opened the way to the Greek mystery religions with their exuberance of emotion, the enthusiastic flight from reality, the longing for an experience. This pattern was conquering the ancient world; allying itself to it, Christianity swept to victory:

> What is called the victory of Christianity was in reality this victory of romanticism. Before Christianity took its course, that through which it eventually became Christianity—or, to put it differently, whatever in it is non-Jewish—had already become powerful enough to be reckoned as a world faith, as a new piety which united the nations. [28, p. 198]

Throughout this work, Baeck tends to ignore the Jewish aspects of Paul, viewing him more as an outside figure from Asia Minor, bred to the romantic mood from early days. Paul is described as wanting to be in both worlds, and thus finding for himself a Jewish messiah who would fulfill the romantic needs of the pagan world. The faith he taught contained the essentials of the pagan mysteries: the romantic fate of a god reflecting man's inexorable lot; a dramatic process of salvation; and the romantic myth. With it, Paul left Judaism; "for there was no place in it for any myth that would be more than a parable . . . this myth was the bridge on which Paul went over to romanticism." [28, p. 203] Baeck recognized that Jewish aspects within Paul kept fighting romanticism;

but he stands in history as the apostle who drew his group into the romanticism beyond Judaism and created the new romantic faith—Christianity. Baeck's basic work in midrashic texts shows the Jewish community resisting the pressure of the outer environment and its syncretism. Paul's life is seen as an example where the outside pressure proved too strong.

In paralleling Strich and Woelfflin, Baeck is not trying to equate aesthetics with religion. He rather contends that the romantic personality takes the aesthetic experience into religion and magnifies it at the expense of ethical action and intellectual knowledge. The moment of revelation becomes everything for the romantic; it changes the nature of faith and makes the moment of artistic vision, the moment of grace and redemption, unrelated to man's striving. It becomes the whole, the essence of life, the full content of existence. The initial instant of reception becomes fulfillment, "romantic magic becomes romantic truth." [28, p. 208] The moment's experience is overvalued, and faith stresses the surrender to that moment at the expense of ethical action.

Baeck's greatest objection to Pauline religion is this experience of faith that brings the romantic into the realm of the transcendent beyond which all strife and movement has ceased. Man in this world has a task to perform and is therefore a creature endowed with purpose and power. Man, transported into the world beyond, is only an onlooker—a consumer, it might be said, of the experience of ecstatic faith; and he does not earn salvation—it is given to him. He does not recognize God, but God recognizes him: the dialogue is one-sided. Romantic religion only experiences Schleiermacher's "taste of infinity": the living experience of the true believer who knows the joy of feeling himself saved or the anguish of feeling himself a sinner.

This theme is developed in greater detail, particularly the romantic espousal of *gnosis* over *chochmah.* Yet Baeck's approach to Christianity is not one-sided; a partial rejection of romanticism in areas of Catholic thought is noted. Throughout, Baeck expresses his sympathy for that Calvinism and Anabaptism which drew deeply upon its Old Testament background and stressed voluntarism and ethical action; appealing to man's will to improve the world by action in God's honor. In "Judentum in der Kirche" [5, pp. 136 ff.], this is clearly expressed: Baeck found Calvinism an open door to the modern world, permitting access for the ethical injunctions of the Old Testament. The influence of Max Weber can be noted here. Weber's thesis on the contribution of English and

Dutch sects of Calvinist origin to the making of the modern middle class helped Baeck find a place for the Jewish contribution to modern life. As Hans Liebeschuetz has observed: "Weber's theory . . . offered the link between Jewish belief and modern civilization."[21] But when Baeck encounters Luther, the polemic is renewed with vigor. Baeck sees Luther renewing Paul's romanticism with the motto *sola fide*; man should wait for salvation and faith *velut paralyticum* "as one paralyzed." [28, p. 205] It is this paralysis which leads to pessimism, to estrangement, making the romantic subject not only to *Welttrunkenheit* but also to *Weltschmerz*.

The Pauline religion here constructed by Baeck is not necessarily Christianity at a specific time and place of past or present. It is a construct of the negative aspects of Christian faith, lurking within, inhibiting Christianity from proceeding on the great tasks shared with Judaism. As we view Baeck's construction, it is once more seen as the polemic against the other, as the apologetic for what is his own:

> One might characterize the Pauline religion in sharp juxtapositions: absolute dependence as opposed to the commandment, the task, of achieving freedom; leaning as opposed to self-affirmation and self-development; quietism as opposed to dynamism. There the human being is the subject; here, in romantic religion, the object. The freedom of which . . . it likes to speak is merely . . . received as a gift, the granting of salvation as a fact, not a goal to be fought for. It is the faith that does not go beyond itself, that is not the task of life; only a "thou hast" and not a "thou shalt." In classic religion, man is to become free through the commandment; in romantic religion he has become free through grace. [28, p. 211]

Once more, we see the essence of Judaism defined through the flaws of the romantic mood within the daughter of religion.

Baeck's critique was not that of an objective, dispassionate observer. Romanticism was an enemy encountered in all aspects of life: in culture, literature, politics. The first version of this essay was written when the romantic position was gaining adherents in German politics; the second, when it had gained control. And it is significant that this collection of Baeck's essays was immediately confiscated and destroyed by the Nazi government: it is not apolitical. Romanticism's mood of subservience to

---

[21] Hans Liebeschuetz, "Between Past and Future: Leo Baeck's Historical Position" in the (1967) yearbook of the Leo Baeck Institute. I am grateful to the author for the proof sheets of this interesting article.

the state is stated in challenging terms. And Baeck's attack upon "the silent coldness with which the Protestant Church in Germany endured . . . serfdom and traffic in human beings" [28, p. 214] is certainly unfair when we review the position on social issues taken by that church in America and Europe during the twentieth century—but had an immediate application in Nazi Germany in 1938. Baeck notes the tendency within all romantic religion—from mystery cults to the present—to come to terms with tyrants. Where the emphasis shifts to another world, accommodation to a world of tyranny is not uncommon (Judaism itself has not been free of this sin). The romantic religion can attempt to stand *outside* of culture, living solely for itself; it can stand *alongside* of culture in an uneasy compromise; but when it really enters *into* culture (as we have noted, this is the preposition operative for Leo Baeck as for Paul Tillich) it ceases to be romantic religion. [28, p. 215] An alternative does exist: Religion can dominate a culture to the hurt of both. The history of every "Christian culture" is seen by Baeck as an example of a crippling, stulti-fying construct. Throughout, this writing shows us the optimism and rationalism of a mood already estranged from its environment: Before the twentieth century began, the romantic mood was a native of Ger-many. Fichte filled the atmosphere of the university tavern; Treitschke's book rested on the front parlor table; and the rise of political romanticism had not been an accident.

The essay returns to the argument with Harnack: if the origin of Christianity is placed outside of time, its history loses its dynamic thrust and becomes captive to romanticism. Once again, polemics juxtapose both faiths:

> Faith is made dependent on the certification of a story. To be sure, it is also characteristic of the genuinely historically revealed religion that it knows about the mystery of the beginning and picks a single event out of the past to determine the course of truth. Yet it makes an essential difference whether, as in this case, a *beginning* is posited or, as in the Pauline religion, the absolute goal and the ultimate fulfillment are posited. In the one case, the idea of further creative activity is posited or at least admitted; in the other, it is rejected from the onset. . . . Classical religion knows living history; romantic religion only a finished story. [28, p. 219]

Baeck would assert here that the Christian understanding of Calvary is that of romantic history: a vision of the past outside of history, an *Urzeit* that will return to *Endzeit*, but not within human history. Judaism, on the other hand, knows only the way of human history that leads from Sinai to the future: only the task is clear, and not the end of days. Judaism is the knowledge of the unending way; Romantic Christianity instead already knows of the ultimate fulfillment and rejoices in that saving knowledge.

In this rejoicing rests a fundamental problem of romantic religion. The life of faith is here tied to a subjective experience which is not a continuous one. How can this be captured within daily life? Pauline religion's answer was that of the sacraments. They objectify the miracle of the religious experience. They are entirely material and objective for the romantic faith—they have to be; for if they become symbols they are no longer the actual miracle which enters the life of romantic faith (Luther is again seen as the romantic, Zwingli and the Anabaptists as the classic tendency within Protestantism striving to come to terms with this problem [28, p. 226][22]). Baeck's Liberal Judaism comes to the foreground here as, contrary to traditional Jewish views, he emphasizes that the sacraments are only symbols for Judaism. Paul makes the sacrament indispensable:

> Judaism, too, created its ceremonies, perhaps . . . too many. But here they were erected only as . . . a "fence around the doctrine" . . . they are symbols and signs which point to something religious, but their observance was . . . not yet piety, nor yet a good work. . . . The religion of the sacraments has its place in the Church of the miracle; and its cult with its ceremonial is the drama of the miracle. [28, p. 227]

Baeck's first writings had been even stronger in de-emphasizing the ritual and the possibility of deriving any meaning for it out of the human experience. But when he rewrote *The Essence of Judaism*, the mystery had come to stand more firmly next to the commandment within that human experience; and the point made above was phrased with great care:

> The idea of the *mystery* is something real in the Church, something which becomes tangible in the sacrament; but in Judaism, it is something ideal. It designates something unfathomable which is of God and not of man, something that can only be intuited. God's being is concealed by a dark remoteness impenetrable to human vision; only pious devotion, with its meditation and its silence, can draw close to Him. Here is where the *commandments* enter the world of man: good action is also the beginning of all

---

[22] Here, as in several other places as suggested to this writer by Wilhelm Pauck, I have had to differ with the text and substitute "Anabaptists" for "Baptists."

wisdom. Man's duty precedes the knowledge of God; and that knowledge of Him is less the act of possession than the process of searching and inquiring. [2a, p. 6]

Sacrament here begins to regain its place as an expression of Jewish existence. Beyond its utility of preserving Israel and sanctifying the everyday experience, it points toward the Divine which can only be intuited. But in "Romantic Religion," Baeck draws a firm boundary between this pointing, indicating sacrament and the Christian sacrament which claims that the curtain has been penetrated and that the mystery is now tangible and real, to be enjoyed, manipulated, and controlled by the sacraments. When the sacrament becomes the actual religious experience, religion loses its dynamic power for Baeck. It leaves life and establishes its own artificial world: the Church.

Dilthey's typological approach and the use of psychological criteria mark Baeck's approach not only in his analyses of individuals but also in his dealings with institutions. Baeck sees the Church less as a historically conditioned institution than as the response to the psychic needs of the romantic who is brought there by the desire for repose, whose romantic faith requires established authority as its necessary complement in this world. The law of "psychic retribution" makes the romantic faith seek an authority in matters of faith. [28, p. 234] Beyond the psychic need of the romantic for authority, Baeck saw the Church as the necessary place where the miracle gains its permanent and continual existence. The kingdom of God is the Church—that is why there can be no salvation outside of the Church. The romantic world is a closed one: Man is complete within himself and his romantic experience.

Inside the Church, salvation is guaranteed to its members by this process: They must be permitted to partake regularly of the miracle. This leads to intercessors: "alongside the men of complete romanticism there appeared the men of the prepared sacraments: alongside the saints and monks, the priests." [28, p. 230] And faith comes to find itself content to be faith in the experience of others. The place of the *fides qua creditur* (the faith *with* which one believes) is taken over by the *fides quae creditur* (the faith *in* which one believes). [28] It lives in a world of dogma, of "frozen feeling" which inhibits the pursuit of truth, where religious life becomes a stately procession divorced from life. We must note here that this position exhibits Baeck's independence. The Jewish community patterned itself after Protestantism in a number of ways: The Protestants were identified with the more liberal trends within twentieth century Germany; Protestant theology seemed a more adaptable pattern for Jewish thought than Baeck was prepared to admit.[28] From the very beginning, Baeck refused the security of a system: His structure of polarities maintains an openness which cannot freeze into dogma and places him in a lonely position, midway between the systems.

In this polemic hammering out the form of romantic religion, Baeck's concept of polarity in religion gained in clarity. Alongside the romantic the classic unfolds: Mystery is confronted by commandment. Yet, because this is polemics, Baeck tends to ignore the interaction between the two. There are exceptions: In the discussion of sacraments, the ceremonies of classical religion are seen as pointing toward the mystery. But on the whole, the sharp critique stands out, directed against romantic religion which is Christianity which is Pauline thought. Ultimately, German Jewry here confronts the German Lutheran Church. *Sola fide* is interpreted as making the just man the creation of Divine grace and not of his own moral actions. When the Church was silent against dictatorship, Baeck mourned for the ethical stifled by the romantic mood surrounding it. He saw romantic religion placing sin and guilt into nature whence it could only be extricated by grace and not by human action. Outside of human life, romantic religion watches the great drama between the redeemer and his opponent, the devil. At that point, man has ceased to be an actor; the struggle is carried on outside of him. Man is no longer a moral subject, an ethical individual; ethics has lost its foundation in life. Once again, Pauline thinking is judged to lack ethical content. The fact that Paul continually made moral demands is ascribed to his honest and deeply ethical personality and to his Jewish roots (Baeck's later position is here clearly foreshadowed). Baeck separates the person of Paul from the faith of Paul. The faith of Paul, as seen again in Luther, is the decisive opposition to ethics: let life be the earth, and the doctrine, heaven—*vitam esse terram, doctrinam coelum.*"[24]

---

[23] Hans Liebeschuetz [145] indicates Geiger's dependence upon Protestant thinking, notably the evolutionism of the Tuebingen school. And he rightly shows Baeck's divergence from Geiger, partially along the lines of the Historical School of the Breslau Seminary. A twentieth century example of Jewish theology patterned after Protestant theology, giving due credit to its inner Jewish spirit, was Kaufmann Kohler's *Grundriss einer systematischen Theologie des Judentums auf geschichtlicher Grundlage* (Berlin, 1910). It was nevertheless unfortunate that Kohler and not Baeck was the theologian studied by the Reform rabbinate in America.

[24] Baeck [28, p. 252], quoting Martin Luther, *Werke,* Weimar edition, vol. XIV, p. 464.

Kant's liberating "you can because you ought to" is then compared with Luther's view that man's will can only be the will to sin. [28, pp. 254–255]

Baeck recognizes that the religious desire for ethics continues to live in the Church; but he sees it acquiring a hollow sentimental pathos, the "false enthusiasm" of Schleiermacher's *Monologe* and the advocatory art in his *Christliche Glaubenslehre*. [28, p. 257] Both are based on an external acceptance of ethics and do not conflict with one another because there are no inner involvements: Pious Church hymns and vulgar love songs have been composed by the same author! The sentimental mood is unrelated to the ethical life. Baeck's judgment is excessive here. The Christian dialectic theology of that time could point toward an ethics devoid of sentimentality. And there were also Jewish authors—Salomon dei Rossi, for example—who could be charged with writing both sacred and profane works.

On one point Baeck remained consistent: The eternal "thou shalt" of Jewish existence was part of its creation from the very beginning—there was a Divine law to be obeyed which could not be controlled by the state or by the individual. Romantic religion, on the other hand, made law an experience, a plaything which was no more than one aspect of a world controlled by dogma and by miracle. Casuistry came into play:

> Where religion confronts the soul as a dream that has come to us and as a vision that is enjoyed, the religious actuality with its commandments is no more than an image that is beheld. It is a message that is perceived dimly, as if from a vast distance, and can mean everything without demanding anything: one can play with it and subtilize it. [28, p. 265]

Baeck saw both casuistry and frivolity as diverse aspects of the romantic faith. His own character is revealed in his response: that touch of austerity, of severity, which carried upon itself the imprint of Kant's religion of duty. Baeck had little contact with children; he did not have to teach them in Berlin. The same mistrust of the romantic mood which makes children forget the goal and rejoice in immediacy, with life a joyous game, also kept Baeck some distance from the intellectual game played by the Talmudist. The *baal ha-Halacha* has the basic task of linking community and individual with the "thou shalt!"; it is a necessary, a vital task—but it contain dangers. Casuistry can reside there. The world of Oral Law, the vast sea of the Talmud, can overwhelm the scholar and sweep him away, far from the realities of historical existence. Baeck was

a *baal ha-midrash;* perhaps, partially, because the Halacha of the Talmud
seeks to subordinate the contemporary to the past; the Midrash, at its
best, gives advice and shares experience instead of laws. The law is here
less likely to be subjugated to external authority. In any event, Midrash
and Halacha are part of the same framework in which the synagogue
can never wholly control and dispense the law—the authority of the
synagogue is derived from the community and is not autonomous.

Speaking out of the same matrix of Jewish experience, Ernst Simon
tries to discover how the individual Jew comes to take upon himself the
burden of being God's witness, which he sees as the Jewish task:

> To bridge this chasm [between the average individual and the mission of
> the community] is one of the main tasks of Jewish law as a way of life—
> Halachah. It enjoins on its believers a discipline from early childhood on.
> It is total because it does not exclude or set free any province of life, but
> forms all of them according to its patterns. However, it is not totalitarian,
> firstly, because it does not possess any supreme authoritarian body that
> could be likened to the papacy, and then because it does not approve of any
> religious hierarchy. . . . Last but not least, Jewish law is based on the still
> ongoing procedure of finding the truth . . . by means of free discussion. . . .
> [179a, pp. 311–312]

This is the same assertion of the openness of a tradition which ever
goes back to the ongoing experience of the people—the law, the Torah,
is not out of reach of Israel; it has been given to them on this earth.
Man is God's partner, responsible, with tasks to perform in the here
and now.

At the heart of Baeck's polemic against romantic religion rests this
concept of man. Baeck felt that Pauline Christianity encroached upon the
universally human. The ideal of the baptized believer, which goes hand
in hand with the sacraments, interferes with the growth of the ethical
ideal of the good man. By separating the saved from the lost, it also
undermines the unity of mankind. The saved person, whether inducted
into a mystery religion or a member of the Church, views the unredeemed
in a manner that can easily lead to active intolerance. For when a church
possesses salvation, it must also have perfect justice—and can abolish opposition by judging it. If the *Mitmensch,* the fellow human being, can
be abolished, he can also be ignored. Baeck sees one danger of this
"finished, perfected justice, this self-assurance of the possessing" in the

expression of smug indifference. [28, p. 274] Indifference is a true mood of romanticism, perhaps even more so than intolerance: And it is entirely consistent with the repudiation of the law.

The final repudiation of the law is self-abandonment, the surrender to the mood of absolute dependence which Baeck finds in both Paul and Luther. He is grim and stubborn in indicting the dynamic Reformer as the voice of passivity, using Luther's own words against him: "What are the Ten Commandments to me? Why should I require the Law or good works for blessedness? When the nourishment of Christ does it, I am not permitted to do any good works to attain eternal life." [28, p. 277][25] Baeck praises Luther for checking the egotism and passivity of hermit and monk in the Church, but feels Luther responsible for a pietistic luxuriating in guilt which brought the Christian faith further into the romantic mood. But in that mood, the romantic faith wants everything now; faith has become a desire, an appetite for happiness. Despair takes hold of the worshipper; faith is attained through fear.

And the faith moves out of this world, leaving the Jewish hopes for a messianic age far behind it. In the last pages of the essay, Baeck stresses that the faith founded upon messianic hopes of the Jewish community has tried to rid itself of much implied by the early messianic vision. Thus, the Augsburg Confession repudiates the "Jewish doctrine... that the pious will have a worldly kingdom before the resurrection of the dead and destroy the impious." [28, p. 285][26] Most of Christianity, according to Baeck, has replaced the Biblical ideal of God's kingdom on earth with the kingdom of the Church, the romantic *civitas Dei*. Missionary activities of the Church, viewed from this position, are only an expansion of an empire and no longer advance the ancient dream of a better world. Baeck sketches the history of Christian missionary preaching after the old Jewish apostles and proclaiming the One God, His commandment, and His judgment; the changes during the second and third century when the Church's dogma and authority changed the character of those missions; and the age of egoistic and vigorous missions that created the worldwide Church. The bridge of doctrine between mother and daughter faith was shattered here; yet Baeck still finds and asserts the link of the human experience. The missionary journeyed for

---

[25] Quoting Martin Luther, *Werke,* Erlangen edition, vol. 48, p. 63.
[26] Quoting the Augsburg Confession, XVII, 5.

the Church; but the concern for his fellow man, which set his feet on the martyr's road, will always bring a warm response from a people who see their destiny in the vision of the Suffering Servant.

Romantic religion with its emphasis on feeling has to be challenged by the classic faith; Baeck never hesitates in his polemics. But here, at the close, the theology of polarity has to include even as it attacks:

> Romanticism is the contradiction and the opposition, often so necessary against that shallow reasonableness which would dispose of everything, against that enlightenment which has knowledge of and answers to everything, and against that activism which would take care of and execute everything. [28, p. 290]

But Baeck's point is that classic religion is not just rationalism or "enlightenment"; it contains the nonrational within itself. The revelation, the commandment, the knowledge of the holy come from outside the rational and yet inside of it, the religion of polarity which is God's covenant with man. And that religion, Judaism, receives the final statement in this great polemic which is also an apologetic. Judaism is shown as the great faith in which the mystery and the commandment join, where the longing for God is not an end in itself but a striving toward a goal of one mankind serving God by the fufillment of the commandment. Judaism knows that it must reach beyond the rational, but that it must find its way back into life. For as it discovers the covenant with God, the Holy that lies beyond reason, it is sent back to the life of the commandment in which man encounters the Divine as he meets his fellow man. Baeck's exploration of the romantic religion has gone full circle: Again he had written concerning the essence of Judaism.

V

Baeck's discussion of Christianity is a key to his theology and his philosophy of religion. It is also a necessary aspect of the Jewish-Christian dialogue in the twentieth century. With the impact of Vatican II, most assessments of this dialogue—if, as we have indicated, there is indeed two-way communication[27]—have occupied themselves with the materials

---

[27] Eliezer Berkovits [77a] has voiced some of the sharpest questions concerning this dialogue. The incisiveness of his polemic has brought new vigor to this discussion.

supplied by contemporary texts. No full assessment is possible, however, until we have gone to that time between world wars, in Germany, where Leo Baeck, Martin Buber, Franz Rosenzweig, and perhaps Hans Joachim Schoeps displayed a dazzling variety of ways in which Judaism addressed itself to Christianity. (Schoeps found an immediate response in those days—partially because he was more of a spokesman for Karl Barth to the Jewish community than a great interpreter of authentic Judaism to the outside world.) Buber—was Martin Buber: thinker and sensitive poet whose language crystallized the moods and longings of his age; philosopher; but not a critic whose sharpness could penetrate the awareness of the Christian and lead him outside his faith and into a Jewish world which could instruct him through its differences.

Important parallels between Buber and Baeck must be noted here. Both confronted Christianity with genuine concern and with creative polemics.[28] Nor was Buber a romanticist. The prophetic mode is clear, the demands he made were immediate. Where he finds Jesus as his "great brother," it is the Jewish figure in the mold of the suffering servant which is acknowledged. Yet there is a romantic mood in Buber which blurs distinctiveness. In his presentation, the world of Chassidism becomes sentimentalized, poetic, more Buber's creation than an accurate depiction of what once existed. Buber must be honored as a poet of existence who speaks of the condition of man. The very emphasis on the universal makes it difficult for him to be a spokesman of that particularity which is Israel addressing the Christian world. The details of that particularity, the ethical framework *and* the encounter with the mystery, come clearest through Baeck. In time, when Franz Rosenzweig's writings are translated, that great and tragic voice may add a still deeper dimension to the dialogue (the very fact that men like Ehrenberg and Rosenstock-Huessy considered Rosenzweig's Jewishness a dangerous aberration, a romantic nationalism, shows that he has not yet been heard). Meanwhile, it is Baeck who speaks clearest out of the time between the wars, and who comes to speak out of the Holocaust.

The "young" Baeck, as we have seen in this chronological survey, approached Christianity through the polemic with Harnack still in the spirit of the nineteenth century. Essences were defined against one an-

---

[28] Martin Buber's *Two Types of Faith* [92] is an important parallel to Baeck's "Romantic Religion."

other; and it is an aspect of apologetics that the opponent shapes the self-presentation of the apologete. To the extent that ecstasy, aesthetics, emotion, dogma, and ritual are placed in the center of Christianity, they must be excluded from Judaism, which comes closer to Kant's religion of duty, to an ethical rigorism where the emotions are at best peripheral. But this criticism of Baeck can be overstated. Baeck's position in *The Essence of Judaism* shows that the opponent, the passive faith of the egotist, was identified as Buddhism; and the family ties between Judaism and Christianity are emphasized strongly. And Baeck showed himself a special type of apologete in this work: It is not addressed primarily to the rest of the world; it speaks to his own people. Rabbi Simha Bunim of Psyshe used to teach: "If I am I because you are you, and you are you because I am I, then I am not I and you are not you. But if I am I because I am I, and you are you because you are you, then I am I and you are you." Baeck's presentation proceeds out of that insight. It is his statement of law in Jewish life which points out authoritarianism in Christianity; the lack of dogma within Judaism which suggests the frozenness of a doctrinaire community; the role of the synagogue, which leads to the condemnation of that church which makes an alliance with secular authority; and the concept of man as the free agent of God which challenges the notion of flawed man as an object of grace.

When Baeck proceeded to the direct examination of the Gospels and of the Christian faith, his writings already were coming out of the context of his developing theology of polarity. Behind the incorporation of Christianity into Judaism there is the assertion of the universal which is encountered through the particular. And the essence of the faith is no longer viewed apart from life, but out of the context of human experience. The Pauline faith attacked so bitterly—and it is certainly a *Zerrbild*, a distortion of trends which were not as strong as depicted in Christianity, not as weak as assumed in Judaism—is still constructed as an essence, as the pattern of romantic faith. But the charge against Paul is not only that he took the Jewish faith of his master into the mystery religions of the environment; more important, he took the community of followers out of the context of Jewish life. Even Jewish ideas within Christianity had to change in this new environment: messianism and its ethical imperatives which place a better world into man's task lost their original meaning. They became a withdrawal from the world; or they merely abetted the building of a Church empire.

Baeck's move from the essence of Judaism to the existence of the Jewish people is gradual. It is already foreshadowed in his early writings; and the framework of polarities contains the difficult middle way which separates Baeck from Buber and Rosenzweig on the one side, from Hermann Cohen on the other. In Baeck's later writings, his treatment of Paul can only be understood in terms of the shift in Baeck's approach to the problems of theology. Baeck's 1952 essay on "The Faith of Paul" [59] was hailed by Reinhold Mayer as a fundamental change in Baeck's judgment which would now also free the Church of the charge of romanticism. [150, pp. 105–106] Mayer is in error here. The basic judgment of Paul and of Christianity remains the same. What has been overcome is the construct of nineteenth century scholarship in this field which saw Paul and his theology as the absolute antithesis of Jesus and his teachings. Baeck still maintains the difference between what Paul and Jesus taught. But, as he had come to affirm Jesus as a Jewish personality, so does he now stress the kinship of the two persons. Baeck's new emphasis on peoplehood which includes Paul as his typology of the Jew in the world takes on new dimensions.

The sympathetic study of Paul does not lead Baeck into retractions regarding Paul's teachings, which he sees as a turning away from monotheism: "The old theocentric faith of Judaism is superseded by a new Christ-centered faith ... Here is a parting of the ways in religion." [59, pp. 146–147] Baeck here confronts a Christianity which conceals God and makes him the *deus absconditus,* surrounded by dark mystery while the refulgent lights shine around the Christ. Baeck cannot accept the center of Paul's teachings as derived from Judaism. But an enlarged feeling for the complexities of Jewish existence, for the various modes and expressions which are the atmosphere for all Jewish life, now brings Baeck to the acknowledgement that many of the images and concepts of Paul come out of Paul's Jewish experience.

Paul is seen as a Jewish personality. Where a Greek would have mused upon a vision such as experienced by Paul, would have cogitated, reflected, and then would have written concerning it, Paul acted at once: "Only the Jew would always be aware that the revelation entailed the mission ... the last Jew in the young Church was its last apostle." [59, pp. 142–143] And Paul acts; and he reacts to Jewish teaching. Jewish problems fill his theology. Jewish methods of Biblical interpretation are used in solving the problems. But he arrives at answers which place him outside of Judaism. For there is a Jewish tradition that the Law will be abrogated with the coming of the Messiah. Once Paul has decided for himself that the Messiah has come, even the Jewish aspects of his theological structure demand that he break with the Law. This does not take him outside of Jewish life in every sense: "The Jewish people remained, however, interwoven with Paul's messianic Christian faith. The 11th Chapter of Romans shows this very clearly. [59, p. 166] It is only when this passionate and stubborn Jew lets his monotheistic fervor enter the mystery cults that the breach becomes unmendable. Baeck must deplore the results of Paul's teaching. But the Jewish scholar who could turn to the Gospels as documents of Jewish history has now also approached the point where the life and personality of Saul of Tarsus are one more documentation of Jewish existence in a world where the particular is ultimately united before God.

There are other ways in which the polemic against Christianity becomes milder in the final writings. Once the emphasis is no longer upon the essence but upon the existential reality as it arises out of life, man's imperfections must be considered. More, there is the love of fellow man which negates separation. Baeck's polemic against Christianity was always infused by the love of parent to child which stresses the ancestral heritage. To this, in the sphere of human experience, is added the love of brother to brother. But in our time, this sharpens the polemic: "Cain, where is thy brother?" Baeck now had different questions for the Church:

> The subject of our questions is not the "what" but the "how," that is to say, not the belief in itself, in its contents, but so to speak the conduct of the belief, not what the belief wants to say, but how it is saying it. Every religion claims its place and asserts its task in the world. It also wishes to strengthen this place and to confirm this task. It cannot dispense with this. [62, p. 104][29]

In asking Christianity about its task in the world, Baeck also asserts its right to that task: it must join its parent in striving for a better world. "Romantic" Christianity and "classic" Judaism are united in the human experience in which the finite reaches out towards the infinite. They share in the flaws of the human experience. But the past history of the Holocaust differentiates between victims and perpetrators (and those

---

[29] See also Walter Jacob [138b, p. 170] on his interpretation of Baeck's late writings concerning Christianity.

sunk into romantic inactivity). And when the Church is now asked by Baeck to account for its actions rather than its belief, the basic question of the Jewish-Christian dialogue comes to the foreground. No full answer has as yet been given. The silence of the Church during the Six Day War (June, 1967) indicated to a deeply hurt Jewish community that the Church is indeed unable to give that full answer. But the challenges of the aftermath of war, when hurts have to be assuaged, provide a new opportunity for Church and Synagogue to strive for a world of peace. Once Christianity has become reconciled to the continuing fact of Jewish existence, it will be able to recognize the Jew as a witness of God. Church and Synagogue can then join together and strive for the kingdom of God. A true dialogue will then commence.

NOTES

This issue raised on page 107 is often obscured by those who would like to claim Buber for Christianity or expel him from Judaism. Buber, Rosenzweig, and Baeck are all committed to the Jewish tradition and opposed to Christianity. Buber's initial statement on Christianity, written in 1909 ("Drei Reden ueber das Judentum": Die Erneuerung des Judentums, pp. 52 ff.), clearly parallels Baeck's position:

> That which was creative and not eclectic in the beginnings of Christianity was unequivocally Judaism. This spiritual revolution flamed up in Jewish land; it wakened out of the most ancient Jewish communal associations; Jewish men carried it throughout the land; they spoke to the Jewish people and none else (as is constantly emphasized), and it solely prophesied the renewal of the religiosity of deed in Judaism.

Seeing Jesus as rising out of this Jewish tradition in his teachings, Buber concludes:

"That which is creative in Christianity is not Christianity but Judaism . . . and that which, within Christianity, is not Jewish, is not creative and is mixed together out of a thousand rites and dogmas." Buber rejects Christianity at the same time firmly placing the Nazarene spiritual movement into the mainstream of Jewish history.

In 1933, Buber and Karl Ludwig Schmidt had a confrontation; published in 1936 as *Die Stunde und die Erkenntnis*. [89] Drawing upon this, Schoeps emphasizes Buber's words that:

We, as Israel, understand our inability to accept this proclamation [of Christ's coming] in another fashion. We understand the Christology of Christianity throughout as an important event which has taken place between the world above and the world below.

But, as Schoeps indicates, there is a difference between belief and acknowledgment, particularly since, Buber continues by stating that "we are not able to define God under any aspect of this revelation" (Buber, as quoted by Schoeps [169, pp. 150 ff.])

In 1950, Buber's *Two Types of Faith* [92] again showed that he accepted Jesus as part of Jewish tradition, but not Paul. And his often misquoted introductory remarks about Jesus must be seen in this context:

> Jesus habe ich von Jugend auf als meinen grossen Bruder empfunden. Das die Christenheit ihn als Gott und Erloeser angesehen hat und ansieht, ist mir immer als eine Tatsache von hoechstem Ernst erchienen, die ich um seinet und um meinetwillen zu begreifen suchen muss. Ein weniges von den Ergebnissen dieses Bergreifen-wollens ist hier niedergelegt. Mein eigenes bruederlich sufgeschlossenes Verhaeltnis zu ihm ist immer staerker und reiner geworden, und ich sehe ihn heute mit staerkerem und reinerem Blick als je.

As Arthur A. Cohen evaluates this [94, p. 65]:

> Contemporary Jewish theology—Buber and Rosenzweig in particular—are no less critical of the fundamental character of Christian thought for all their appreciation of the authentic witness of the Synoptic Gospels. Buber's affirmation that "from my youth onwards I have found in Jesus my great brother" attests only to the consistency of Buber's position and his unqualified honesty. The Jesus in whom Buber finds companionship is he whom Buber considers the inheritor of the prophetic tradition of the "suffering servant."

Buber, Rosenzweig, and Baeck consistently reject the essence of Christianity; but their approaches do differ. Baeck, with all "positive neutrality," is sharper.

6

Leo Baeck and the Religion of Polarity

The recognition of the polemic core which is the heart of Baeck's presentation, the exhaustive survey of his writings which in the end identifies them with the literature of apologetics, lead to a basic problem in the evaluation of Baeck's presentation: Can Baeck achieve a fair presentation of Judaism in the framework of apologetic writing? When the goal is self-defense rather than self-realization, an overlooking of one's own faults and an overstressing of the opponent's weaknesses is almost unavoidable. And there are other dangers in the apologetic approach that must be examined and applied to Leo Baeck before we can proceed with our presentation.

In 1923, Franz Rosenzweig's criticisms of Baeck's work centered on this point.[1] Apologetics, according to Rosenzweig, had been the legitimate method of Jewish thought concerned with the totality of Judaism throughout the centuries. Either the Jew *learned* within Judaism and took the framework for granted; or he moved to the outside, to the periphery of Judaism, and then his thought was determined by the outside forces and took on the strength and weaknesses of the apologetic

---

[1] Franz Rosenzweig, "Apologetisches Denken; Bemerkungen zu Brod und Baeck (1925)" in [163, pp. 31–42].

mode. In the writings of Baeck and Max Brod, Rosenzweig saw both: the *weakness* of apologetics that depicts Christianity in its ideational structure and abstracts it to the point where it loses its warmth and its life (Rosenzweig's own existential commitment comes through here), the desire to believe the theologians and not the saints and nobles of Christian life, and the corresponding weakness of designating that which speaks to the author out of his Jewish tradition as "specifically Jewish" rather than recognizing in it the universally human; and the *strength* of apologetics which turns to the ancient tradition with new vision and becomes a renewed testimony. [163, pp. 36–39]

Speaking specifically about Baeck, Rosenzweig has reluctant praise for the representative of an opposing group within Judaism:

> It may be noted that Baeck says some very fine things about Law; but he does so incidentally and without giving them a central emphasis. In the same way, the liberal rabbi (particularly in the second edition) says things about the Jewish people and about Jewish history which are of a depth scarcely reached by that which the Zionist poet has to say. There is perhaps no more hopeful symptom in contemporary Jewish existence than this reversal of roles. [163, p. 41]

Baeck's writings had parried an attack from the world of letters, just as Brod had responded to an attack within his own experience. Rosenzweig does not find Brod's passion in Baeck's *Essence of Judaism*. Instead, the deep and quiet love of a man at home in all of Judaism parallels Brod's genuine ecstasy with a great classic statement. Baeck's polemical misunderstandings of Christianity do not show themselves clearly in this work, according to Rosenzweig; but they do speak out of the later essay on romantic religion. Baeck is also seen as having a faulty understanding of Law in Judaism. And the opposition between Rosenzweig's and Baeck's approaches becomes clear when Rosenzweig states:

> Baeck fails to realize that the critical point is found at the point where the essence of Judaism recognized by him is more *essence* of Judaism than essence of *Judaism*. Just as with Brod, it may happen that at this point, where the deed rises out of the faith, the Christian reader will follow Baeck without hesitation; but the Jewish reader will pause. [163, pp. 40–41]

In the end, Baeck's failure to understand the essence of Judaism is seen by Rosenzweig as the result of the apologetic character of thinking. The apologete's theme—his own essence—is determined by the outside attack. For the thinker examines that which is inmost in himself, sees it—but does not see himself. For he does not see his outer self which combines with the inner core, lacks the knowledge that the innermost which he equates with himself is rather the inner core of every man; when he thinks that he is speaking about himself, he is rather speaking about every human being:

> And his own self, the binding of the elements of humanity into the interwovenness which he is—this remains a mystery to him. Apologetic thinking cannot cross this barrier. The final strength of recognition is denied him, just as he is spared the final pain of recognition. For final recognition no longer defends: Final recognition judges. [163, p. 42]

There is some truth in this charge against Baeck. Baeck became the great apologete of Judaism in his time. Confronting the ultimate attack launched against his people, he would not and could not dwell on the flaws of a people that needed the knowledge of its inner strength and not its inner weakness. Time after time, in *The Essence of Judaism* and in *This People Israel,* he saw the flaws of Judaism and of the Jewish people as "momentary aberrations," a stumbling, an understandable reaction to outside pressures from which the faith and the people quickly recovered. Even where Baeck judged, it was in order to defend: The individual should not become the prototype of the people and enmesh the people in his own guilt. Rosenzweig could not foresee the future; but he did mark a tendency in Baeck's early writings which was to become more pronounced in the years ahead.

There are other ways in which Rosenzweig's criticism can be not only accepted, but also extended: The polemics in *The Essence of Judaism* is even stronger than Rosenzweig indicated; and, with all its insights, the essay on romantic religion shows the flaws of apologetics and polemics noted by Rosenzweig. The concepts "romanticism" and "classicism" are present for Baeck before anything else. Christian existence is sifted through them, and the classic aspects are separated and labeled the Jewish heritage of Christianity. On occasion, the worst is considered the norm and the best is viewed as the exception. If the essay, with all its exaggerations, still speaks to the conditions of religious life, it does so because it is a passionate polemic and not a reasoned presentation of two contrasting ways of religious thinking.[2]

---

[2] Professor Walter Kaufmann of Princeton, who translated Baeck's essay on romantic religion and many other writings by Baeck on Christianity, told me that his first reading of this essay was a profound experience which affected his life. In retro-

Nevertheless, it must be said that Rosenzweig never fully comes to terms with Leo Baeck. Teaching in the same tradition, they use the same words for different purposes, in particular, the word "Law." Both of them are disciples of Hermann Cohen, and their way parts with their interpretations of their master's words. We are confronted with a curious phenomenon. On the one side, we have Franz Rosenzweig, one of the great existential thinkers of the twentieth century, whose system is presented to us in the elaborations of that profound idealistic construction he called *The Star of Redemption.* On the other side, there stands Leo Baeck, one of the last spokesmen of German Judaism firmly established on the teachings of idealism, a leader of the Liberal Jewish community which was in search of a system—and he does not really present us with a system.

Rosenzweig clearly defined God, the world, and man, and the relationships between—but they are the content of experience for which he tries to find a conceptual form. But there is a dialogue within existence, one that rises out of revelation to creation and redemption; and the passionate experience of that revelation in every moment of existence turned Rosenzweig's system back into a personal testimony. Baeck's total experience of the Jewish faith as the religion of the Divine "Ought," the ethical commandment that rises out of every encounter with the Divine— these in the end make for a system in which the moment of experiencing the revelation (the heart of Rosenzweig) becomes suspect and is subordinated to the ethical way that leads from there. In the end, Rosenzweig celebrates the existence of each individual human being who experiences the Revelation; Baeck speaks of the People Israel and the Revelation vouchsafed to it: the Eternal Task of ethics, the Mission of Judaism. At that point, the existentialist confronts the idealist. Rosenzweig would break through and know God; Baeck is content to know His will.

"Where the deed rises out of the faith . . . the Jewish reader must pause" had been Rosenzweig's charge against Baeck. And he was right. This was the point on which they differed. Rosenzweig felt estranged from this liberal rabbi who could not go along with him into an

---

spect, he feels less impressed. It might be argued here that the mood, more than the argument, drew the reader into Baeck's book. A true confrontation leads men to choose sides, even when the argument is imperfect.

existential realm of law where men meet all the *mitzvot* as an objective reality which they must first experience before freely accepting or refusing all or part of the law. Baeck's liberal faith preceded and thus excluded such encounters. Rosenzweig felt the passion of Jewish existence, and saw detachment in Baeck's view of the *essence* of Judaism. There, Rosenzweig was wrong. Quite correctly, Rosenzweig had seen Baeck's writing as part of apologetic writing. It was a response to an attack taking place in the world of ideas—and the reality of that attack was felt in all its intensity by the pupil of Hermann Cohen. Baeck's reply was *The Essence of Judaism,* and its hidden polemics must be appreciated before it is fully understood.

When Rosenzweig speaks of the election of Israel, he notes that the works that deal with Jewish theology never mention it. Prayer, poetry, mysticism, and legend all deal with it, but not the philosopher—with one exception: Jehuda Halevi. [163, pp. 31–32] Rosenzweig does not come back to this idea; but he does suggest, later on, that Baeck speaks about the Jewish people with a depth going beyond the finest Zionist poet. Taken together with the knowledge that the election of Israel is central to *The Essence of Judaism,* we move to the suggestion that it cannot be fully understood until it is recognized as the great work of Jewish apologetics of the twentieth century, paralleling that masterpiece of the twelfth century: *The Essence of Judaism* may be bracketed with the *Kuzari: The Book of Argument and Proof in Defense of the Despised Faith.*

Baeck is not Halevi. The *Essence* is not the *Kuzari.* But it does speak of the Jewish people as the people of the Revelation, of Judaism as the great source of religious truth. It challenges the other interpretations, Buddhist, pagan, and Christian, and opens the way of mission for all who would join Israel and its faith. For those who look at the outer framework, it might seem that it would be more apt to compare Baeck's *Essence* with Maimonides' *Moreh Nevuchim:* Both can be seen as metaphysical interpretations of Judaism that rise out of the metaphysical challenge to the faith. Indeed, Baeck's *Essence* has only been read and understood along those rational lines, and it *is* a reasoned interpretation of the Jewish faith. But within that reason, already evident in the 1905 edition and becoming quite clear in the revised version, there is the not unromantic sense of the mystery. The book does not argue its way toward the existence of God. God is known. And this knowledge is not established by appeal to doctrine but out of the experience of the Jewish people: It is not the prophet's word but the prophetic experience that brings us to the confrontation of the Divine "Ought" of human existence. The living reality of Israel is asserted in the passion of the polemic, carrying within itself the knowledge of the tragic dimensions of humanity, of Israel within humanity, of created man confronting his Creator in the tension of existence. Because the polemic was concealed, this aspect of what is certainly a rational work schooled in the philosophy of idealism has also been hidden. But when the 1905 edition of *The Essence of Judaism* is set alongside the 1955 *This People Israel: The Meaning of Jewish Existence,* this inner aspect of Baeck's work breaks through.

There is one other reason to stress this reading of Baeck's work, one that rises out of the nature of the Jewish tradition. Baeck was a *baal ha-midrash,* one who specialized in the rabbinic homiletics of the first centuries and showed how to break open the structure of the rabbinic homily so that the hidden polemic could be found and seen as the basic motivating force behind the words. Baeck's own writings are part of that tradition and respond to the hermeneutical principles of an oral tradition in which not only the reading but also the listening to the text becomes basic to full understanding. And there is a certain stubbornness to the rabbinic tradition, grounded on the experience of Israel more than on the meditations of its thinkers, which does not permit itself to be fitted into an idealistic structure without letting its own existential reality be known. Baeck's words apply here: There is a twofoldness to Jewish life. That same twofoldness must be appreciated in the teaching of Leo Baeck.

II

The early Baeck, i.e., the young Jewish scholar who wrote *The Essence of Judaism* in 1905, contains this "twofoldness" just as much as the matured scholar of the twenties and thirties; but it took on a different form. At the turn of the century, Baeck found himself part of a large group of thinkers, Jewish and Christian, who attempted to overcome the historicism which had dominated the later nineteenth century by redefining their own religious tradition through a new theological statement. Baeck learned from Troeltsch and Dilthey in this struggle but also sees, within Jewish thought "the individual ideas and even the terminology of Hermann Cohen finding a continuation." [46, p. 274] What was now wanted was a theology and not a history of Judaism. For the old ways of life no longer gave support to the Jew. Torn out of his traditions, pressured to give his intellectual and even spiritual loyalty to the outside world, he had lost much of his connection with the past. The "scientific study of Judaism" which marked Jewish scholarship denoted the objectivity of those who could view it from the outside, who were objective because they were no longer subject to it. Judging those days, Baeck later felt that the science of Judaism had achieved a great deal, had even supplied a foundation for the Jew at a time when it was desperately needed—but at too high a price.

> Judaism was often regarded as merely an area for research, not as a matter of concern, not a problem of the seeking, thinking human being. History was studied for its own sake. . . . Aggadah . . . and Midrash . . . were only belatedly understood. [46, p. 278]

Baeck noted earlier attempts of the past century to frame a theology for the post-emancipated Jew, and he names Geiger and Steinheim. They could not and did not serve his needs. Nor could Christian theology help. Baeck saw Judaism as having its own peculiarity—the basis of its origin and its inner motivation—rising out of its special, characteristic problem which he defined in this manner:

> This problem, through and on account of which Judaism in all of its particularity has become universal—this specific problem of world history—is that of the incursion of the Infinite, Eternal, the One and Unconditional into the finite, temporal, manifold and limited, and of the spiritual and moral tension of the human fiber which is its result. [46, p. 281]

It is worth noting that here again the Revelation is a given fact, which does not have to be proven. It is given in the tension of the human fiber, i.e., Baeck is still speaking out of the experience of the Jewish people, out of the knowledge of man touched by the Divine and not out of the direct encounter with the Divine. But the two, the Infinite moving into the finite, and the resultant response, are here set next to one another. The roots for that teaching can be found in Baeck's work from the very beginning.

In Leo Baeck we see the Jewish scholar who wants to make a

specifically Jewish statement, but must make it in terms of the contemporary intellectual community in which he had found his training. At this point, there was only one teacher to whom he could turn: Hermann Cohen.[3]

It has been suggested here that the experience of Judaism cannot easily be fitted into the framework of idealism, that there is a stubbornness to the material that finds the opposite expression.

This may even find some support in the final work of Cohen: *The Religion of Reason out of the Sources of Judaism* [98]; but it must be granted that the Hermann Cohen who influenced Leo Baeck and supplied much of the framework for the 1905 edition of the *Essence* had succeeded in finding his place within idealism. The "early" Hermann Cohen had seen critical idealism completely in terms of absolute idealism and had excluded transcendental reality. Reason was also the creator. The idea of God existed within that system because it had the independent function of connecting the teleological realms with each other and binding them into a unity: A necessary congruence of natural and moral theology arose out of the presuppositions of the system. It was a calm and reassuring system: The eternity of ethics was guaranteed by the eternity of nature, which in turn necessitated the eternity of humanity as the subject of ethical action; and the God-idea stood over all. The God-idea guaranteed historical humanity and was the basis for the unity of nature and ethics; it could not be absorbed in either field but, in effect, had to stand "outside" the world—which denied pantheism. But the transcendence of that God, in this system, could only be the transcendence of an idea.

Baeck was a theologian, not a philosopher; a representative of religion, a rabbi, and not a university professor. Religion had not yet achieved an independent place in Cohen's system, and so he could not give his assent to it. Baeck could respond to Cohen's mood of reason, of optimism, and to certain postulates that seemed to be drawn out of the Jewish tradition cherished by Baeck. For Cohen's system was ultimately based on the postulate that ethics is realized in nature, and he drew upon Jewish messianism and upon the ethics of the prophets. Cohen's confrontation with Treitschke in 1880 was an experience into

[3] None of the others, like Moritz Lazarus's *Ethics of Judaism*, achieved any real resolution in which his problem could find proper treatment.

which Baeck could enter; and, while Cohen's apologetics seemed much too mild and overly defensive, his stress on the Jewish ideas of ethical autonomy and the uniqueness and transcendence of God[4] could be accepted by Baeck who did not necessarily have to follow Cohen in equating the spirit of Judaism with the spirit of Germanism. Baeck follows Cohen completely in permitting the sense of the ethical to suffuse all aspects of his approach, to see in Judaism the expression of the categorical imperative. Kant's "pure consciousness of duty" is cited in the *Essence*. But Baeck is not Cohen. When Cohen sees Judaism as *a* religion in which ethical life is stressed, Baeck sees it as *the* religion. Alongside the ethical teachings of Cohen, that of ethical realization as an "eternal task" and, conversely, "eternity" as the ethical perspective, we find in Baeck that passion of the Jewish tradition which we can name the "Biblical love of God." (It is always a mistake to deny the idealist position its own passion, which is profound and deep. Cohen's love of the idea of God is very real, but it is confined to the knowledge of morality.[5] We find a different love of the Divine in Leo Baeck.) Cohen's personal warm friendship for Baeck, in whom he saw his successor within the Jewish community (at least in terms of the German-Jewish confrontation, this hope was realized), help us link these two rational thinkers through their personalities as well as through Cohen's teachings. But the differences persist. Cohen was the more profound philosopher, but the complexity of Baeck's thought is only partially found in the neo-Kantianism of his great teacher.[6] In Cohen, there is more of the serenity of the complete system, in Baeck, the tension of the unfulfilled that is still in quest of the answer.

The intellectual clash and turmoil of the first three decades of the

---

[4] Hermann Cohen, "Ein Bekenntnis in der Judenfrage" (1880) in [96, II], in which Cohen challenged Treitschke's position.

[5] Hermann Cohen, "Die Liebe zur Religion" in [96, II, 142]: "Love of God is . . . the recognition of morality" (quoted by Arthur A. Cohen [95, p. 99, n. 35]).

[6] Baeck [22, pp. 134–151] indicates something of this when he writes: "Often, only the conflict in contemporary Jewish thought is seen. But they find their unity within Jewish individuality, the unity of the basis of life and the contents of life. Their relationship is not controversy but tension . . . viz., the idea of Hermann Cohen which once again places Judaism into intellectual world history and reclaims its place among the world religions and the idea which sometimes fights this in presenting the foundation of our particularity the special depths of our life, our religiosity. Tensions give life."

twentieth century, which also entered all phases of the political life of
Germany, formed the common background to the development of
Martin Buber, Franz Rosenzweig, and Leo Baeck.[7] At the same time,
one must keep in mind that Cohen's own development continued right
up to the moment of his death, and that he primarily occupied himself
with the questions of Judaism from 1912 until 1918. Certainly Rosenzweig, and also Leo Baeck, were particularly affected by his attempts to
win an independence for religion alongside logic, ethics, and aesthetics;
and his concept of "correlation" has a relationship to Rosenzweig and
Baeck that still presents puzzles. Franz Rosenzweig and, in our time,
Samuel H. Bergman, see the "correlation" concept as the break within
Cohen's idealism that leads to the new thinking, to existentialism.
Julius Guttman and Alexander Altmann, on the other hand, feel that
this significant change of Cohen's God-idea took place within his idealistic system.[8] The acceptance of Altmann's analysis here also aids us in
understanding the difference between Rosenzweig and Baeck.

Put into its simplest form, "correlation" is the interpenetration of
the idea of God and of man in Cohen's system. Man, as a shareholder
of reason, is created by God; the correlation between them runs in that
reason. Man cannot be properly thought without God; God cannot be
properly thought without man. Within their internal relationship their
experience of each other affects and defines both. Out of this there comes
a new understanding of such terms as creation, revelation, and redemption (which are at the heart of Rosenzweig's system): God creates; man
is created. God reveals; man receives (in Baeck's terms, the receiving
of that revelation constitutes his mission). God redeems; man is saved.
And the Divine movement of action is correlated to the human movement responding to it.[9] But is this correlation, as Rosenzweig and his
followers indicate, a true dialogue between a transcendent God who
has emerged out of an idealistic system and engages individual human
beings? Or do we still deal with definitions of the idea of God and the
idea of man as they appear in Hermann Cohen's idealistic system?

[7] Cf. Leo Strauss's *Spinoza's Critique of Religion* [181] where the introduction
by this Rosenzweig disciple deals with these stirrings.

[8] Cf. Samuel H. Bergman [79], Julius Guttman [131], and Alexander Altmann
[70, pp. 377–400].

[9] Arthur A. Cohen [95, p. 98] ends his summary by stating that "to correlate man
and God is to hold that man and God—individual man and personal God—seek and
address one another." Before reaching that conclusion, it must be clear whether
ideas or realities are correlated.

Certainly, correlation grew out of the idealistic system. Reconstructing its history, Altmann notes that it makes its first appearance in 1907: "The idea of humanity is the correlation of the unity of God. [70, p. 379][10] And the full statement of the concept of correlation appears in the 1919 work *The Concept of Religion in the System of Philosophy:*

> Neither the concept of God nor the concept of man can be thought of as standing by itself. When I think God I must at the same time think man; and I cannot think man without thinking God (p. 96). . . .[11] God is conditioned through the correlation with man. And man is conditioned through the correlation with God. (J. Schr. III, p. 191). [70]

In the "early" Hermann Cohen, religion's ultimate value had been its ability to be dissolved into ethics; the God of religion had been replaced by the "idea" of the realization of morality in the Messianic Age. Now, religion was shown as irreducible to ethics—through the use of the concept of correlation. For it is not possible for ethics to satisfy all aspects of this correlation; but religion does have "its own combinations in this correlation."[70, p. 383][12] And Cohen proceeds to prove religion *sui generis* by means of the correlation not only as this applies to the field of ethics, but also in the fields of logic, aesthetics, and psychology. In Altmann's summary, we are again reminded of the great teaching Cohen gave to both Baeck and Buber: The *Nebenmensch* who becomes the *Mitmensch*. And we come to see this in the framework of the correlation:

> The concept of God is enlarged to that of the loving God. Just as human love "is the religious form of the social relationship between man and man" rising out of (Mitleid) pity, so "only within religion does the God concept find power for love" (Begriff der Religion, p. 79). The love of God is thus as conditioned through human love (p. 80). The sense of correlation lets God's love to man be "an additional contents" of human love: God must love the poor man, since man ought to love his poor Mitmensch fellow man. [70, p. 388]

And when Hermann Cohen relates correlation to the field of aesthetics, we find expressions that relate directly to Baeck's fight against romanticism and against Schleiermacher's approach that would transfer the

---

[10] Quoting Cohen's *Religion und Sittlichkeit.*
[11] (p. 96) refers to Hermann Cohen [79, p. 378].
[12] Quoting *Begriff*, p. 44.

aesthetic feeling into religion. Cohen attacks this "feeling of absolute dependency" which does not truly describe the religious realm:

> In this expression it is only the indeterminateness of this kind of awareness that lets itself be known, one that has no other objective content but itself. . . . The full indeterminateness of pantheism reveals itself here, and, just as much, we see romanticism's lack of concepts. [Against Schleiermacher's feelings, Cohen stresses] God and man, as religious concepts, are genuine logical abstractions whose values as ideas cannot be generated through any form of feeling (*Begriff*, 95–6). [70, p. 392]

The correlation, as we see it here, is fully identified with Cohen's idealism; it does not reach beyond that, into the realm of the metaphysical. Since its full exploration lies outside our scope, Altmann's summation serves to indicate its full extent in Cohen's system:

> It has been shown to us that the concept of the correlation fulfills itself in three areas, depending whether we study its relation to logic, to ethics, or to aesthetics. There is the temptation to characterize it as metalogical, meta-ethical, and meta-aesthetical. As metalogical concept it is mere concept (creation, revelation); as meta-ethical it enlarges itself into the idea determined by the purpose (redemption). As meta-aesthetical it is psychologically tangible in pity and in longing, but not, because of this, reducible to psychological phenomena. [70, p. 394]

We can then determine, with Alexander Altmann, that for Cohen religion remains the religion of reason. It is constructed, not received through revelation. Both content and validity are determined for it a priori by reason. And having determined that, we can recognize that both of his disciples, Franz Rosenzweig and Leo Baeck, went in ways that differed from their teacher. Rosenzweig, who felt the idealistic framework almost as a prison from which he had to escape, saw a way out of idealism in terms of the concept of correlation and thus admitted Cohen posthumously into his own world of the "New Thinking." Baeck differed from Rosenzweig; by temperament and in terms of his own studies, he found himself much more at home in the world of idealism that Cohen had created. But Baeck was a rabbi with an absolute involvement within the Jewish experience. He had come to understand Judaism and the Jewish people as a living chain of tradition; and the ancient teachers of the Midrash and the Aggada came to contend not only with Hermann Cohen, but also with Dilthey. His modern teachers had taught Baeck how to overcome history. With Hermann Cohen, Baeck entered the domain of the Absolute, and discovered the integrity of the intellect. It was this very integrity which made Cohen resolutely repress his personal emotions, which made him accept the categories of the mind and follow them to their ultimate conclusions. Out of the integrity of his teacher, Baeck came to know the total commitment to the ethical task, and its extension to all areas of life. In the concept of the correlation, Baeck came to appreciate the overwhelming importance of the relationship between God and man, and between man and man. Cohen taught him the concept of the *Mitmensch,* the fellow human being who is part of the ethical life which is the core of existence. Forcefully and logically, Cohen showed him the correlation in the world of ideas. Baeck could accept this.

But Baeck could not stay solely in the world of ideas. The "God of Abraham, Isaac, and Jacob, and not the God of the philosophers"—to use Pascal's words—was more than an idea to Baeck, even the great idea in which the ethical task reached to the end of time. Revelation was more than the creation of reason for Baeck. He joined Cohen in accepting the categorical imperatives of the ethical commandment that came to mankind, and stressed the rational aspects of Judaism that gave the clearest expression to the commandment. But more and more, he saw the mystery behind the commandment, a dimension of the Holy that was not part of a rational system and yet had to be confronted. The correlation of God and man, if it is more than the correlation between ideas, leads to a tension of the religious life that he could ultimately only resolve through the polarity of the mystery and the commandment. At that point, Baeck stepped outside the world of Cohen's system. He did not become part of the "New Thinking" of which Rosenzweig spoke; nor did he follow the path being established by Buber (who had also learned far more from Cohen than his disciples are ready to admit). Baeck's way was his own, in some ways resolving the conflict between Buber and Rosenzweig on the one hand, and Cohen on the other. It was theology, defined by himself as a "reflection" (*Besinnung*) upon the great tradition in which he was firmly rooted:

The systematic reflection upon this problem by which an age renders its account of its Judaism and by which it seeks to express its own connection with the basic problem and its forms—this is *theology* in Judaism. [46, p. 282]

With Cohen, Baeck goes back to the sources of Judaism for his religion; but it is no longer just the religion of reason. It contains the paradox, and it becomes the religion of polarity.

III

Cohen's concept of the correlation of God and man brought the confrontation between the Creator and the created into the domain of the intellect. For Cohen—and for Baeck—the fundamental concern of theology was man's ethical response to the Divine revelation. But Cohen was satisfied once he had equated the Divine revelation with the creation of reason. Reason itself was the link between man and God. Baeck moved away from Hermann Cohen at this point. The writings of Rudolf Otto had directed his attention toward the "peculiarly irrational within history . . . which had to be appreciated by religion," [46, p. 275] and there grew within Baeck the sense of wonder concerning the mystery behind the commandment. God was more than an idea. If his essence could not be known, if all that man could know were the categorical imperatives of the moral law in which God manifested his will, the moment of encounter with that commandment still drew man toward an infinity which left its mark within man, which left a tension, a yearning, the utter humility of the finite confronting the infinite, the pride and exultation of finitude feeling itself in the arms of the infinite. Schleiermacher's theology instructed Baeck, but he felt much more at home in Cohen's religion of reason. Yet he could not rule out emotion, the encounter with the infinite that lives on in every act of justice. Both were needed. And Baeck turned away from Cohen's philosophy of reason, as he had been taught by his master to reject history. He looked for an answer within Jewish theology.

Baeck's theology builds upon the contemplation of that revelation which is at the beginning of Jewish history and which is continuous throughout all Jewish experience. In contrast to the historicism which had made revelation a predicate of history, history here became a predicate of revelation. We go back to the basic quote from Baeck's "Theology and History" at this point, to that incursion of the Infinite, Eternal, the One and Unconditioned into the finite, temporal, manifold and limited, and of the spiritual and moral tension of the human fiber which is the result. [46, p. 281][13]

Moving through all of Jewish experience with the knowledge of that continuous revelation reflecting upon it and making that reflection part of the total tradition and part of the revelation, Jewish theology then becomes the *theologia viatorum,* the theology of travelers. [46, p. 280][14] Baeck moved into Jewish experience, into "this people Israel, and the meaning of Jewish existence."

Baeck entered the stream of Jewish life in quest of an answer to what his earlier writings had called "the paradox" between the mystery and the commandment. And as the categories of Jewish existence became part of his framework of theology, he came to the answer which he named "the polarity." The commandment was very clearly framed in his mind, instructed by the neo-Kantian religion of duty which saw it everywhere. There was the need now for Baeck to come to terms with the mystery. And he found it, in its concealed form, in his studies of the Midrash, where he eventually isolated what he termed the oral tradition of mysticism. In its clearest form, he found it recorded in the texts of Jewish mysticism, notably in the Kabbalah.

When Baeck started upon his study of mysticism, the scientific study of Judaism (*Wissenschaft des Judentums*) viewed the Kabbalah and other texts as mystification and fraud. The Kabbalah in parts of Eastern Europe was still a way of life to which one dedicated oneself in full surrender and without criticism; in Western Europe, it was practiced surreptitiously, if at all. [172, pp. 359–377] Nevertheless, Baeck's research can be viewed in the frame of reference of the new scholarship which included Buber and an emotional involvement with the material studied, and the more objective and withdrawn scholarship of Scholem. (By now, the indefatigable work of Scholem has led to a whole school of Jewish mysticism which studies the mystic concepts as powerful motifs in the migratory movement of the Jews, and has restored a proper

---

[13] Cf. the quotation on page 147, above.

[14] Baeck notes the espousal of this theology by Bultmann, Gogarten, and Karl Barth at this point, but indicates the Christian solution differed from Judaism since the concepts of the Church and of the Revelation here created a different frame of reference. Max Gruenewald [129] analyzes this in detail.

perspective to this aspect of Jewish thought.[15]) Baeck cannot wholly be identified with Scholem in this connection. He does approach the Kabbalah without surrendering to it, with the scientific apparatus of the twentieth century. But he is still the *baal ha-midrash*, the exegete, who wants to discover the idea behind the text. Within the Kabbalah, Baeck notes the experience of the Jewish people in its encounter of the mystery; and this experience is to become part of his theology in which the categories of Jewish experience record Israel's reaction both to the commandment and to the mystery.

Baeck's first study of mysticism has been made available to us through the research of Kurt Wilhelm [189]; it dates from the year 1911. At that time, Baeck published an article in a Protestant journal entitled "The Historical Bases of the Parties in Present-day Judaism"[16] which stressed the importance of mysticism within Judaism and placed its origin in the spontaneous yearnings and hopes of the human heart which confronts a dismal world with optimism for the future. Baeck did not see mysticism as the absolute opponent of rationalism:

> Mysticism claims to represent true tradition and therefore adopts the term "Kabbalah" . . . as far as rationalism is concerned, there was never such a great opposition, since both of them were of a speculative nature. They differed more in the system than in the method. . . . However, philosophy tended to overestimate the role of knowledge, and it is against that intellectualism that mysticism insisted on the rightful claim of its secrets. [189, pp. 124–125]

In the speculative nature of the Kabbalah, Baeck found a corrective for the tendency in medieval religious thought which worked at achieving the purity of the concept of God by emptying it not only of all anthropomorphisms, but of its living reality. In the gigantic Kabbalistic speculations concerning the *Sephirot* ("the *Spheres* surrounding God"), it is the fullness of God and His living reality which is stressed. The near God is stressed as against the far God; while he cannot be entered in the sense of a Christian or Buddhist *unio mystica*, man can cleave unto Him. [189, p. 125]

At this point, an area of Baeck's thinking opens before us which deserves the closest consideration. The "New Thinking" of the 1920s rises out of the confrontation of the data of existence, the *Gegeben-*

---

[15] Max Gruenewald [129, p. 9] expands on this.
[16] Quoted by Wilhelm [189, p. 124].

heiten. Baeck shares much with Rosenzweig and Buber, including the analysis of the life situation.—"The world is twofold to man . . ." is the first sentence of Buber's *I and Thou.*[17] Buber, Baeck, and Rosenzweig share the insights and teachings of Hermann Cohen.[18] But once the existential aspect has been asserted, and the encounter with the mystery has been recounted—how can it be communicated? *Quid juris* —how judged? As long as the Cartesian quest for a universally valid basis of rational thinking is not considered an unwarranted intrusion into human *Existenz* (and, indeed, there is one answer to this question), the builders of the theological system must turn back to it.

In contrast to his two colleagues, Leo Baeck returns to Hermann Cohen at this point. The encounter with the mystery is not just given as the fact of existence, but is to be discerned out of the commandment which lives in the world of reason. The tension of religion is not the *Angst,* the knowledge of death, but the recognition of the correlation between the emotional experience of the mystery and the rational recognition and assent to the ethical imperatives of the commandment. Baeck's system here builds upon Hermann Cohen's concern with the ethical progress that gives meaning to the world of existence, and attempts to enlarge it by including the "irrational encounter" with the mystery. Baeck's work then becomes the attempt to reconcile the worlds of Buber and Cohen. This is done, not by attempting a synthesis between two antitheses, but by an assertion of both in a system of polarity.

The clearest exposition of this is found in Baeck's fundamental essay "The Mystery and the Commandment" [25, 25a] which was first published in 1922.[19]

[17] "Die Welt ist dem Menschen zwiefaeltig nach seiner zwiefaeltigen Haltung." [88, p. 9]
[18] Buber's dependence on Cohen is often enough forgotten to warrant quoting the *Religion der Vernunft* [98, p. 17]: "By the side of the I arises, different from the It, the He. Is this He naught but another occurrence of the I which would, therefore, already be implied in the I? Language itself guards against this error: before we get to He we come to Thou. But is the Thou only another occurrence of the I, or does the Thou require a separate discovery even after I have become aware of my I? Perhaps it is the other way around—that only the Thou, the discovery of the Thou, can bring about my awareness of my I, the ethical cognition of my I" (Quoted by Steven Schwarzschild [174] in a full analysis of this problem).
[19] It is worth noting that Baeck suggested this article be included in the collection *Judaism and Christianity* [28], and supervised the translation. *The Essence of Judaism* [2] was also republished then; and Ernst Simon's "Geheimnis und Gebot" [178] gives an incisive analysis of the changes in the two editions.

The opening sentence of "Mystery and Commandment" parallels the opening of *I and Thou:*

> There are two experiences of the human soul in which the meaning of his life takes on for a man a vital significance: the experience of mystery and the experience of commandment; or, as we may also put it, the knowledge of what is real and the knowledge of what is to be realized. [25a, p. 171]

The various sources from which Baeck draws his understanding join together here. Baeck starts with the experience, with the human condition in which man senses something lasting, a fundamental reality that speaks to him of his createdness. And out of this reflection of what he is, there arises the knowledge of the ethical task which he has to do, which is inherent in man's nature. But if we move out of this world of experience and re-enter Hermann Cohen's idealism, the language re-translates itself into the God Who is Being and man who is becoming, into the messianism of the ethical task that reaches to the end of time. The theology of reflection gives its assent to both: The mystery under-girds human existence and is the assurance of life; the commandment gives certainty to action and is the assurance of the self.

Toward the end of his life, speaking of Jewish mysticism's search for the Divine spark, Baeck wrote: "The soul is given by God to be discovered by man." [57, p. 26] For Baeck, theology is man's search for the Divine within the realm of man, the content of life in which man discovers the foundation of life. It is the assertion of rationalism which is in the service of the Revelation. And Baeck does follow Schleiermacher here in grounding the Revelation in human experience, as we see in the description of that experience of the soul in "Mystery and Commandment":

> This twofold experience could also be called humility and reverence. The humility of man is his recognition that his life is framed by infinity and eternity . . . ; that his life is absolutely dependent; that the unknowable and unnameable . . . enters into his life. Humility is the feeling for that deep and mysterious sphere in which man is rooted; the feeling, in other words, for that which remains in being and is real—the great quiet, the great devotion in all philosophy and all wisdom. And reverence is man's feeling that something higher confronts him; and whatever is higher is ethically superior and therefore makes demands and directs, speaks to man and requires his reply, his decision. It . . . can manifest itself in the other

as well as in oneself. Reverence is thus the recognition of the holy, that which is infinitely and eternally commanding, that which man is to accept into his life and realize through his life—the great impelling force, the active aspect of wisdom. [25a, p. 172]

In man's experience, the Revelation does engender the knowledge of man's absolute dependence. But this knowledge is the ground of man's being, not its contents. Emotion underlies reason; the world of scholarship is the driving force of the intellect, of man's self-assertion which is based upon the knowledge that he is supported by eternity; his absolute dependency is also his reason for self-assertion. And so one aspect of wisdom is the acknowledgment of its roots, the quiet reverence with which wisdom confronts the Infinite which is its foundation; but the active aspect of wisdom correlates the feeling engendered by the mystery with the knowledge of the commandment that sounded through the mystery and must be realized in life, with the fact of man as an ethical being who must realize himself through the ethical tasks which the commandment says to him at the moment of the mystery. The experience of the mystery is not the sole content of the revelation. For Schleiermacher "every original and new communication of the universe to man is a revelation. . . . Every intuition and every original feeling proceeds from revelation." [165a, p. 89] But Baeck placed his acknowledgment of human experience as the source of the revelation into the framework of Jewish existence where the historical experience had encountered the *unique revelation* to which this people Israel had responded. To an extent, Geiger's definition of revelation as "the peculiar Jewish *genius* for religion" [119] is continued in Baeck, who explains this genius in terms of Israel's ability to live within both mystery and commandment, in a religion of ethical awareness that has remained conscious of its ultimate roots in the Infinite.

Baeck places the consciousness that man has been created next to the consciousness that man is expected to create. The finite also addresses itself to man as a task to be fulfilled. The way of life brings man to the foundation of life, and man cannot have knowledge of that foundation without at the same time finding the way: always, there is that twofoldness in which the one is not balanced against the other but contained in the other. And this religion of polarity, absent in other religions because of the split introduced into them through their concept of God, is the religion of the Jew:

Judaism lacks any foundation for the conflict between transcendence and immanence. Jewish piety lives in the paradox, in the polarity with all its tension and compactness. That which is a contradiction in the abstract world of mere theory is made a unity and a whole in the religious consciousness. For this consciousness there is no such thing as this world without any beyond, nor a beyond without this world . . . whatever is on this side is rooted in the beyond, and whatever is beyond demands completion on this side by man. The infinite appears in the finite, and whatever is finite bears witness to the infinite. The life of man leads from God to man and from man to God. . . . The human dwells in the Divine, and the Divine demands of every man his humanity. This unity of both . . . alone is truth. [25a, pp. 174-175]

The human dwells in the Divine. But this is not the immanentism of the nineteenth century. God speaks to man and man speaks to God in the framework of a personal religion that is closer to the Biblical faith than to philosophical systems of post-Enlightenment Europe. It is a religion of personal experience and of the Jewish experience. And it always asserts both God and man.

As Baeck saw the rational aspect of Jewish mysticism, so did he stress the ethical content of that mysticism. In Baeck's Judaism, all ethics has its mysticism and all mysticism has its ethics:

All absorption in the profundity of God is always also an absorption in the will of God and His commandment. And all Jewish ethics is distinguished by being an ethic of revelation or, one might almost say, an ethic of experience of the Divine: it is the tidings of the Divine. . . . Ethics is here rooted in the profundity of living experience, and it is significant that in the Hebrew language of the Middle Ages the same word is used to designate an ethical disposition and a mystical absorption. [25a, p. 175]

The term Baeck has in mind here is the word *kavanah*, particularly as it exists in the process of *tikkun,* the continuous process of Restoration [170, pp. 276 ff.] within the universe. Kurt Wilhelm [189, pp. 126-127] here comments on Baeck's ability to translate Kabbalistic terms into his own language without falsifying them. *Kavanah* is used in the legal texts of the Talmud in reference to the ethical intention which is to accompany the fulfillment of a commandment. But in the Kabbalah, especially that of Luria, where prayer is more than the free outflow of religious feelings, *kavanah* leads to a virtually cosmic broadening of prayer. The pious man who prays in the spirit of mystical meditation moves the divine spheres; he penetrates all darkness which separates man from God; he changes the chaos into cosmos; he fulfills a messianic task. [189][20] And, using this mystic term, Baeck is able to speak out of the fullness of a Jewish tradition in which the language and life of those who affirm the mystery above all else still sounds the commandment clearly and unequivocally. In an article written within a year after the publication of "Mystery and Commandment," Baeck affirmed his conviction that

> In the development of mysticism the Jewish mysticism has its special way. All other mysticism in its essence seeks to show the release from the will and all that determines it, that obligates, that guides, that makes demands. . . .
>
> It is the speciality of Jewish mysticism that it wants to confront that mysticism of death, this passive mysticism seeking release, as the mysticism of life. It is the mysticism of the reconciliation, the mysticism of the will, of the command and its realization, an active mysticism. It is stamped by the special aspect of Judaism in which it is the deed that is decisive. For Judaism there is only one entrance into the meaning of life and only one way from man to God: the fulfillment of God's commandment. All commandment comes from God, out of the depth of the mystery. Whoever forces himself into the commandment forces himself to God, he has brought that which is clear into that which is hidden and has brought the hidden into the open. . . . The pious of every age achieved this: they overcame the distance and established the holiness of God in this world. [29, pp. 340–341]

Questions can be raised here concerning the degree of accuracy with which Baeck assesses Jewish mysticism. There were many for whom the Kabbalah was a refuge from the world, not a path that led into it. Ecstasy and sinking into the mood of surrender were not unknown in the Jewish community, particularly during the long stretches of darkness and persecution. But this does not materially affect Baeck's thesis. Baeck sees Judaism out of the totality of the Jewish experience; as in his apologetics, he can always bracket an individual or even an era as being an aberration not characteristic of the fundamental mood of Judaism. Mysticism is part of the religious experience; it is part of Jewish

---

[20] Scholem [170, p. 278], says: "The task of man has been defined by Luria as the restoration of his primordial spiritual structure or Gestalt. That is the task for everyone . . . every soul contains this potential of its spirit. . . ."

existence and must appear in the full dimensions of its color spectrum, which includes the ecstasy and the passivity. All of it becomes part of the rhythm and tension in which the mystery and the commandment become the polarity of Jewish thought. Now one was stressed, now the other. And

> Judaism ceases where the mood of devotion, that which is at rest and restful, would mean everything; where faith is content with itself, content with mystery. . . . The religion of mere passivity, devoid of commandments, is no longer Judaism. Nor is Judaism to be found where the commandment is content with itself and is nothing but commandment. [25a, p. 176]

Again, the full statement of Judaism as the faith of polarity becomes a challenge to Paulinian Christianity which overstressed one aspect of this faith and thus broke away. Baeck sees Paul as leaving Judaism when he preached *sola fida,* when mystery became everything to him, when sacraments and dogma were used by Christianity as the tangible mystery which men could touch and mold. But as Baeck finds Paul one who abandoned Judaism by discarding the commandment and exalting the mystery, so does he warn against the Judaism which sees only the commandment, which views religion as mere ethics devoid of that foundation which is the mystery:

> When [Judaism] becomes a mere edifice of ideas, a doctrine; or when that which the mystery intimates is no longer supposed to be the foundation of man's life, but merely some postulate of his thought—when Judaism is taken to be a religion without paradox. There is no such thing as a Judaism which is nothing but Kantian philosophy or ethical culture . . . or where the abundance of its laws may still prevail . . . but severed from its roots in the mystery, void of devotion. [25a, pp. 177–178]

Baeck finds the resolution of the paradox within human existence; for man naturally experiences both the foundation of life (the mystery) and the ethical task (the commandment) in a unified way that is not a synthesis, not a syncretism, not a mere connection of ideas—but a revelation. One thing is grasped and experienced through the other, and each receives its meaning only through the other. The mystery and the commandment proclaim each other and sustain one another: "The commandment is a true commandment only because it is rooted in the mystery, and the mystery is a true mystery only because the commandment always speaks out of it." [25a, p. 178] Religion is here based upon man's ability to perceive the twofoldness of his experience. And Israel's history is produced as the proof that this ability can proclaim itself in the life and thought of a people whose awareness of the revelation helped them create the distinctive pattern of a classic religion in which the commandment and the mystery find expression as the ethical awareness of a people that knows these laws to come from the ground of being.

A comparison with Tillich comes to mind here. And, indeed, Tillich does define his basic teaching of "ultimate concern" in two ways: both as the existential engagement and as the awareness of the unconditioned. [149] But there are differences between the Biblical man of faith and the ontologist that are connected with Tillich's self-awareness of the ontological search. And while there are strong resemblances between Baeck's *theologia viatorum* and Tillich's way of ultimate concern, there are similar differences of emphasis that rise out of their diverse backgrounds. Baeck cannot separate himself from the totality of Israel and its continuous awareness of the revelation through the oral tradition. In Israel, as in the *Mitmensch,* the Divine is encountered. The Biblical revelation is also the election of Israel, and active assent must be given to it. For Tillich, the Biblical word between God and man is a metaphor symbolizing the nonsymbolic reality of the Ground of Being in which one participates through knowing oneself accepted and therefore acceptable. Baeck would already view this as part of the Christian approach in which the mystery becomes abstracted into dogma and can be manipulated within a system. In his own approach, Baeck gives his assent to Israel's encounter with God which is not a metaphor but a reality of life. The mystery is within the commandment, the commandment within the mystery. In the will of God, the ethical imperative, man comes to encounter the holy mystery from which it receives its absolute authority. And this dual encounter, Israel's experience through the ages, in a way comes to substitute for Tillich's system. Ontological self-knowledge is as important for the people Israel as it is for the individual human being. But in that process the reality of a personal God comes to be part of Israel's faith which is never the Greek *pistis,* but always the Biblical *emunah.* [110, pp. 241–243] In its life of ethical action which is the reality of total Jewish experience, Israel always encounters the living reality of the mystery which undergirds the universe.

In affirming Israel, Baeck always affirms God. The individual experience is shown as marked by the impress of eternity. But Baeck finds history to contain the same meaning. The unity of creation and future necessarily makes for history. Hermann Cohen's thinking is evident in Baeck's statement that

> Creation is unthinkable apart from a future, and the idea of the future is inseparable from the certainty of the divine creation. Every commandment that issues from God . . . has its own infinity, its everlasting future. It creates and begets, it commands on and on, it transcends itself. . . . A commandment that can be fulfilled completely is merely a human law. The commandment of God is a commandment which leads into the future and involves a mission which, in the words of the Bible, continues "from generation to generation". . . . [25a, pp. 179–180]

Israel's mission is part of the revelation through which Baeck comes to establish man's role in the world. And it is part of an optimistic approach in which the framework of Cohen's thoughts gives assurance of an ultimate reconciliation that must be part of the ethical law, leading to what Baeck calls the "realism of Israel," its trust in the world. Reconciliation and redemption are correlatives for Baeck, and testify that there are not two worlds which oppose one another, two different realms, but that they belong together and are unified in the one God. Again, the stress rests on the fact that there is no mystery outside of life and no life outside of mystery; life is contained within the holy and the holy within life.

Earlier, we had examined Baeck's defense of the Pharisees in the *communio sanctorum,* the function of all of Jewish life to establish the holiness of existence. As apologetics and the presentation of Judaism interact, we come to understand that the defense of Jewish life is also the defense of the revelation within the Jewish people. And this revelation has its inner and its outer manifestation: The inner religious life is expressed through those customs and ceremonies of Judaism which some see as the only aspect of Jewish life. Life is given its style here by "causing religion to invade every day and penetrate the whole of every day." [25a, p. 182] Every partition of life into the profane and the sacred is to be avoided. Out of the awareness of the holy in all of life, Judaism comes to guard man against a life devoid of the tension of polarity. For

> Thoughtlessness is the true Godlessness; it is the homelessness of the soul. And the Law would guard man against this state in which he is without

mystery and commandment; it would give every surface its symbolic function and every bit of prose its parable. [25a, p. 182]

It is most characteristic for Baeck to stress "thoughtlessness" at this point: His type of mysticism is so fully involved with the ethical and rational implications of the encounter with the Holy that it must first waken thought for those who would turn to life only with their emotions. If man cannot acknowledge the Infinite that shines through all finite aspects, he is indeed homeless in a world devoid of meaning. And Baeck applies this kind of analysis to the institutions of Jewish law, to the Sabbath, which is to keep awake the Jewish awareness of both mystery and commandment.

In writing about the Sabbath as the great example of the Law and its full application to the Jewish experience, Baeck once again sounds the major notes of his theology which takes its instructions out of the incidents of the Jewish experience within life:

> As the day of rest, the Sabbath gives life its balance and rhythm; it sustains the week. Rest is something entirely different from a mere recess, from a mere interruption of work, from not working. A recess is something essentially physical, part of the earthly everyday sphere. Rest, on the other hand, is essentially religious, part of the atmosphere of the divine; it leads us to the mystery, to the depth from which all commandments come, too. It is that which re-creates and reconciles, the recreation in which the soul, as it were, creates itself again and catches its breath of life—that in life which is sabbatical. The Sabbath is the image of the messianic; it proclaims the creation and the future; it is the great symbol. [25a, pp. 183–184]

The poetry of Baeck's presentation—about which we shall have more to say—gives us a picture of the Sabbath in which the ethical imperatives of Jewish life that reach unto messianic times are once again found within the mystery as it reveals itself in the ceremonies of Judaism which are more than ceremonies. In our day, Abraham Heschel's work on the Sabbath [136] is linked to this presentation. But it is Baeck's final emphasis that this tradition of the Sabbath and the over-all awareness of the Law for the mystery result in creating a different man, a man in whom the capacity to be different has been developed:

> Whoever experiences mystery and commandment becomes unique among men, different, an individual within the world. Whoever knows only mystery becomes merely unique and knows only the day of silence. Who-

ever knows only the tasks is only among men and knows only the days of work and times of recess. But whoever experiences both, both in unity, lives in the world and yet is different, is different and yet is in the world, lives for other men and with other men and yet within himself, within himself and yet also for other men and hence also with them. This is the gift and possession of Judaism. [25a, p. 148]

Baeck's great poem of the mystery and the commandment as it reveals itself in all human experience comes to men out of the context of Judaism. The Jew, as the great dissenter of history, as the discoverer of the way that all should walk, comes to mankind with the faith that can release within all the energy to achieve the messianic age. Some religion —again Baeck confronts Buddhism in this assertion of the active as against the passive way—can only assuage the hurts of life, can teach submission to the world. Judaism strives for the creation of the kingdom of God in this world. And its strength, its ability to attain the creative act, comes out of the encounter

where the soul experiences its depth and its task, that which is concealed and that which is evident, each in the other and each through the other. It is found in the religion of paradox and reconciliation, that religion which lives on the strength of the unity of mystery and commandment in the soul of man. [25a, p. 185]

IV

"Mystery and Commandment" can only be fully understood when it is seen as the great poem in which the tension and the paradox of the Jewish experience becomes the great confession of the Jewish faith. It appeared almost simultaneously with Buber's *I and Thou* and occupies the same position in relation to Baeck's other works as *I and Thou* does to Buber's writings. There is the same discovery of the twofoldness of life, the same appreciation of the mystery as a dimension of the human spirit that does not separate man from man but brings him to the position of dialogue. But where Buber comes to a universal statement of the human situation, Baeck stresses Judaism, the particular faith in which the universal experience has become the religion of polarity. And this religion of polarity attempts to include both Buber's awareness of the mystery as the dimension of human existence and

Hermann Cohen's emphasis on the ethical imperatives which make the religion of reason the true area of man's existence in the world. The essay builds on Baeck's statements of the past. Unlike *I and Thou,* which did have its predecessors in Buber's writings (e.g., *Daniel*), but is a fundamental, new statement initiating the later developments of the religion of dialogue, "Mystery and Commandment" is more of a summation, a final statement of a position initiated by Baeck in *The Essence of Judaism.*[21] It is not complete in itself, and has to be seen as the first of a series of statements which we will come to examine. But it does contain the end result of what Leo Baeck had accepted from Cohen's ethical idealism. It speaks out of Baeck's experience with the Kabbalah and rabbinic texts (although it must be added that Baeck examined these texts with an eye for what they shared with the larger Jewish community, and minimized that which had brought them to their separate situation); and in its statement of the religion of polarity it arrives at a position from which Baeck never retreated.

The essay must also be understood on the basis of Baeck's personality.[22] And, conversely, it tells us a great deal about Baeck. The few studies of Baeck's life that have appeared (the one edited by Reichmann [159] is the best) and the reports of contemporaries have all stressed the rational thinker who followed Hermann Cohen: cool, somewhat detached, ironic and irenic. But behind that rationalism there was the burning knowledge of the revelation. A recent discussion of the rabbis whom Baeck followed in so many ways reminds us that

> The legalists whom we encounter as the champions of Reason used rational methods for the classification of laws . . . but in reality, and this fact has until quite recently been ignored, the savants themselves were "pneumatic" personalities, mystics whose true source of enlightenment lay in religious experience.[23]

Baeck was such a personality. He was not a mystic, not in the sense of the ecstatic who stammers of his special experience to the world and

[21] Cf. Chapter 4, above, where the 1905 edition of *Essence* [1] is shown to contain the clear statement of the "paradox" which becomes the "polarity."

[22] Abraham Heschel states in [198] that "Baeck can *only* be understood through his unique personality."

[23] Jacob Petuchowski in [195, p. 37, n. 34], citing Y. Baer, *Israel Among the Nations* (Jerusalem, 1955), pp. 99–117; and Gershom Scholem, *Jewish Gnosticism, Merkabah Mysticism, and Talmudic Tradition* (New York, 1960).

wants it to share his insights. Nor was he the ascetic who withdraws from the world and lets the flame of his experience consume his soul and take it into some higher, distant sphere. Baeck was a rabbi and a teacher. As such, he participated in the prayers of Israel; the integrity of his personality assures us that it was a full participation. Baeck prayed daily—as Rosenzweig prayed on the day he returned to Judaism. And he gave sermons. Most rabbis open themselves to their congregation at this moment. Baeck was different. One of his students and colleagues reports of the board member who grumbled that those sermons were "Baeck's private conversations with God"—and adds his own impression that it appeared as though Baeck did not expect a response to his words from his listeners but from somewhere beyond. [76, p. 2]

The most important self-revelation to be noted in Baeck is his suppression of his personal aspects whenever he confronted the public. When he left his first pulpit, he could remind the congregation that the personal pronoun "I" had never been used in the pulpit, that the man had always receded behind the message. And his two major works, dealing with the essence of Judaism and the meaning of Jewish existence, do not once employ that personal pronoun. Yet behind that calmness—which could sometimes be cold, and that Olympian detachment—which sometimes appeared almost too far away from life, there blazed a passion and an excitement which could and did communicate itself to others. His private life gives full testimony of an inner warmth and a personal commitment to the *Mitmensch* that made him reach out to student or congregant or friend with deep concern for the other life. The public life was different, *had* to be different when Baeck knew himself to represent German Jewry as it was being liquidated. But to some extent there does exist a personal testimony, even a mystic testimony: Baeck's writings. Identified with Judaism and with Jewry, his apologetics become an *apologia pro vita sua*. And his description of the mystery and the commandment as it exists in the Jewish experience is a delineation of his innermost self. When Baeck describes Jewish mysticism in terms of its ethical impulse and its rational system, he is again describing an aspect of his self which cleaves to this type of mysticism within the Jewish experience. When he shows the hidden polemics of the rabbinic texts in the centuries of Christianity's first development, he gives us an insight into his own works where the polemic is now open, now concealed. And when Baeck talks about the strength rising out of the unity of mystery and commandment, he is delineating the religious type discovered within the Jewish experience and in rigid self-examination. Jewish experience is the basic source of authority for Baeck's *theologia viatorum*. Alexander Altmann rightly criticizes this emphasis on the prophetic experience instead of on the Divine word given the prophet:

> This untheological approach leads of necessity to a certain reduction of religious concepts to a humanist level, and is not without danger. It not merely demythologises but somewhat robs the religious concept of its specific character. Thus the concept of revelation assumes a humanist aspect which is not altogether satisfying. . . . Revelation, Baeck says, is the theological expression of the fact that Judaism possesses a sacred literature and history . . . that in the religion of Israel an entirely new idea of God first manifested itself in history. . . . [71, p. 200]

But we find this weakness in systematic theology partially rectified when we see history made subservient to theology, and when the Jewish people's experience with the revelation that speaks out of its existence is recapitulated in the individual life. The commandment speaking out of the mystery, and the mystery speaking out of the commandment come to every man; but they were placed into history as that special revelation which is the people Israel. This is Baeck's inner knowledge, is the core of his personality. And that conviction makes him a *homo religiosus* whose rational inquiries are rooted in religious faith, who is a defender of his people because they are a revelation in this world which must be preserved—a man who in his innermost being feels himself separate, standing apart, a witness to the world.

This innermost, nonrational core of Baeck's thinking—let us be clear that his position as a representative of the neo-Kantian approach within early twentieth century German Jewry is not negated by this—has not been stressed sufficiently. One problem has always been his identification with the liberal Jewish movement which stressed his rationalist, anti-mystic, and nonnationalist thinking. But Baeck's self-identification with the Jewish people grows stronger throughout the years, and there are touches of nationalistic feelings even in the 1905 edition of *Essence of Judaism*, where the Jew begins to become a theological figure, a witness —which ultimately means a martyr. Ernst Simon has noted this in his comparison of the two editions, when he stated that the 1905 edition already evidenced.

A somewhat timid emphasis upon the national element as an aspect of Jewish existence and upon the figure of the martyr, the religious witness; these emphases keep re-appearing with a force that is almost anti-systematic, showing both the individual and the collective martyr, all Israel and its mission for which it is sent into the world. . . . [178, p. 31]

By 1922, when Baeck presented "Mystery and Commandment" to the non-Jewish scholars, leaders of European culture, at Darmstadt, he spoke with a self-awareness that makes this essay both autobiographical and a short restatement of *The Essence of Judaism*. The religion of polarity presented here is clearly identifiable with Judaism—just as the man who presented this study was viewed as one of the leaders of German Jewry. But "Mystery and Commandment" was only one of a number of studies presented by Baeck at the meetings of the *Gesellschaft fuer freie Philosophie* which met in Darmstadt during those years (1922–1925) when Baeck arrived at the clear and mature formulation of his thoughts. A full understanding of the religion of polarity as enunciated by Baeck requires an examination of the two lectures that followed "Mystery and Commandment": "Perfection and Tension" given in 1923, and "Death and Rebirth" given at the autumn sessions of 1924.

"Mystery and Commandment" was the description of the inner human experience, man's inner feelings as he encounters the commanding mystery of the holy, as he learns from that which is real that which is to be realized. And now Baeck turns to a discussion of this experience as it reveals itself within two specific cultures: in Hellenic and in Jewish *Weltanschauungan*. It is, again, the confrontation of the infinite by the finite that is Baeck's concern, now narrowed down from the universal human experience to two types of men who loom behind their respective civilizations. It is a polarity: that which has reached its ultimate form, which has fulfilled itself, is finished, done, come to rest, is placed against the unfinished, the search, the action that can never rest, the constant tension of life as an eternal process of becoming which can never rest in the contemplation of what it has become. He terms it the polarity of "Perfection and Tension"; and the translation of *Vollendung* as perfection is stated clearly:

> The existing as the artistic creation is the perfect, that which is terminated. It is apart from all possibility of becoming different, of growing. It remains what it is. It is that which is *finished*. It is a perfection and to that

extent something concluded. As a terminated thing it is a thing of the past. It is significant that the Latin word *perfectus* designates all three as one: ended, past, and perfect. [31, p. 11]

Seen in this light, Baeck's use of the term "perfection" designates what seems to him to be the dominant aspect of Greek thought: the capture of the fleeting impression into a finished artistic creation that can henceforth be contemplated with the assurance that it will not change its form, will not dissolve—that it has achieved its fulfillment in this form. Only art exists and is real; all that exists and is real is art—this is what Baeck terms the underlying motif of Greek thought.

Kurt von Fritz makes a similar distinction between Greek and Judaeo-Christian thinking when he states that

> the development of Greek religious thought finds its natural conclusion in the belief in a god or gods who are and should be loved but do not love (cf. Aristotle's first mover), while God's love for man, or as Kierkegaard said "That God has loved us first" is the very center of the Christian religion. . . . [117, p. 14]

The calmness of contemplation here can be compared with the passionate involvement which must and does keep man in anguished tension. Baeck turns to Plato in order to stress the oneness of logos and *eros* in Greek thought, the basic likeness between the dialectic and the erotic. Aristotle's Metaphysics speaks of the harmony of the spheres, how the spheres are moved by the highest idea, namely, God at rest: "It moves the constellation, the spheres, by its being loved by them"—and Baeck would add "by its being seen, by its being thought." [31, p. 12] And Baeck places Greek ethics into the same area as Greek thought: as essentially aesthetic and intellectual, the viewing and thinking upon the existing and the enduring, i.e., the concept, the law, the work of art —and not as the unconditionally commanding, pressuring, dynamic ethics of the Bible. The Greek ethics carries with it the concept of the ideal ethical personality; once more, it is the artistic creation that rules in this field of thought. And the ethical life becomes a work of art which the wise present to God: a play for gods and men.[24] The life of the Greek scholar becomes contemplation; it is subject and ultimately the object of the religious ethic. Contemplation becomes adoration. And

---

[24] This element of Greek religion is also stressed by Fritz [117, p. 26]: ". . . the activity of man, itself and directly, is the most appropriate offering to the gods."

all that is left for the needs of the day, for politics, is Aristotle's median way or Plato's dictatorship. Alongside of it, there walks the sophistry which plays with all, denies all, and becomes nihilism.[25] It is the idea of finality, says Baeck, which leads to nihilism.

The idea of that which is finished became the only answer for ancient Greek thought, according to Baeck, because the Greeks arrived at it from two sources:

It was not only the result of the apollonic view of art, but also the dionysian-orphic mystery of the Beyond leads to it; not just that aesthetic rationalism, but just as much the empiricism of the religious experience. . . . The viewer of the drama became its object. As he was transported, the moment became fulfillment, the ultimate; he was granted something ultimate which sig-nified a lasting possession, something eternal. [31, p. 16]

Once again, Baeck found the experience of redemption in the mystery cults to be the source of a *Weltanschauung* which was fundamentally opposed to the Jewish point of view. The flight from the transitory be-comes the flight from life into the world of experiences, the apotheosis of the moment.

Both mystery and Greek philosophy shared the possession of the ultimate, the final, and in the certainty that they had the truth. They walked together, and, in the Church, found themselves united: philos-ophy and experience, gnosis and sacrament united in the certainty of the finished, absolute man, the savior and the saved; they became one— the mystery as the artistic creation and the artistic creation as the mystery. This union lived on in the Church, and conquered the Middle Ages. [31, pp. 19–20] Once again, as we listen to Baeck, the polemic reappears. And with its reappearance, we also find a restatement of the position of Judaism.

When we come to the Old Testament from the Greek antique world and from the Middle Ages, we enter into a different world. From the temple of ideas, and out of the house of the cult, we step into the world of life, into the driving force of the ethos and the pathos, out of the cosmos of being into the becoming that wants to be a cosmos, out of the peace-bordered space out into the eternal way. . . . All that can speak against that which is finished here speaks and demands. The coming-into-being and the strug-

25 A comparison of this passage with Baeck's views on dilettantism encouraged by the "romantic religion, Christianity" (cf. *Romantic Religion* [27]) is here valid.

gling, the constant confrontation with the way and the future, with the task and the designation, this constant *tension* here wants to signify the life of the world and of man. The soul comes to grasp its being here. It has grasped it in a twofold experience: that of the creation and that of the commandment. [31, pp. 20–21]

We are back to the basic position of "Mystery and Commandment" here. In the evaluation of the Jewish experience we hear the language of Baeck's contemporaries, notably Buber: the stress on the pathos of Jewish existence, affirmed here as a driving force of Jewish life in which the infinite path of becoming affirms both the individual ethical task of the individual and the mission of Jewish existence that reveals itself in the tension of moving toward that which is the infinite touching the life of humanity and giving it purpose. The strength and weakness of Baeck's theology become apparent at this point. The infinite presses so strongly upon the life of man, twisting his existence in a tension born out of the yearning to follow this impression to its source. But Baeck cannot permit the existential breakthrough of faith that would carry man into the secure knowledge of the heart of the mystery, the "leap of faith" that finds the true knowledge of the Beyond in the moment of encounter. It is not the love of God, and it is not the knowledge of God, nor even the impressions of the Infinite upon the world of man that bring man unto God. Man is brought to God by the ethical action. Whenever he reaches toward the Infinite, the moment of its encounter thrusts him back into the world of man. There is "a certain reduction of religious concepts to a humanist level" [71] and it is a weakness in his theology. Theology can ill afford to jeopardize its authority by questioning the transcendental. Its rational system depends upon the given revelation. Baeck places the revelation within the historical Jewish experience—but it is found there in a chain of transmission to which the contemporary Jew can bring assent or skepticism. And man is to find the revelation in his own experience. He cannot simply give his assent to a system of dogma and move toward the infinite on its rungs.

Perhaps this is a strength in Baeck. The ontological self-examination does lead to the awareness of the ground of being, to the Infinite that supports the finite; but out of this experience, man must find his way to the ethical action that validates it, that affirms his role as an active participant and denies the passive surrender to the Tao or the mystery god who would only be adored, who alone acts by reaching forth in his ultimate grace. The fact that Baeck has a way here—the way of Jewish existence, of an ethical approach to all aspects of life which is declared as a revelation in which the Divine entered history—this fact does give Baeck's *theologia viatorum* an additional strength within the humanistic area into which it has been placed. But then it cannot depend upon intellectual assent to it. The validation of the religion of polarity is the experience of it, the self-conscious experience: man sensing the Infinite within his finiteness and discovering in this the imperatives of ethical action. In one of the great poetic passages contained in "Perfection and Tension," Baeck describes this experience:

> Man experiences his belonging to an infinity. It presses upon him, whether he goes into himself or goes beyond himself. He lives in space without end and is a part of it, in time without stop as a segment of it. Space and time are fundamentally one here, they come from the one, omnipresent, eternal God. World and eternity are here one word, both signify the same unendingness [translator's note: i.e., the Hebrew word עולם]. Man lives in this unendingness and from it. His domain is the opposite of mere location, of that which has its boundary and its written description. His day is the opposite of finality, of fate. His domain is a going outward that points to the faraway, his day is the direction that leads into the distance. All that has come into existence and has been given becomes a path to the beyond, and to that which is in the process of becoming, to the world beyond and to the coming day. All creation wants to be revelation, all of the past becomes the future. Revelation and the future in its way without end, life in its constant onward surge and its constant openness—these have been discovered here. All experience here is the experience of the infinite, the tension; and the finite grows out of it. [31, pp. 22–23]

In this description of the human experience of the Infinite, we find a bold attempt to reclaim the infinite for man in a way diametrically opposed to Greek thought, which viewed the transcendent as isolated in the beyond, to be contemplated by the intellect or by love. Baeck does not so much place the Infinite into the finite as the finite into the Infinite: *he opens the beyond to the incursions of man.* There is an open road leading into the beyond: all that has come into existence becomes a path into the beyond; life is the constant onward surge. The world is the place in which creation realizes its creativity: both creatureliness and creativity are experienced by the finite that confronts the infinity. The tension between the near and the far, between that which is in the process of becoming and that which is, between the beginning in time and the eternal goal—this makes for a dynamic, not a static existence. The distance remains—this was important for Baeck—but he sees an elasticity in it: "One may dare to call it an elastic distance which becomes that which is dynamic, kinetic in the world." [31, p. 23] Man is the creation of the Eternal One, the revelation of the infinite. And tension rises upon tension, since the Divine creation is continuous. There is no finality. Baeck turns to the Jewish tradition here:

> An ancient Jewish word says: God creates, in order to continue to create— Gen. 2:3 was thus interpreted which speaks of God's work which "God in creating had made." All creation has its force, its constant birth. Creation and revelation, becoming and designation belong together; they determine one another. The world . . . is not mere fate . . . nor a mere likeness of an urform which man should only contemplate. . . . It is the world of God: a world; and nevertheless, God's domain. Space; and nevertheless, unendingness. Time; and nevertheless, eternity. Just so an ancient Jewish word again says: "God is the space of the world, but the world is not the space of God. . . ." It is the creation and revelation of God and therefore a world filled with tension. Standing apart from God and belonging to him designate it. It is an interweaving of opposites, an immanence of the transcendent, a being at one with the other, the covenanting of the finite and temporal with the infinite eternal. Both become one within religious feeling, the current moves between the poles . . . but man does not only possess (to use Schleiermacher's terms) "the taste of infinity" and "absolute dependency," but he has the tension toward the infinity—the oneness in the antithesis, the antithesis within the oneness. [31, p. 24]

It is worth noting that modern traditional interpretation makes the same point, including the stress on ethical action.[26] And, in this presentation to the general rather than Jewish community (it must be kept in mind that these are the Darmstadt lectures), Baeck continues by stressing this Jewish tradition, this time with the Talmudic stress on man's ethical action as being "something even greater than the creation of earth and

---

[26] Cf. J. H. Hertz, *The Pentateuch* (London, Soncino, 1964), p. 6: *"in creating had made* לעשות אשר ברא ה' literally 'which God created to make,' i.e., to continue acting through time (Ibn Ezra, Abarbanel) by the unceasing operation of the Divine laws . . . or, as the rabbis say, the work of creation continues, and the world is still in the process of creation, as long as the conflict between good and evil remains undecided. Ethically the world is thus still 'unfinished,' and it is man's glorious privilege to help finish it. . . .' "

sky." In every task demanded of man, he experiences the commandment; and this is also the experience of the infinite. The commandment
is God's commandment, filled with divine unrest and with divine movement. Every duty creates a new duty, for each is a step on that eternal
way, part of the infinite demand upon the finite life, the tension of the
polarity. Again, Baeck finds a word from the Talmud in this: "The pious
person is a man without rest in this world and in the world beyond."
[31, p. 26]

Out of this experience of the tension between the finite and the infinite, Baeck adduces the ethical action as it must arise out of the confrontation between man and the commandment:

> God commands, in order to continue commanding. And herein the tension
> enters the domain of the human task, gains its activity, its drive and its
> force, its moral longing: it becomes the commanded tension. The experience
> of eternity becomes the will unto eternity, becomes a duty, a designation
> assigned to it which becomes the way of life. God demands the infinite
> from the finite. And at the point where this decison for infinite enters,
> the ethical begins. It lives where man seeks to possess his life within this
> infinity, this constant unfulfilledness of the commandment—in the holy.
> The ethical is the categorical, infinite commandment: "Ye shall be holy,
> for I the Lord your God am holy." [31, p. 26]

God has left his mark upon his creation, and that mark, which is part
of creation, is his will. The Infinite manifests itself to his creatures in
the categorical imperatives of the ethical, man's Infinite dimension is the
ability to hear and to act upon God's commandment by becoming the
creator of the ethical act which moves him toward the Infinite.

The tension here becomes more than just the experience of the tension between creature and creator. The experience becomes life, action,
witnessing, and striving. Man struggles with God. Again, the Talmud
is brought forward as the witness of Israel's particular engagement with
God: "God says: My children have conquered Me." [31, p. 28] And
Baeck continues:

> All moral heroism as well as all moral patience is this struggle with the in-
> finite. A further step has been taken along the road of humanity when a
> man let eternity enter his life . . . when he "conquered God." It is a victory
> which means the overcoming of the tension, which lets life be born out
> of that tension. It is the greatest aspect of human life, the victory of the

moral, the creative, the ethical and its logos and eros contained within it. [31, p. 28]

Wrestling with God, man wins his redemption; in one moment, he gains eternity. His life is broader. Since he does not live within that which is finished and perfect, he is more tolerant and able to turn to the unlimited possibilities of existence, toward his fellow man:

> Where tension is experienced as the sense of life and is lived as its commandment, the will to history begins. All history is the manifold in its strife and disputation; and here history gains its activity with all its unrest which, after all, is its life. Nations here enter into infinity; and it is here that the reconciliation of the nations finds its indication, reconciliation within that great tension which is called world history. [31, pp. 29–30]

History then becomes a paradigm of the tension, a way of showing its activity in the lives of men. And if one nation lives in the quietness of contemplating the perfection, and the other in the tension of a way that consists of the great creation drama of God and man that never ends—both have their place in the world.

Which will endure? Baeck grants the strength of that civilization which can transmit a perfection from generation to generation. It stands in the world upon a firm foundation. But when something crumbles, everything goes. And it cannot return. That which is final also dies the death of finality. The civilization that affirms the tension, on the other hand, has no possession; but within it there is the constant possibility of rebirth:

> Whoever experiences the unending and the eternal through his life experiences it without end and without a close. Whoever wrestles with it fights the battle that always begins anew, is always new, and in which he himself becomes renewed. He does not see God, but he sees the way to Him, the way of the unending commandment, the way which God demands from man and which is unceasing where man wrestles every day with the commandment. He tires, and yet conquers. In the process of wrestling he is always reconciled, is renewed and reborn. There is no end or cessation in the reconciliation. All tension has its renaissance. There is no enduring rest in it—but also no death. [31, pp. 31–32]

The finished perfection, once broken, has no way of returning. But where the link between infinity and the finite is the tension that wrestles with the future, there is always rebirth: "Return, O children of men" is the Biblical word of God to man.

The confrontation between Judaism as the religion of polarity, as the religion of the tension and the unending ethical activity, and Hellenism, as the religion of the contemplation of perfection (or the ecstatic surrender to it), is conducted on a high level; Baeck wants to speak to the best of Hellenic thought and not to its weaknesses or excesses. He does not really present the full form of Hellenic thinking. The reaches of *hybris,* of Promethean rebellion and tragic heroism are not brought into this confrontation. But it is really not two civilizations which are here compared, but two moods, two modes of thinking. And where Baeck stresses the activism of Jewish life, and its preoccupation with that better world that is ever coming into being, he does establish the tension of Jewish thought within Jewish existence. The closeness between Hellenism and Judaism, as Baeck points out in numerous places, enabled Israel to learn much from Greece; but the similar can be quite different. Baeck's stress upon "ye shall be holy, for I the Lord your God am holy" is not the contemplation of the perfection, but upon the demanding mystery. And the demand is the ethical action in which the tension of Judaism wins its enduring rebirths while the great god Pan dies and the great civilizations surrounding Jewish history crash into oblivion.

The final statement in this special presentation of Baeck's religion of polarity to the scholars who met at Darmstadt in Count Keyserling's School of Wisdom was made in 1924, when Baeck lectured on "Death and Rebirth." [32][27] The theme of death and rebirth, sounded and resounded in the last pages of the previous essay, here moves into the center of Baeck's observations, and becomes one more way to express the nature of polarity in religion.

The 1923 meeting at Darmstadt had explored the question of the unity of thought between the Occident and the Orient. The following year, continuing along those lines and seeking to determine the basic meta-

[27] Attention must also be directed to other statements by Baeck in *Der Jude*, notably the 1930 "Geist und Blut" [44] but going back to the early (1917) "Lebensgrund und Lebensgehalt." [21]

physical motif in which East and West concur and clash, the School of Wisdom listened to papers dealing with the meaning of existence. The processes of coming into being and of dissolution were expressed in the language of Eastern and Western thought. The speakers representing Western thought spoke more in immanent terms, understanding the "being" of "becoming" more or less as the absoluteness of its inner structure: Hans Driesch ("Organic Development") saw the "totality" as the form and goal of individual life; Hans von Hattingberg ("Between Death and Life") emphasized the "proper rhythm" between consciousness and unconsciousness; Count Keyserling ("History as Tragedy") looked for "meaning" realizing itself in the human cosmos; all had a "this-worldly" emphasis in contrast to Paul Dahlke who lectured on "Samsara and Nirvana" and Nikolas von Arseniew who spoke on "Resurrection." The last two scholars placed the "being" longed for by the "becoming" into the absolute beyond, which it could only attain by ceasing to be "becoming."[28] Between these two positions, Leo Baeck represented (according to a well-known scholar) the high point of the meeting:

> Between the two attempts for a solution, one of them representing the immanence tendency of the West, the other the transcendent tendency of the East, Leo Baeck stood out as the undeniable high point of these sessions. He stood there as the great Jew, the classic scholar of the scientific study of the Essence of Judaism, in whom the antithesis between Hermann Cohen and Martin Buber found its solution. [157, p. 625]

Baeck's presentation here built upon the one certain knowledge which man possesses that touches not only upon the present but reaches into the future: the fact of man's death. The past tells man that he was born; the future, that he will die. And so death is a true and enduring fact in the metaphysical sense. According to Baeck, all true facts point beyond themselves and have a dimension of the "beyond." This is the question and problem of life: Is death just that which happens on that straight line running between coming into being and moving into dissolution—or is there a relationship between death and the unending and unknowable? Or does it stand between these two alternatives

---

[28] Cf. *Der Leuchter: Weltanschauung und Lebensgestaltung. Jahrbuch der Schule der Weisheit* (herausgegeben vom Grafen Hermann Keyserling), VI Band, (Darmstadt, 1925), pp. 1–293; particularly Keyserling, pp. 5–25.

forming the middle between fact and happening . . . between that which belongs to eternity and that which is owned by the hour: on the one hand, an occurrence like a happening, but an occurrence coming from extraterrestrial powers, from the beyond; on the other hand, something determinate, existing, like a fact, a determination and an answer like the fact . . . but a meaningless answer . . . a door that only receives and locks in, but leads to no beyond. This is *fatum*, fate. Death can also announce itself to man as fate. [32, p. 52]

Most men, from the very beginning, viewed death as fate. All dreams for redemption were dreams for the deliverance from death which destroys all of life. Philosophy attempted to give the two other answers: Death is a simple happening, a natural occurrence which has no ultimate meaning; or, death is not a happening, but the final dictum of necessity against which there is no answer and no rebellion. Men were not reassured. Death remained the *fatum*, the happening in which the beyond reached into the here to destroy; and the determined fact in which all sense is lost.

Only the mature thought of the Bible found a way of confronting the concept of fate and conquering it so that death became a true fact containing its revelation of the unending and eternal, together with its problem and its task. In contrast to others who formed their concept of life and (often) of their gods from the idea of death, Biblical man started with the recognition of the meaning of life; through it, death was defined.

Out of the life of man something twofold speaks. One, that he was born, born without his own participation, into a determined existence, into his weaknesses and his strengths, into his form and into his structure, born into air and arbors, language and history, into sojournings and wanderings, home or homelessness . . . but this not yet the totality, the essential part of life. Something essential enters to give it sense and meaning. Our life is not only born, it is also created; created by God. It has not only its origin, but also its foundation; not only its effect, but also its value . . . it is a fact rooted in the beyond. All origin comes from the One, the Eternal, Unending, is a createdness, is the origin out of God. In it, the manifoldness of life has its connection with the oneness; in it, the interwovenness of days and years with eternity appears; its becoming has its foundation in being. . . . It is a creation. It is not only an existence, but also a life. [32, pp. 52–53]

Life as creation—Baeck's structure of the polarity religion is now restated in a number of ways—contains the task of creating in obedience to the commandment for the sake of which the world and each creation is called into being. Baeck's definition here does not find the commandment in the mystery. The mystery *is* the commandment: "Life itself becomes the commandment: Thou shalt live, thou shalt fashion thy life." [32, p. 54] The paradox and the polarity are part of the definition. Life is the created which has its creativity and therefore its freedom. It is set into the world to fashion the world. In this concept of the origin of life and its meaning, Baeck sees the conquest of the idea of death as the *fatum*.

Our careful look at Baeck's treatment of the fact and concept of death helps us restore the balance between the mystic of "Mystery and Commandment" and the activist of "Perfection and Tension." Both must be seen as expressions of a pupil of neo-Kantian idealism. When we compare this article, "Death and Rebirth," beautifully written and with deep insights, with Franz Rosenzweig's awareness of death as the category of existentialist thought, we become aware that there is still a vast separation between the two. In the essay before us, Baeck conquers the idea of death. Rosenzweig affirms death itself in order to win his victory.

Nevertheless, it would be wrong to place Baeck against Rosenzweig as his antithesis. Baeck's teaching of polarity really does stand in the middle, between idealism and existentialism. It is a precarious position to maintain; but there is a subtlety and inner consistency in Baeck's system that expresses itself in these three essays—which should be read as one—in every area into which Baeck brings his definitions. The authority is always derived from the transcendent, the infinite that breaks through and reveals itself; but the revelation is found in the finite, in man's existence, his inner moods, the outer facts of his life.

Drawn into this network of Baeck's system, death, too, becomes a polarity. It describes something in the state of becoming—dying—and yet stands in the world of being; it is fact of life, part of the way that moves from origin to creativity, and therefore touched by this:

> Every being born received its meaning through its being a creation. Death also receives a meaning through this origin and foundation of life; it remains in a relationship with the creative, with that which man achieves. The fact of having been created and the commandment of creation are not dissolved by death. [32, p. 56]

Baeck takes the notion of death into the total development of human experience. And death is redefined. No longer a force from the outside, death becomes one aspect of human existence. Existence has meaning and purpose from the beyond, and so death shares in that meaning. But its independent authority over mankind as man's fate has been broken. There is not one death in man's existence; there are many deaths.

Baeck follows the riddle of the sphinx in his exposition of death in life. Death is a caesura, a cutting into life. The first caesura is the death of the child, overtaken by puberty. The child lives in immediacy, with nothing between the self and the world, the here and the beyond. It looks at the world with great eyes, and feels itself viewed by all. Art and originality, the ability to ask and to wonder belong to the child.

The child dies as the grown man looks around the world. Intellect and doubt now stand between man and the world. Man stands within his thoughts, confronts the world, battles it, tries to vanquish it or to flee from it. Another caesura, another death; and man the provider, the worker, the established member of that world stands before us. Man has possessions. He is again within the world, but only that very small part of the world in which he has established his stake. He is at home. His farm and his house are the world. Much later, another caesura, another death; an old man moves away from the world and his earlier enthusiasms. He is tired, worn out, disappointed, estranged from the world; and he retreats into himself. The final caesura. But each death need not occur; and there is constant rebirth: the artistic passion of childhood, the creative doubt of the young man, can and do find rebirth as long as the origin and foundation of existence has not been lost. And that ability of re-birth is the true religiosity, found in Biblical man and in the Jewish faith. The antithesis of the pious man is not the atheist but the philistine in whose life everything dies, who was young only once, who may have memories but no enduring life, no true rebirth.

Our life is made up of these deaths and rebirths. And when death comes, which is the deepest caesura, so deep that the body disintegrates and the soul loses its unity—should not the same pattern of rebirth apply to it? Should it not also be thus here, that the happenings do die in this caesura, as in the previous ones, but that the direction which started from the origin continues to go on? Man, reborn out of the other deaths—should he not be reborn out of this deepest cut into life, in a still deeper sense than all the others? For the events of life, this death is the happening of the end, the end of all periods, the end of all possibilities, the final fate. In the facts of life, death too, it above all else, becomes the revelation of the eternal, the unending. Should it not also be thus here: Man who only has his birth but no longer an origin only has his dying; but where he continues to stand within creation and his origin remains within him as a quality, is he not reborn and lives on? [32, pp. 61–62]

The quality of rebirth is part of Jewish man and of Judaism. Baeck uses the image of the Sabbath here: It is the rebirth of the week, its constantly renewed creation. "The allegory of the Beyond is the Sabbath"—this is how the rabbis understand it. There is a reminder in this that Baeck always writes with a profound dependence upon the Jewish sources even when, as in this instance, the general framework of the essay does not permit the elaboration of this Jewish background. Rabbinic teachings see the Sabbath as the picture of the messianic age—the messianic age *is* the Sabbath properly observed by all Israel for the first time;[29] and the full ethical imperatives of the Sabbath place the beyond into the terrestrial realm through the creative acts of justice and kindness which are the true meaning of Sabbath *menuchah,* the Sabbath rest that is never cessation from activity.

The dangers in the Sabbath, which are the dangers of human existence, are found in the fact that the commandments can die. Baeck stresses that life is not only a matter of new experiences, but also of actualizations, of creativity. Creativity can die, just as the commandment can die, when man departs from it: Man is free to reject the meaning of life. Man can sin; but man is also free to return to the commandment, to the creativity of existence.

For Baeck, the pattern of individual life is repeated in the history of nations. Nations can also be reborn; and they can also die. The enduring character of a people comes to it through the idea which formed it and through the commandment which fills it. When it forgets this, a nation dies. (Much later, Baeck was to pick up this idea and make it the heart of his final work dealing with the meaning of Israel and its existence.) Nations die through thoughtlessness and through lack of spirit. They die through idolatry. The Talmudic word applies: A nation's gods die before the nation dies. And Baeck again closes his presentation with an eloquent statement of Israel in confrontation with the other nations:

In the book of Isaiah, we find a painting of the fall of a nation. Its idols have sunk to the ground, and the people load the broken images upon their

---

[29] That is, "The Sabbath will come on that day on which all Jews will observe one complete Sabbath perfectly" (B. Sabb. 118b).

shoulders and break down under the load. The prophet views this image and he hears the voice of revelation, God's word addressed to the people to whom the prophet belongs: "When you become old, I remain the same. I have created you, I carry you and I make you free." That is the word of the rebirth of men and of the people. [32, p. 71]

The concept of death and of rebirth thus becomes the final Darmstadt statement on the religion of polarity. The grim intrusion of death is dissolved in the totality of life, in the polarities of the mystery and the commandment, of createdness and creativity which make up human existence. Baeck's system of the polarities places the actuality of death into the activism of an existence where the many deaths are followed by the many rebirths. And underneath that process is the validation of life as the created and as the creating. In the life of the individual, and in the history of a people, death has the meaning of rebirth: The valley of dry bones is there to testify to the underlying ground of being that can and does give life to those who would affirm the meaning of existence, who are in the process of becoming, walking the unending road of ethical action linking the terrestrial with the infinite beyond.

V

The Darmstadt presentations—except for "Mystery and Commandment" —have neither been translated nor evaluated in terms of their significance in Baeck's theology. Viewing them as one unit, we have come to see them as the most characteristic expression of Leo Baeck's thinking. There is even a touch of the apologete and the polemicist that can be noted, particularly in the second lecture, where Judaism confronts not only Greek thought but also the Church as the inheritor of the Greek tradition of perfection. The twofoldness that spoke to Baeck out of all aspects of the universe is here seen as the basic mood of man, as the underlying motif of civilization, as the creative bond uniting even death and birth. All is established out of human experience; but existence does not precede essence, nor essence existence. Each is contained in the other, and each defines the other. And there are intricate polarities within polarities in which revelation secures and maintains its authority within human experience without requiring the sacrifice of human reason or of independent action. Much of this system is mirrored in these lectures, particularly in "Mystery and Commandment," where the prose poetry is a definite attempt to take the listener into the heart of the system. But the final exposition of the system is found in the one systematic presentation of Baeck's theology: *The Essence of Judaism.*

The examination of the 1905 edition[30] tried to indicate that at least the framework of the system of polarity was already evident. The particular had been set against the universal, Israel against the nations, optimism against pessimism. Nevertheless, the ethical commandment, the great "Ought," loomed strongly over all; the emphasis upon the mystery as its complement was added only in the 1922 edition. What must be noted, even in passing, is that the new edition did not differ only in major matters; the nuances were different, the tone was stronger and more convincing; there *was* a movement from Cohen to Rosenzweig.[31]

In the revised edition, Baeck brings the concept of creation into the center of his system. The creation *is* the revelation. [2a, p. 105] Man becomes aware of having been created, and it is the awareness of the mystery of the near and far God that fills him. The feeling of the dark mystery also carries within itself the feeling of complete security: Man is carried by the ground of his being. Learning that the one God is his God, man discovers the meaning of life:

> The manifold is now connected with the One, the transient with the eternal, the apparent with the unfathomable. The Biblical word of allegory—filled with deep symbolism—of the Covenant which God establishes with man and with the world and with all of the future, could here be enunciated as the word of the Creation. Between God and man and between God and the world there is the covenant; the world, as man, is placed into religion. [2a, p. 106][32]

---

[30] Chapter 4, above.

[31] Ernst Simon [178] points out many of the small stylistic changes: *Volk* is changed to "nation"; "religion saved from mysticism" is changed to "from fantasy"; *experienced much and learned much* is inverted; *martyr of conviction* becomes *martyr of conscience; standpoint* becomes *foundation;* "no one will defend the psalms of vengeance" is omitted; the "attributes of God" are put into brackets as philosophy becomes more personal; a nationalism, a warmer feeling for the Jewish people, a deeper appreciation for the mystic experience becomes evident. This short (two newspaper pages) article by Simon, in its empathy and profound understanding, must be ranked at the top of all studies in the evaluation of *The Essence of Judaism.*

[32] The Schocken translation [3] omits half of this passage (cf. pp. 99–100) including the important reference to the future. Too often, the desire for clarity results in oversimplification.

Much of Baeck's system of the polarities, to which the above serves as a preface, is clearly influenced by Hermann Cohen's concept of the correlation in which the human response is part of the Divine action (i.e., God reveals and man receives; God creates and man is created; God saves and man is saved—the first two as metalogical concepts and the third as the meta-ethical idea). But for Hermann Cohen, correlation came through man's reason; the dark mystery that now speaks to Baeck alongside the commandment and connects the known with the unplumbed depths of the unknown is something new. And man does not know only his own response to God; somehow, he knows of the response of the world, knows that there is a twofold covenant here in which man is to redeem the world. And this comes to Baeck from Rosenzweig and not from Hermann Cohen; Rosenzweig's concept of covenant enters the framework of the correlation, just as Buber's words of the pathos of Jewish history sound strongly through this revised edition. It is not to be forgotten that Cohen's basic importance is here accentuated: all three of these Jewish thinkers base themselves upon Cohen as their teacher. Yet the interplay between these contemporaries is significant: Baeck's system of polarity, and his own personality, had to make the attempt to see in these various positions the manifold that was yet a basic unity; and so the covenant of Franz Rosenzweig and the extra dimension of the Jewish people, in which pathos becomes a category of their existence, enter into Baeck's system.

There are a number of ways to sketch that system as it shows itself in the *Essence*. Baeck keeps approaching the same aspects of Jewish experience from different directions. A number of paradoxes seem restatements of earlier observations, and a large variety of polarities (i.e., mysticism and ethics, man and humanity, optimism and pessimism) appear and disappear. Yet these can always be resolved (mysticism and ethics, for example, in the mystery and the commandment); and it must be kept in mind that the heart of the system is the twofoldness that is found in all aspects of the world and man.

Baeck lists the *first great paradox* of life as the confrontation between the near and the far, the transcendent and the immanent, the here and the beyond. [2a, p. 107][33] And, out of the fundamental experience of

---

[33] In Chapter 4, above, the treatment of this theme in the first edition of *The Essence* indicates both similarities and differences. Certainly, the foundations of the system are already there.

the mystery and the commandment, he comes to what he calls the *second great paradox* of life, man as a creation who is yet a creator, dependent and yet free, form and former, within a life that exists only through God and that is yet to have its own independence. Wonder and freedom confront one another. [2a, pp. 131–32] Life becomes a tension here in which life itself becomes a great longing for the Divine revelation; and man comes to experience both the love of God and the justice of God, the foundation of life and the path of life. Both exist in the One God; and the contradiction of life that brings Baeck to his third statement is the tension between what our life is and what it should be; what has been given to us and what is demanded of us. The *third great paradox* is that of God whose essence is endless love, and Who yet finds his definite expression in jealous justice. God has given eternal value to our life; but at the same time the justice of the universe demands that we, by our own actions, give to it any value that it may contain. God gives life, but he also demands life. Man is man because he was created by God, but he is also man only to the extent he keeps the commandment. [2a, p. 155] The world is both immanent and transcendent in terms of the good; created by God it truly becomes God's domain through the work of man.

In drawing these paradoxes together into a system, we must recognize that Baeck presents us with a religion of experience, taken out of human existence and building upon Dilthey's understanding and approach to the human condition. The first and fundamental polarity then rests within man, in his *createdness* which comes to confront man in his aspect as a *creator*. But each of these poles contains within itself another polarity. In man's createdness, we find the confrontation between *the near and the far* God. Man, the created person, recognizes within himself that feeling of utter dependency when he reaches toward that which gave him being. But then he also comes to see that the absolute greatness of his ground of being infuses him with a meaning and purpose that set him into the world as but little lower than the angels. The presence of God touches him and fills him with God's nearness. In his createdness, man experiences the mystery of the Holy, of God the creator.

At the other end, man has the experience of being a creator who in his creativity confronts another polarity that is found in the field of activity. As a creator, he feels the value of creation resident within him. And yet, he knows that in terms of God's justice he cannot achieve anything. He is told to redeem the world by his actions, but the task is an endless one. But he is called to this task without end by the commandment that never ends. As man the created encounters the mystery, so does man the creator encounter the commandment. It is his reason for being, and his only chance to continue as that which exists in order to reach out to eternity.

Stating the structure in this manner is something of a disservice to Baeck, since the whole thrust of Baeck's teaching presents us with an indivisible unity in which the mystery is not next to the commandment but the one is contained in the other. The near is in the far, and the far is in the near. It is found in the nearness and farness of moral life, in the activity of the unending task of ethical action in which the Divine enters the human experience and the human experience enters the Divine. Man and the world are too far away from God and cannot be redeemed, and yet are redeemed by the moral act. *Yet life is tension:* The moral act cannot be frozen into the permanence of perfection; it is one step upon an unending way, and step after step must be taken as man gives assent to the ground of his being by making it the content of his being. In just the same manner, the encounter with the mystery is the assurance of the worthwhileness of life. But, as was brought out in the Darmstadt lectures, man cannot live in the permanent experience of that encounter. The true moment of wonder brings within itself a definite commandment, and the righteous action encounters the mystery in the inner reaches of the soul. Awareness of the polarities gives life its tension, and in that tension man realizes the covenant that unites him with his Creator: He fashions the redemption of the world and of himself.

It would not be impossible to take Rosenzweig's star of redemption and press the categories of God, man, and the world, with their interrelationships of revelation, creation, and redemption upon Baeck's polarities. But it would not be true. Nor can the following sketch do any justice to a system where the immanent is contained in the transcendent and the transcendent in the immanent; its only function is that of a visual aid to summarize the outline that is suggested in the last two pages [see below].

What must be noted about the polarities is that they all resolve themselves in the world of human experience, through the ethical action that affirms life and the world in the optimistic messianism that is a lasting inheritance from Hermann Cohen. The twofoldness of man and the ten-

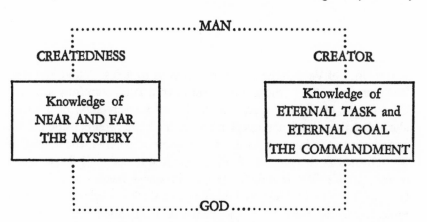

sion of human existence reach out toward the transcendent. As long as this is stated only through the ethical tasks, it can be suggested that Baeck's system is really that of immanence, and does not reach beyond the world of human experience. And, in the final Darmstadt lecture there is indeed the suggestion that man's immortality takes place in the constant rebirths of humanity which he shares as the *Mitmensch*. And the Jew, with his special mission and his revelation of the task, finds himself bound within history as the "suffering servant" of God; but it is history without end, task without cessation. Rosenzweig placed the Jewish people with God, as a metahistorical people outside the flux of the occurrences. Baeck places the people of Israel within history, as the yeast, the spark of continuous revolution and rebirth, upheld by the mystery, drawn onward by the commandment, achieving themselves in serving mankind and testifying to the revelation.

Nevertheless, Baeck's theology, closely examined, does not resolve itself into humanism, into immanentism, or into a pale ethical idealism where the Divine is neither denied or affirmed. The Divine, the infinite, and the revelation are firmly placed into the sphere of human existence; but human experience is not the judge of the Divine; the Divine judges it. Faith in God precedes all of the structure. And the affirmation of the revelation opening itself to the world in the life and destiny of Israel is a continuous act of faith in Baeck's theology that may create some difficulties in terms of the content of the revelation, but fits in perfectly with a religion of polarity in which the mystery and the commandment do not deal only with the inner and outer aspects of human existence, but are the true way in which the Holy addresses itself to finite man.

VI

The critique of Baeck's theology came from many areas. Within the Jewish community, the Orthodox who would read Baeck carefully accepted the fact that he did not speak for the liberal interpretation of Judaism alone; but they could not accept many of his basic presuppositions. We come back to the fact that in Baeck's religion of polarity, the revelation was affirmed as the ground of being; but it was not spelled out as the content of life. The traditional Jew could accept Baeck's teaching that God selected Israel for a special mission, that the knowledge which Israel presented to the world, this knowledge of God called "ethical monotheism" was indeed true revelation. But when the existence of Israel, and Israel's knowledge of the commandment and feeling of the mystery become so strong as vehicles of the revelation that they push against the traditional standards of Halacha and ceremonial, when, indeed, the function of the ceremonial is seen as the preservation of Israel, as a useful but not everlasting experience of Jewish life—then the Orthodox Jew had to take his stand against Baeck.

There were any number of additional reasons why this should be so. As we have briefly indicated, Baeck emphasized midrash and Aggadah more than Halacha; and he espoused an ethical and a rational mysticism that was in many ways unknown to the leaders of traditional Judaism. He was a product of a liberal seminary, and a leader of the Reform group within Jewish life. His religion of polarity, even as expounded in the Darmstadt lectures, drew deeply upon Jewish sources. Baeck lived in the Bible. But the Bible was not a revelation because each word came from God. Rather, it was revelation because it recounted the history of Israel, God's revelation to the world. And when Israel itself becomes the revelation, the Halacha becomes only one constituent part of that revelation and loses the authority Orthodox thinking must claim for it. Baeck's polarities give assent to the manifoldness of Jewish existence, and this is the truth that is his possession, and he cannot but feel uncomfortable within the elasticity of the polarities.

Jeschajahu Aviad-Wolfsberg (that is, Oscar Wolfsberg, who adopted Driesch's "philosophy of organism") is a spokesman of Orthodoxy whose criticism of Baeck is significant because it is bound up with Wolfsberg's full appreciation of Baeck as an authentic voice of Judaism. In the "elasticity" of Baeck's thoughts [196] he sees a positive aspect of the Jewish tradition, but warns of its inherent dangers which weaken the solid structure of the Halacha. Baeck's great talent is seen as that of the exegete who sees the manifold in the Jewish tradition; but his framework of interlocking polarities is that of a liberalism which does not fully appreciate the Tannaitic world and its respect for the law (the affirmation of the Jewish elements in Christianity is seen as a misreading of the historical situation: Christian opposition to Jewish law is a more characteristic expression of early Christianity than the shared aspects of midrash and Aggadah). Wolfsberg notes that

> the good interpreters of liberalism—to which Baeck certainly belongs— did not deny the rank and the validity of the Halacha. But they honored it too much as concept and idea and not sufficiently as the force of life that constantly proves itself through its effect in daily life. [196, p. 147]

There is an excessive mildness in Baeck's system; it lacks the decisiveness of the Halacha. Where the Aggadic is central, it is difficult for Halacha to act as the constitutive principle of thought; and it must be that for Orthodoxy. Baeck's nonrejection of Biblical criticism, his lack of enthusiasm for the exquisitely rabbinic aspects of the Oral Law—these also separate Baeck from Wolfsberg.

We come back to the question of mood and personality at this point. The openness of the polarity, the affirmation of so much that seemed contradictory, the very hypostasizing of adjectives in which the tension of the open definition expresses itself ("there is a twofoldness," for example, moves away from the solid statement of "the twofold"; "there is something great" states less than "the great") here kept Orthodox thought at bay. And it is significant that the same aspect of Baeck's style is affirmed as an essential quality of Baeck's teaching in which the liberal students could recognize the openness of their position (compare Bamberger [76]). Wolfsberg (and Alexander Altmann's criticism tends to go along with this) feels a weakness in Baeck's position of polarity. He demands the decisiveness, the clear, and ready affirmation of principles. Wolfsberg sees Baeck as too soft, too indecisive in these matters. And he concludes his critique by seeing Baeck as too open to Christianity and the outside world, too optimistic in his relationship to mankind. One's own vineyard must be kept, and the fence around it must be preserved.

There is a misunderstanding of Baeck's position in this critique, which

is already evident in the facts of Baeck's life which was a rock of un-
yielding decisiveness and an exulting declaration of Judaism. Wolfsberg,
and the other critics of Baeck, in recognizing this, separate the life from
the teachings and pay full respect to the authentic Jewish life in which
the commandment spoke in all its decisiveness. But that same decisiveness can be seen in the theology. Wolfsberg does not fully recognize the
polarity of Baeck's system that sets *Lebensgrund* ("the foundation of
life") against *Lebensgehalt* ("the contents of life"). In that context,
Baeck absolutely affirms the revelation that undergirds life; but he refuses
to isolate the aspects of that life, the Halacha and the Aggada, and to
affirm one part—Halacha—as the authority out of which the revelation
speaks. The revelation speaks out of all aspects of man's life. But in
answer to those who would then say that it speaks out of nothing, Baeck
isolates Jewish existence at this point, as the polarity of Israel and the
nations, and sees Israel as the revelation. Orthodox Jewish critics could
accept this point, but with the reservation that Baeck stops short of the
traditional emphasis on the Law; non-Orthodox critics, particularly
Christian theologians, could not accept Baeck's point at all. By its very
nature, the position of the theology of polarity stands midway between
other systems. It enters into other systems, affirms aspects of it, but stub-
bornly sees the antithesis as well. For that reason, it is constantly under
attack. But the maintenance of that position is only possible out of
strength, not out of weakness. It is not the bland acceptance of all
values, but the affirmation of the unending and eternal that is the foundation of the universe which gives its character to the *theologia viatorum*.

The sharpest critique of Baeck's system does come from traditional
Christian theology, in the writings of a Jesuit [157] who showed a much
greater awareness of the importance of Baeck's theology than that shown
by Baeck's Jewish contemporaries. Przywara acknowledges the depth of
Baeck's vision, the truth of the polarity; indeed, he would see in it the
essence of Christianity. But when Baeck declares the interwovenness
of mystery and commandment to be "a religious reality and not a postulate of philosophy, not just a statement of faith but the life of man,"
[2a, p. 173] Przywara has to challenge Baeck:

> At this point, there is an irreconcilable parting of the ways. If this polarity
> is man's gaze into the unexplorability of God who is above his creatures,
> the spiritual possibility of the salvation belief has already begun: man,
> to whom the "polarity" is *the* revelation of the absolute incomprehensibility
> of God, will not hesitate before the still more mysterious "polarity" which

unites the true nature of God and the true nature of man, without mingling them, in the one person, the Christ; nor will he hesitate before its ultimate unfolding in the "polarity" of the Church's existence as that of the onliving Christ. [157, p. 657]

Przywara, who lived within this "Christian polarity" and placed it at the center of his teachings,[34] was deeply aware of the revelation of God within the Old Testament—a revelation which he also saw as the polarity. As long as the Jew lives in the religiosity of the Old Testament in which the polarity shines forth as the *one* form of religion, the experience of the polarity is concretized in the Jewish religious existence which centers upon the deed. But then, according to Przywara, the Jew can experience in Christianity the undreamed of fulfillment of his existence by finding in the Christian polarity the gaze into the mystery, the breaking of the barrier. His closed existence is broken open as he unconditionally surrenders himself and his faith to the "God of the unexplorable paths." [157, pp. 657–658] In some ways, Przywara, like Baeck, goes back to the early centuries and links the Jews together with the first Christians through a mutual experience of the polarity. When he comes back to modern times and the confrontation with Baeck, he finds the Jew divorced from this Biblical experience in which the polarity was truly felt as the transcendent entering into the immanent. He must attack Baeck in almost the same manner as Wolfsberg, the Orthodox Jew:

> If this polarity—as is indeed true for today's Judaism—is no more than a deep formula for the immanent closedness of human life in which "God" is somehow linked to the "human ideal" in some inner manner, then Christianity with its basic demand of "faith" (i.e., the breaking open of all human attempts to stay enclosed within themselves) is indeed *the* vexation and *the* foe. The Jew who experiences this kind of dissolution of the divinity of his immanent polarity with "God" of necessity becomes the untiring "revolutionary" of the Christian world. [157, pp. 657–658]

Przywara sees this kind of Jew as the untiring activist who is driven by his inmost religiosity to the Ahasverus existence of the "Wandering Jew." All must be realized in this life, and there is never any rest, because the Jew experiences the eternal God as the "eternal striving." Buber's words apply here: "We are the slaves of many earths, and our thoughts fly unto many heavens. But in the utmost depths of the soul

---

[34] In *Gott* [157a], where he constructs his polarities.

we have no earth and no heaven." [157][35] Just as Baeck's system of a closed immanentism leaves no opening for a challenge by the Christian or Jewish traditionalist who wants to present the truth of his transcendental revelation, so Israel stands impervious in today's world. Anti-Semitic attacks can only shift the tremendous force contained in Israel's drive for realization into peripheral fields. And Przywara sees only the Catholic faith, the faith of the absolute belief in Jesus Christ and the Holy Apostolic Catholic Church, as able to confront the tremendous figure of the Jew in the world. It alone, in its inmost essence, is the God-created fulfillment of the innermost longing within Judaism. For Judaism's drive for the unification of mankind is bound to fail: A colorless internationalism destroys all individuality, including that of the Jewish people. Baeck's optimism for the world and faith in man is here confronted by Przywara's pessimism and his rejection of man's ability to achieve a messianic age by his own efforts:

> The union of all nations can only come into being beyond the human sphere, in Him Who as Creator called each nation by "its" name and gives each people a special radiance of countenance, in Him Whose becoming human within the mystery of the "head and body of the *one* Christ" aims for the meeting of "the *many* parts of *one* body," i.e., a union of humanity which really demands the differences—"when all would be *one* limb, where would be the body?" [157, p. 660]

Judaism, according to Przywara, is hopelessly locked into its task within human existence. Ever since the advent of Christianity, it has insisted on viewing God in the immanence of human existence: no matter which way it proceeds, all of its energies must come to concentrate upon mankind. The result has been tragic:

> Since the goal that Israel has to present to mankind is ultimately—no matter which approach is used—its own Jewish humanness, every nation eventually experiences this Judaism as a presumptuous disturber of its own national spirit [*Volkstum*]. The antisemitism of world history is basically the necessary Ahasverus fate of the people which has dared to set itself into the place of the God Who rules creation. It is Christianity, on the other hand, which is the patient creator of the unity of man. The all-decisive fundamental structure of Christianity is its faith in the God above creation; and the unity of man rises out of the differences of the indi-

[35] Quoting Martin Buber, *Die juedische Bewegung* (Berlin, 1916), I, p. 63.

vidual nations, a unity that is not called man but God: "Head and body of the *one* Christ." [157, pp. 660–661]

The challenge of Christianity then becomes the bringing of all men to that unity, to the Christ. And the anguish of Israel is that it will remain the wandering Jew until it has found its fulfillment in the Holy Catholic Church.

The facts of German history in the two decades that followed this statement cast a dark shadow over some aspects of it; they need not blind us to Przywara's very real attempt to come to terms with a Judaism that did, indeed, stand in ultimate opposition to what he believed and taught. It was not only Baeck whom he opposed. Buber's Zionism, with its hidden depths of humanitarianism and messianism, its insistence upon this world as the place of realization, seemed just as much an aspect of the immanentism with which Przywara identified the Jew. Przywara confronts Baeck as a Christian theologian who insists upon the truth of his own revelation. In this revelation, the transcended God manifested Himself to man in Jesus at Calvary. When Baeck rejects this and places the revelation—and Przywara has doubts about the transcendent aspects of the God of Whom Baeck witnesses—into the existence of Israel, Przywara has no choice but to attack this revelation, i.e., the people Israel. Przywara gives his full assent to the description of polarity as the essence of religious life. But in his assessment of the religious enterprise, the stress must ultimately be upon the mystery, to the point of surrendering to it in order to break out of the immanent and its limitations. In Baeck he finds the exposition of a polarity that ultimately places its emphasis upon the commandment, upon the enlargement of the possibilities contained in the immanent so that it can open itself to the transcendent as the place of the messianic age. Przywara rightly understood that Baeck's system, at least implicitly, placed Israel into the world as a messianic figure: The revelation as the mission of Israel admits of no other ultimate conclusion. The deeper the understanding, the deeper the opposition; in a way, the sharpness of Przywara's attack is a testimony to the strength of Baeck's position.[36]

[36] Professor Ernst Simon (now at Hebrew University, Jerusalem), who is one of the foremost authorities on this period of Jewish thought, feels that Przywara profoundly misunderstood Baeck when he charged him with an absolute immanentism. Baeck believed in a transcendent and in a personal God (i.e., with Franz Rosenzweig that "God is at *least* personal!"). Simon attacked Przywara's position on Judaism at that time as "infamous!" (private conversation with Dr. Simon, December 23, 1965, New York).

Wolfsberg and Przywara both have significant criticisms of Baeck that rise out of their background. Wolfsberg, speaking as an Orthodox Jew, recognized that there were basic liberal suppositions behind Baeck's statements even when Baeck felt that he was speaking for the totality of Judaism and not just a segment of it. The Law meant something else to Baeck than it did to Wolfsberg. Even when it was placed within the same chain of transmission, the traditionalist would turn to the authority of the earlier generations, while Baeck would emphasize the ability of the present to make drastic changes. But Wolfsberg erred when he felt Baeck assenting to so much in contemporary Jewish life that there is not enough left for a great central affirmation. As indicated, there is a narrow ridge, the religion of polarity, that Baeck affirms absolutely. Przywara recognizes this religion of polarity; but he also sees Baeck's approach as a challenge to traditionalism and to the specific Christian revelation. There, the transcendent revelation which has broken into the immanent continues in the world through the Church, fenced in and protected by the sancta, the sacraments, and the authority of the Church. Baeck places the revelation into the continuous existence of Israel. This weakens the concept of authority, since Baeck refuses to see the synagogue as an analogous institution to the Church and will not put rabbinic authority beyond criticism.

But Przywara's charge of immanentism cannot be sustained, since it does not rise out of the nature of a Baeckian system that is completely humanistic, but rather out of Przywara's conviction that the transcendent revelation can no longer be part of Israel's existence: The revelation now belongs to the Church. Israel can only regain it if it returns to the Church. Baeck's affirmation of the ground of being from which the contents of life take on meaning is overlooked by Przywara, who simply cannot accept a dimension of Jewish existence that would reach out to the transcendent revelation without going through the Church. Baeck may acknowledge the mystery as the source, but his emphasis is on the commandment. And this commandment is not channeled through traditional interpretation and traditional authority, but is part of the revelation that comes through human experience, through the secular life. At this point, traditionalist Judaism and Christianity join in their fight against the liberalism which is at the heart of Baeck's position. But Przywara's antagonism is even stronger than Wolfsberg's because he fears that a humanistic Judaism, engaged in ethical action for the benefit of all men, will usurp the role of the Church which must enter this field and bring all nations to the realization that the one humanity can only come into existence in the Christ Who stands beyond history.

Przywara was correct in pointing out that Baeck's religion of polarity places its greatest emphasis upon the ethical action, the commandment; and he rightly sensed the liberalism upon which Baeck's religion was built. But it must also be noted that there was no full endorsement of Baeck's thinking by the liberal Jewish thinkers. Baeck's ethical idealism clearly fitted into the liberal framework, and Baeck's position at the Lehranstalt and his presidency of the liberal rabbinate identified him with Liberal Judaism. Even his polemic against Christianity can be seen against the liberal background: Such stalwarts as Abraham Geiger were far more prominent in Jewish apologetics and the polemic against Christianity than the traditionalists. Orthodox Judaism tended to ignore Christianity; where this proved impossible, the polemic was either stated in language resembling the disputations of the Middle Ages, or it was buried deeply in the text. But, for the liberals, the polemic was generally one more tool to gain complete equality within the Christian community; and Baeck's confrontation with Christianity was on a completely different level, a radical challenge to all aspects of the Christian revelation, the Christian mood of religion, the nature and function of the Church.[37]

From the very beginning it becomes evident that Baeck is not espousing a clearly liberal position. The 1905 edition of *Wesen des Judentums* had already abandoned the safe path of theological statements that fitted the liberal thinking and could be announced as dogmas. A different kind of Judaism is found here than that of the liberals, of

[37] It must be noted here that Baeck's judgment of Christianity tends to be extremely harsh—if viewed *solely* within the polemical framework which by its very nature avoids qualifications. Pointing to the uncompromising ethical strain within Bonhoeffer, Eugene Borowitz asks: "What has happened to the anti-Christian polemics of the Jewish neo-Kantians (Leo Baeck's *Romantic Religion* . . . is a classic example) that Lutheranism emphasizing salvation by faith alone, cannot be morally oriented as Judaism?" ("Bonhoeffer's World Comes of Age," *Judaism*, Winter 1965, p. 85). But if this is rightly noted as a flaw in Baeck's understanding, his statements of the 1920s must be seen against all of the events of the next two decades. The moral failures of the Church loom larger than the successes. Baeck predicted the failures; he also expected the moral greatness of men like Bonhoeffer who would respond to the commandment of Christianity which could not but shine through its sometimes obscuring mystery.

men like Kaufmann Kohler who taught a system of dogmas.[38] Nor are
the prophets seen as the primary expounders of Judaism: Alongside of
them, the Pharisees appear with all their attention to the daily details
in which the prophetic vision is to hallow all of the people in all their
ways; and there is a wealth of Talmudic quotations which, once again,
was strange to the liberal pattern.[39] The revised version of 1922, in
which the mystery takes its place alongside the commandment, is an expression of Baeck's system of polarities, emphasizing an area of Jewish
experience which had generally been outside of the liberals' commitment: the field of mysticism. (Scholem *does* relate Shabbataism to Reform Judaism.) Baeck's approach to it is dominated by a liberal attitude
and the commanding sense of the "Ought." Drawing upon the mystical
sources, Baeck found the same ethical rigorism and rationalism in these
texts which he had previously discovered for himself in Hermann
Cohen's philosophic system. But it was still a field that was viewed with
suspicion by liberal Judaism. In the end, Baeck's clear-cut ethical activism
was accepted by a community which tended to see in Baeck the successor to Hermann Cohen. Few probed beyond the commandment to
find the mystery. There was assent to the intellectual aspects of Baeck's
system, but the personal religion of experience in which the mystery of
the transcendent entered into daily life found few listeners.

The religion of polarity, then, stands between traditional and liberal
thought. And this leads naturally to the charge that it was not so much
a clear-cut position as an indecisiveness or an unclearness on the part
of Leo Baeck which makes it difficult to classify him. The existence of
any kind of a system in his teachings—outside the attenuated inheritance
from Hermann Cohen—has not received much consideration from the
majority of scholars in this field who prefer to view Baeck as a great
religious personality rather than as a systematic thinker with a particular
contribution in the field of Jewish theology.[40] Our close survey of

[38] As indicated before, Ernst Simon's "Geheimnis und Gebot" [178] is followed
here. He indicates Baeck's break with standard liberal thinking: "Baeck here embarks
—apparently without a rudder—upon the open ocean of a new Jewish adventure of
faith." [p. 31]

[39] The liberal scientific study of Judaism had maintained the traditional defense of the
Talmud against its calumniators, but more as a matter of self-defense than out of
enthusiasm for its contents.

[40] In a number of interviews with Abraham Heschel and Ernst Simon, I found a
continual emphasis upon Baeck as a great religious personality, as the outstanding

Baeck's writings in the first three decades, on the other hand, indicates that there was this central thought of polarity in which a movement from ethical idealism to the affirmation of Jewish existence gains a particular expression not found in other Jewish writers of this period. It is found in the development of *The Essence of Judaism,* in the unity of the Darmstadt lectures, and in a variety of other places. One last example (from 1931) indicates its centrality for Baeck's thought:

> One concept . . . has become important and directive within Judaism: that of the paradox and the antimony, of the polarity and the tension. Thoughts of the same necessity stand in conflict to one another, a conflict that cannot be resolved by philosophic logic. The controversy remains within the world of the abstract, but for religious thought there emerges, out of it, a unity and a closedness. . . . [44a, p. 275]

Again, religious thought is here seen as an aspect of human experience in which the paradoxes of abstract thinking find their resolution. At this point, we move from neo-Kantianism to the affirmation of the people Israel as a paradigm of human existence in which the revelation and mystery are encountered in daily life, within the ethical action through which the beyond enters into the now. (The final section of this book, dealing with Baeck's postwar writings, particularly *This People Israel,* is intended as a documentation of this movement.) But in so far as we can speak of a system of polarity—and if we affirm such a system, it is by no means an attempt to force all of Baeck's writing, much of it fluid and indeterminate, into a Procrustean bed— it is a system that begins with Baeck's first writings and finds its full expression in the 1920s.

Baeck's openness to the *Zeitgeist* must be kept in mind. The 1920s were not only the days of Buber and Rosenzweig, but also of Karl

---

communal leader, as a great moral hero rather than as an important thinker. (A fuller evaluation of these sources is made in Chapter 2, above. Arthur A. Cohen [95, p. 104] representing the next generation which knows Baeck through his books touches on an important point when he writes: "Baeck . . . cannot be dismissed. Though his thought may lack the abstract brilliance of that of his co-workers Cohen and Rosenzweig, it has an adamantine stubbornness and realism on which moral courage—never a virtue solely of the mind—is formed. . . . That we cannot learn as much from his thought as from his life is not to denigrate his thought but to praise his life." Life and thought must be joined, but it is also a fact the judgments here are not based on a full evaluation of Baeck's thoughts.

Barth and Emil Brunner, of Tillich and Schaeder. In the preceding
chapter, we indicated that Baeck's use of "classic" and "romantic"
drew upon Strich and other scholars. Baeck's use of "polarity" need not
be considered as completely derived from these men. Rather, it paralleled existing developments within all areas of European thought then
coming to the realization that the synthesis of Hegelian dialectic needed
a new formulation in the cold winds of the twentieth century. In
"Theology and History" [46] Baeck emphasized the theological fer-
ment within Protestantism and the strong influence of the "dialectic
theology" upon Jewish thought:

> It has gained its strength from a variety of sources: . . . the renewal
> of Old Testament thinking; from the experience of what is undogmatic
> in religion, the encounter with the ultimate impossibility of expressing
> the inexpressible, the paradox and "dialectic" of all religious attestation;
> . . . the religious idea of Creation . . . and of Judgment . . . and from
> a clear understanding of the tension between present and future, between
> dependence and freedom . . . to the affirmation of the "sanctity" of God
> . . . and the "sanctification" of man. And it is unmistakable how much of all
> this speaks out of and to Judaism. . . . [46, p. 274]

Baeck recognizes his kinship and indebtedness to the Protestant
theologians who also want the *theologia viatorum*, the systematic reflection of the theologian upon what he is doing when on the basis of
revelation he speaks of God. The point of separation between them is
his turning to the Jewish experience as the place where the Infinite
enters the finite, where the people Israel come to experience the polarity
of mystery and commandment as the nature of their existence.

Within that Jewish experience, ultimately, we also find the sources
of both commandment and mystery as Baeck understands them in his
system. It may be argued that Baeck brings some aspects of the ethical
imperative into his reading of mystical texts; but that charge cannot
be made against the Biblical sources—the Torah, Prophets, and Writings which speak out of all his major statements. Nor can one question
the ethical timber of the Pharisees with whom Baeck identifies himself
—Biblical scholarship has advanced too far in this century to repeat
the old charges against these men of religion. Baeck came *from* these
sources to Hermann Cohen. Out of Cohen's system, particularly out of
the concept of the fellow human being, the *Mitmensch*, and Cohen's

theory of correlation, the ideological foundations of Baeck's religion of polarity were established. The all-pervading twofoldness, man's necessary response of ethical action to the eternal commandment of God, and the nature of the rational mind that must give its assent to the ethical imperatives—all find their place in Baeck's system. But underneath it there stands the covenant at Sinai; and the covenant of Sinai contains the mystery as well as the commandment.

The *Gesetz* ("law") of Sinai only becomes the *Gebot* ("commandment") within human existence at the moment of assent. And, in that assent, man encounters the mystery within the commandment. As Baeck comes to stress this aspect of man's nature more and more, he moves away from Cohen. We have previously pointed out that there are similarities between Baeck and Schleiermacher at this point, where theology seems to concern itself more with man's consciousness of God through his feelings of dependency, and much less with a transcendent God. Indeed, Professor Leon Roth has been quoted as saying: "Baeck tried to transfer the teachings of Schleiermacher into Judaism; in this, he was unsuccessful."[41] This statement is simply not correct. The differences between Baeck and Schleiermacher, as enunciated by Baeck in numerous places, particularly in "Romantic Religion," do not permit this kind of identification. As the disciple of Dilthey, Baeck was certainly influenced by the psychological approach to religion; and Schleiermacher's "theology of feeling" taught him to understand and value one aspect of the religious mood. But Baeck's firm commitment to the revelation within Judaism and to the ethical act that can reach from the here to the beyond could not but make him an opponent of Schleiermacher. The polarity of the created who is also the creator affirms a fundamental difference from the position of absolute dependency. Baeck's stress on the commandment as the framework of the mystery makes the sustained feeling of utter dependency impossible: The knowledge of the Creator always brings with it the awareness of an action man can and must do and brings him to the awareness of his own worth. Baeck also acknowledges his indebtedness to Rudolf Otto through whom "the peculiarly irrational within history came to be more appreciated from

[41] Ernst Simon recalls a lecture at which Roth made this statement. At the same time, Simon felt that Roth was completely wrong on this point; at best, only superficial similarities exist between Baeck and Schleiermacher (interview with Professor Simon, December 27, 1965, New York).

the vantage point of religion." [46, p. 275] But this does not mean that Otto's concept of the holy came to dominate Baeck's thinking about the mystery in his system of polarity. Throughout, we must come to see both the mystery and the commandment as aspects of the Jewish experience in which the tension of the universal that has entered the finite is resolved through the covenant and its mission that reaches out to all mankind. Once again, we return to the suggestion which opened this chapter: Baeck follows in the footsteps of Jehuda Halevi; and he sees a prophetic quality within this people that hears both mystery and commandment. It is a classic quality. Not surrendering to the bliss of the moment, it confronts the holy as the vision of Isaiah, demanding "Here am I; send me!" And so it is the Biblical vision of the holy which Baeck seeks to rediscover in the writings of Jewish mysticism.

In Chapter 8, the consistency of Baeck's system will be evaluated, together with its weaknesses and strengths. At this point, it suffices to state that Baeck's religion of polarity, traced through his early writings, is indeed drawn out of his Jewish sources. It is a religion of creation, revelation, and redemption in which the Infinite is affirmed within human existence without being limited by the finite. God is found in human nature and in individual experience. But the fact of the transcendental revelation, if not its full contents, is affirmed by a fundamental faith that is the essence of Judaism. Refusing to stand exclusively within either traditionalism or liberal thought, Baeck at this point presents us with a religion that survived the most profound crisis of Jewish life—and here the man and his ideas interpenetrate and cannot be divided. Yet we have come to recognize the important function of the idea of polarity in this religion. On the one hand, it enabled the liberal religionist to affirm ethical activism, man's rational knowledge of the will of God which is the moral imperative—and to link this up with the irrational aspect of the man of faith who finds the encounter with the mystery a basic mood and ultimate experience in religion. Through his system of polarities, Baeck can affirm the categorical imperatives alongside the transcendent revelation that becomes apparent to man not only in reason but also in feeling. The liberal faith can claim the foundation of revelation without being forced to accept the authority of the tradition that claims it alone assures the knowledge of that revelation. And the affirmation of Israel as a special revelation in history is based upon the system of polarities which can affirm the contradictory trends of Jewish life and seal them together with the rabbinic concept of *ele v'ele divre elohim chayim*—"The words of both are the words of the living God."

NOTES

Przywara's judgment of Baeck, Buber, and the German-Jewish community of the twentieth century is clearly within the context of his Christianity. It can in no way be compared with the Nazi attacks of the next decade. Nevertheless his emphasis on the individual spirit of each nation as against the desire of Jewry to achieve one humanity (which to Przywara can only happen in the Beyond, in Christ), and his suspicion of the dynamics of Jewish life which result in a secular messianism—are echoed by the Nazi scholars of the 1930s. Obviously, A and B are not equal because they both say C. The same source can be used or misused. But it may be said, following Baeck's observations in this area, that the common denominator between the two is the romantic element.

The distortions and failures of Nazi scholarship prevent a full use of its criticisms of twentieth century Jewry. One example out of many may suffice:

The Bibliographical Institute in Leipzig, for almost a hundred years, published one of the better lexicons in Germany (Meyer's *Lexikon*). In the 1924 edition (Meyer's *Lexikon*, 7th ed., Leipzig, 1924, column 1293) there is a concise and accurate account of Baeck, who is described as a Jewish scholar, rabbi, and lecturer at the Lehranstalt, with three of his major works listed. Under the rubric Buber, both Salomon and Martin are listed, with a fairly long description of Buber's writings and editorial work on *Der Jude*. Buber is hailed for "his work of enlightenment and his fructifying influence upon the development of modern Judaism" (Meyer's *Lexikon*, volume II).

The eighth edition of Meyer's *Lexikon* appeared in 1936, with the Gothic type-script replaced by a different type preferred by the Nazis. Baeck's name is dropped completely. Buber, on the other hand, is honored with seventeen lines (the seventh edition used nine lines) while his father's name is dropped (Meyer's *Lexikon*, 8th ed., Leipzig, 1937, vol. II, p. 207). He is described as follows:

A Jewish philosopher of religion and author. At first he tended toward as-similation-Judaism, but moved through Zionism and came thus to chassidism and its Eastern Jewry mysticism. He makes a virtue out of the Jewish rootless-ness and *Zerrissenheit* by using it to proclaim the Jews as the people of a synthetic drive and of a messianic hope for the future which is extended to all humanity. However, it is precisely his Jewish adherents who emphasize the relationship between Buber's messianism and the teachings of Karl Marx. Together with Franz Rosenzweig, Buber achieved a new translation of the Old Testament (*Die Schrift, verdeutscht* 1926) in which the German language is raped by being fitted into the Hebrew rhythms and its bombastic expressions.

It should also be mentioned that after the war, the Bibliographical Institute in Leipzig published a new lexicon (Meyer's *Neues Lexikon,* Leipzig, 1961). Baeck is restored (*ibid.,* vol. I, col. 557) and his stay in the concentration camp is mentioned. Buber is also brought back into the work in a proper manner.

Both Buber and Baeck had found their way into the major lexicon (Brockhaus) by 1929. In postwar Germany, such reference works as *Die Religion in Geschichte und Gegenwart* ("Baeck," vol. I, col. 840; "Buber," vol. I, col. 1452–1453) deal with them. *Der Grosse Herder,* 1953–1954 deals with both. Baeck (vol. I, col. 856) has his work *Das Wesen des Judentums* praised as "the fundamental and definitive description of Jewish religious ideas." Buber (vol. II, col. 428) is one of the few honored with his picture.

In the end, the reference books of a land say less about the men they describe and more about the culture from which these reference works emanate.

7

The Later Teachings of
Leo Baeck

A full appraisal of Leo Baeck must come to terms with the fact that Baeck's basic teachings did not find many listeners in the twenties and thirties. From 1933 on, special circumstances prevailed which placed Leo Baeck in the center of German-Jewish existence. This leadership did not come to Baeck by chance; it was the inevitable outgrowth of his activities over the past three decades which—as described earlier[1]— had placed him at the head of the leading religious, cultural, and philanthropic organizations of the Jewish community. But while Baeck's activities within German Jewry receive a fuller dimension of understanding when placed against his theology explored here, the fact remains that this theology was largely ignored by Baeck's contemporaries, who saw only the great community leader, the rabbi, the symbol of German Jewry—but not the teacher of a religion of polarity which could speak to their needs.

Some of the reasons Baeck's writings were not read lie readily at hand. To start with, his major writings were few. Theodor Wiener's bibliography reminds us of the steady outflow of pamphlets and articles [192] which shows us that Baeck remained a constantly creating scholar

---

[1] Cf. Chapter 2, above, dealing with Baeck's biography.

despite the tremendous demands made on his time by his other fields
of endeavor. But when we turn to Baeck's major writings, we really
find only one book for each of the major epochs of his life: The young
Baeck wrote *The Essence of Judaism* in 1905, and again in 1922.
Baeck's major statement of his "middle years" was his *Wege im Judentum* in 1933; five years later (1938), when German Jewry stood at the
end of its thousand year history, Baeck published his *Aus drei Jahrtausenden*. And at the end of his life, half a century after his great
1905 work, there appeared *Dieses Volk: Juedische Existenz* in two
volumes (1955 and 1957). The 1933 and 1938 publications were both
collections of essays, all scholarly and profound, but difficult for the
expert, let alone the layman.

Baeck's *Essence of Judaism* could be found on most Jewish book-
shelves. But it had attained the status of a "classic," to be praised and
venerated, but not to be taken directly into life. The style was too
formidable, the demands made upon the reader were too exacting. The
consummate control Baeck exercised over his emotions placed the
dynamic core of his writings, often even the polemic, deeply underneath
the outer structure. Much of his work shows a lack of color, so that the
most revolutionary things he had to say were often ignored. Baeck
had his disciples: scholars and young rabbis who were touched by the
depth of his thinking and the greatness of his being; he did not have
a following.

By contrast, both Buber and Rosenzweig had disciples and a following. The tragic death of Rosenzweig deprived the world of an important
message. The difficulties of his style, time after time, have frustrated
the translation of his great *Stern der Erloesung* [162]; but that the book
will appear in English, and that it will have an impact upon contemporary Jewish thought, is more than a hope.[2] There was also the
legend of Rosenzweig, even in his lifetime, which gained him a hear-
ing. Above all, there was an institution: the Lehranstalt in Frankfurt,
through which Rosenzweig could speak to a larger public. And the
Buber-Rosenzweig translation of the Bible had an incalculable effect
upon German Jewry; with the death of German Jewry, we can only
speculate upon the harvest that could have arisen from the fruits of this
labor.

[2] A translation will appear in the near future.

The same thing could be said about Buber, who published volumi-
nously and had the poet's gift of expression which won him a worldwide
public. More, he had the personality and charisma of those who attract a
large following even among those who do not really enter into the teachings of the leader they chose for themselves.[3] At one time, there was the
additional framework of a movement—the Zionist group—which assures
the scholar and teacher of a larger public. And while Buber has been seen
to have had a greater impact on the non-Jewish world than on the Jewish
community itself, the response of the outer group always has some effect
on the inner group; to the extent Buber became known to the general
public, the Jewish community found the need to return to him and listen
to his message.

Buber, Rosenzweig, and Baeck *were* the leading voices of German
Jewry. On a different level, we must mention leaders of Jewish Orthodoxy like Isaak Breuer, N. A. Nobel, Joseph Wohlgemuth, and Oscar
Wolfsberg, all of whom responded to the philosophic trends of their environment. But it must be kept in mind that "all these efforts arose not
so much from a genuinely philosophical impulse as from a desire to
fortify the faithful. They provided intellectual embellishments of the
faith rather than new philosophical approaches." [71, p. 211] Buber,
Rosenzweig, and Baeck spoke to all the groupings of Jewish life; yet
Baeck's intellectual influence (in contrast to the enormous impact of his
life) lagged behind that of his colleagues. And the basic reason, quite
clearly, rests in the philosophical positions taken by these men.

Rosenzweig and Buber represented the "new thinking" of twentieth
century Jewry; and Baeck represented the old ways. Baeck's language,
and many of his concepts, were clearly taken from the neo-Kantian framework of Hermann Cohen. He seemed to espouse idealism at a time when
existentialism (not yet named or catalogued as such) was taking hold of
men's minds. The fact that Baeck's system of polarities enters into the
existential realm was not recognized; and the very nature of a system of
polarities with its espousal of two opposites dampens enthusiasm—dur-

[3] Ernst Simon, who is one of the foremost Buber disciples, has a somewhat different
appraisal of the relative differences between Buber and Baeck. Baeck, according to
Simon, was the leader of German Jewry because he was not that far removed from their
thoughts. As befits a leader, he walked one or two steps in front of everyone, but
was still within their range. Buber, an authentic genius, moved in an area that was
beyond the reach of most (conversation with Professor Simon, December 23, 1965,
New York).

ing its birthpangs, the new always tries to reject the old, even if it comes to terms with it later on. The middle way is suspected by all the factions. And Baeck's teachings, quite simply, were not recognized for what they were.

During the second and third decade, until 1933, German Jewry lived an intellectual life which ultimately showed itself to contain many self-deceptions.[4] General Jewish culture, education, and social life had created a self-contained existence in which much was taken for granted which afterward proved illusionary. But, illusion or not, it often provided the German Jew with the possibility of realizing the messianic hopes of the nineteenth century through a career within the general society. Przywara's charge against Baeck[5] as representative of a secularized messianism which seeks its fulfillment now, within present-day society, is more understandable against that backdrop of German-Jewish life. From the standpoint of his Zionism, Ernst Simon had arrived at a similar characterization of the German-Jewish community:

> The Emancipation—though it may be said to have lasted less than one hundred years—nevertheless exercised a decisive influence upon the life feelings of German Jewry. The Emancipation had become the secularized substitute for the messianic faith in a redeemer. It had given the Jew the inner possibility to view his career, his own personal rise within society, as a blow for freedom which he was striking on behalf of all the Jewish community, particularly when he succeeded in occupying important positions in the economic or intellectual life of Germany without becoming baptized. [177, pp. 24–25]

In that connection, it is relevant to point to Baeck's last series of lectures, shortly before his death, delivered in Darmstadt in 1956. Lecturing upon the types of Jewish self-understanding of the past two centuries, Baeck selected Walter Rathenau and Moses Hess together with Moses Mendelssohn and Franz Rosenzweig! [63a] But if Baeck understood the secular aspects of German-Jewish life, this does not mean that he can be viewed as the representative of that position. Przywara's misunderstand-

---

[4] Cf. Ernst Simon [177, p. 22]: "The German-Jewish bourgeoisie, to the extent that it was not Zionistic, lived in the dream world of a fool's paradise. Its German assimilation, paradoxically, was not sufficient to let it recognize the reality of its surroundings."

[5] See Chapter 6, above.

ing of Baeck was grounded upon Przywara's failure to credit Baeck with the religious dimension in which the transcendent is fully received together with the immanent: The ethical activism for a better world within human society did not preclude the existence of the mystery in the beyond for Baeck. And we come back to the fact that those who were most active in the realm of secular Jewish life respected Baeck but did not think of him as their spokesman. Baeck was one of the leaders of the Central Verein where secularism and assimiliation found a greater expression than in the other major Jewish organizations of that time. But he was a rabbi; neither Baeck nor the German-Jewish community ever lost sight of that fact.

The upheaval of 1933 destroyed the secular messianism of assimilation without conversion; but there was no return to the religious leadership or teachings of the rabbis. (Baeck's election to the Reichsvertretung presidency, as previously indicated, was an unusual recognition of the greatness of his personality—as well as an acceptable compromise to all parties concerned.) The new messianism was also a secular faith: Zionism. The *Juedische Rundschau*, as the voice of Zionism, greeted the events of 1933 with its proud editorial "Wear It with Pride, the Yellow Badge" [186, pp. 131–132] and reached out to a young generation looking for a dimension of existence in which action led to tangible results, and to their elders who had seen the foundations of their existence shattered. The new leaders were the Zionists, with only one or two anti-Zionist voices maintaining themselves.[6] Baeck, once again, stood in the middle. He was president of the Keren Ha-Yesod and had worked for a Jewish future in Palestine from early days. But he was not a Zionist theoretician, or a spokesman whose writings could be considered part of Zionist thinking. He was still identified with Hermann Cohen, and Cohen was remembered for his uncompromising anti-Zionism. Baeck did not come to German Jewry with an intellectual or religious program. His writings between 1933 and 1938 were examples of profound—and sometimes esoteric—scholarship. Hans Liebeschuetz is undoubtedly correct when he sees the 1938 publication of *Aus drei Jahrtausenden* as an attempt to speak to the present crisis (but even if the Nazis had not destroyed the

---

[6] Max Naumann and the Verband national-deutscher Juden tried to remain within the German community at the risk of becoming Nazis; Schoeps and his splinter group from the Jewish youth group, the Vortrupp, must also be listed here, but in no way as identical with Naumann's group.

book and its printing plates at once, it is doubtful that it would have been interpreted as such a program by German Jewry):

> The date and place of publication . . . already indicate that scholarly knowledge is placed directly into the service of life here; and a reading of the book substantiate this surmise. The highest official of German Judaism wanted his interpretations of old texts to be used by his readers as a possibility for finding meaning in the spiritual experiences of many generations which could be applied to their own struggle for existence. The immediate confiscation and destruction of the whole edition by Hitler's police . . . prove that the thoughts of his superficially completely un-political book were felt in their living strength by the opposition. [6, p. 1]

The collection contains some of Baeck's earliest works, and much of his writing of the late twenties and of the thirties. With a self-knowledge acquired by Baeck over the course of the years, he could rightly indicate in his preface that this occupation with the small details of Jewish life and thought had a special relation to the vision of the whole which his major works had attempted; and that "special methods have been attempted in these studies with the hope that they will open new paths." [6, p. 10] In this book were contained the great polemical writings and his studies of midrash and mysticism evaluated earlier. Certainly, it was an important publication, marking the end of an epoch in Baeck's thinking. But, as we have already indicated, the book could not speak to its audience. It was destroyed—and so was the Jewish community to which it had addressed itself.

Baeck's life as the leader of German Jewry was his teaching of those days. We gain a clearer understanding of this when we look at a prayer written by Baeck in 1935, in which he tried to give strength to his community by answering the stream of constant lies and humiliations which came to the Jews from the Nazi government. Again, the Nazis suppressed this prayer, which Baeck had sent out as a "pastoral letter" to all Jewish congregations. Nevertheless, it was read by many; and the language of prayer is clearly the language of defiance in words like these:

> We stand before our God. With the same fervor with which we confess our sins, the sins of the individual and the sins of the community, do we, in indignation and abhorrence, express our contempt for the lies concerning us and the defamation of our religion and its testimonies. . . . All Israel stands before her God in this hour. In our prayers, in our hope, in our confession, we are one with all Jews on earth. We look upon each other

and know who we are; we look up to our God and know what shall abide.[7]

At this point, if nowhere else, Baeck did become the spokesman for all of German Jewry.

There is a large area of Baeck's life here which must be recognized, but which lies outside the scope of our study. The work of adult education, of running the charitable institutions, preparing those who were permitted to emigrate for new types of occupations, the whole structure of the Jewish school system—all of this was part of Baeck's task in the years between 1933 and 1938. Baeck was a head of state, with all which that entails. But in tracing the full development of his theological structure, we must turn to the time when he started writing his final works, recognizing the historical events, the successes and the failures, which pulsate underneath the written word.

Baeck's last major book was written (most of the first volume, at least) in the concentration camp of Terezin (Theresienstadt). Time after time, Baeck had refused to leave Germany and his community.[8] But as there came fewer and fewer opportunities to work actively for the Jewish community—the schools had been closed, the hospitals taken over, the people themselves had been deported, the Reichsvertretung had been buried in its successor organization, the Reichsvereinigung, which was supposed to serve only a puppet function—it became apparent to Baeck that only one more action remained: to join his people in the concentration camp. Meanwhile, when it seemed evident that the end was close at hand, he turned back to his writing to give himself an account of this

---

[7] Leo Baeck, "Kol Nidre Prayer 1935," in Nahum Glatzer (ed.), *The Dynamics of Emancipation* (Boston, 1965), pp. 108–109.

[8] There is ample evidence to show that Baeck received invitations from the United States, and that he could have left Germany without any trouble—the Germans wanted to see him leave. Professor Baron (conversation, January 2, 1966) described a number of conversations he held with Baeck in which Baeck stated that "he could not leave his flock." Professor Abraham Heschel also described a conversation he had with Baeck on the Sunday before the war broke out. Heschel had just arrived in London from Warsaw, and met Baeck, who was on his way back to Germany. Both realized that war was imminent; yet Baeck felt it his duty to return (conversation with Heschel, December 17, 1965). This was in 1939. As to whether or not Baeck would have left in the forties, Dr. Max Kreutzberger of the Leo Baeck Institute in New York has been engaged in research that should soon give us clearer information on the role played by the American Consulate in Berlin, and a number of related issues which, again, could not be encompassed in the scope of this work.

Jewish life, this Jewish people. He started writing while still in his home in Berlin. In 1943, when he was deported to Theresienstadt, the small bundle of pages accompanied him. Somehow, Baeck found quiet moments in the midst of that inferno during which he wrote on scraps of paper, adding them to this manuscript.[9] Its survival was as much of a miracle as the survival of the author. Baeck kept this manuscript until he felt that its time had come to act as a witness for those days. In 1955, it appeared in Germany under the title *Dieses Volk: Juedische Existenz*. [7] A second, longer volume was added to the first in 1957; and the English translation appeared in 1965.

Baeck's life in the concentration camp has already been discussed in Chapter 2. What must be recognized here is that scholarship was not a place of retreat for Baeck, and that the writing of a book dealing with the nature of Jewish existence was a considered act of moral resistance against the outside world—and an act of love, a reaching out toward his fellow prisoners as well. Baeck was described by a fellow prisoner of those days as a loved and respected figure:

> He never withdrew from the camp, but it did not seem to exist near him; none of its filth could touch him. Peace emanated from him. He was incorruptible. [69, pp. 249–250.]

This must be evaluated with the utmost care. It is impossible, from the outside, to understand what really happened in the Nazi concentration camps; all judgments must be hedged about with the greatest qualifications. But for a man to remain untouched, he would have had to be in a state of withdrawal such as was part of the *"muselman"* syndrome —the walking dead who moved about like automata until their life flickered out. One could have been a saint. But this, too, would have been an indictment which Judaism could press against the person who in becoming a saint has ceased to be part of the existential Jewish community with its common fate. Baeck had his frailties and weaknesses, his passions and his pride. Since he did not shut himself off from his people, there must have been moments when he faltered under his tremendous load. What matters is that he did not fall. It is entirely possible that his calm-

---

[9] As it happened, Baeck took one other book manuscript into the camp with him. The speculations and some confusion about this were cleared up by Hans Reichmann, "The Fate of a Manuscript," *Leo Baeck Institute Yearbook III* (London), 1958, pp. 361 ff., where we find that Baeck wrote a book between 1938–1941, "The Legal Position of the Jews in Europe" (as yet unpublished) which can be found in the manuscript archives of the Leo Baeck Institute.

ness which brought peace to many brought anger to some who felt him to be distant and remote. In the same way, his lectures at Theresienstadt, whether given in secrecy or as public addresses permitted by the Nazis for propaganda purposes, at first glance seem to exhibit a calm indifference to his surroundings. But life and teachings do interpenetrate here. Adler is right when he notes that "Baeck never withdrew from the camp, but it did not seem to exist near him." In the end, Baeck brought so much of his inner certainty and self-awareness into the crisis situation confronting him that he dominated it. And this certainty can be found in the writings of the concentration camp days which now become our concern.

II

Prison literature—whether poems or utopias, philosophy or autobiography—is sometimes accorded special privileges by those who evaluate this type of material. And this is a mistake. The writings always rise out of a previous context; and while we cannot forget where they were written, it is more important for us to inquire concerning their antecedents. The writings of Leo Baeck, as we have examined them within the first four decades of the twentieth century, show themselves to contain a profound polemical strain. They use the concepts of neo-Kantian idealism, but in a way that would certainly not be acceptable to Kant and that would often go beyond Hermann Cohen's intentions as well. Not human reason but human existence is the matrix of creativity; and the nonrational stands alongside and within the rational and has its place in every religious definition: the nature of God, the meaning or revelation, the mission of Judaism. But both the polemics and the admixture of reason and nonreason rest upon a foundation of classical Jewish texts that dominate Baeck's writings—the sermons of the first centuries which had become Baeck's special area of concern. Baeck's writing is midrashic literature. And his work done in the concentration camp may well be labeled "The Terezin Midrash." [177, pp. 76 ff.][10]

In his studies of the Midrash, Baeck stressed the elements shared with Greek preaching: the pedagogic intention, the general structure. But he saw one major difference in what was to him the essential aspect of the Midrash: it was the polemical tool through which Judaism asserted itself

[10] Chapter 4 of [144].

against its opponents. Viewing the Jewish sermon in the context of its time, Baeck saw this as the central function of the Midrash:

> The theme of the sermon attacks that question which was an existential problem of Palestinian Judaism of those days: Who is the people of God? Is it the Jewish people, or is it the Church? With the Church having become rooted in Palestine at that time, the question came to the Jewish preacher out of the very space in which he lived.
>
> The primary roots of the Jewish sermon rise out of the necessity of battle . . . and it received its strongest impulse by constantly finding itself brought to the confrontation of the commandment to guard Judaism from all attacks and enticements, against apparently related as against foreign thoughts. . . . Its task and its theme was always renewed in this. [33, pp. 173–174]

And what was seen as central for Jewish thought in the first centuries became the core of Jewish expression in the middle of the thirties in Germany—and the only mode of expression for concentration camp literature. Baeck's own writings make us look for the polemical core in his works written in Theresienstadt. And we know that they are midrashic works, just as the German-Jewish writings of the thirties found its outlet in the "new midrash" indicated for us by Ernst Simon:

> Whoever tried to participate in the Jewish work within Germany during the nineteen thirties discovered that there were political presuppositions, part of the midrashic language, which touched his own activity even when he never had the occasion to acquire a theoretical understanding of this. But the most important and far-reaching renewal of this midrashic language took place through men to whom this connection was completely clear. These men, relating the new situation to past situations that had been similar, consciously created the new midrash or interpreted the old text in the light of the actual conditions. This was even more valid for the written than for the spoken word and characterized some outstanding Jewish publications out of the time of the persecution. . . . [177, p. 77]

And Simon points to the work of Buber, Rosenzweig, Dienemann, Baeck, and others.

The writings of Theresienstadt are part of this literary stream. The many midrashim published at that time[11] never openly named the oppressor. They could be read as straight literary works. But the scholarly

11 The Schocken booklets published at that time, namely, Buber-Rosenzweig's Deutero-Isaiah translation, Dienemann's *Midrashim of Comfort and Sorrow*, and the almanachs are among the many texts that could be cited.

Jew always knew that "Edom" was not just Esau, or the Edomites—but after a certain moment in time, always Rome, always the oppressor. And the nonscholarly listener made the implicit connection. Whether imprisoned by the Nuremberg Laws or by the guards of the camp, the silent language of the oppressed became part of the communication between Jew and fellow Jew. All aspects of Jewish life were touched by this awareness. At Theresienstadt, Baeck lectured on Plato, on Kant, on the great historians from Herodotus to Ranke; and each lecture had in it that aspect of spiritual resistance. It was not only the self-assertion over the grim conditions of the camp that denied the humanity and the intellect of the Jew; there was also that inner polemic core which we have come to know in the works of Leo Baeck.

One of these lectures, somehow preserved from those days, bears out this contention. It was entitled "Academic Address, given on June 15, 1944, at the Community House, Theresienstadt." [63] Apparently, its task is the presentation of historical thought from ancient times to the present. Yet in the context of the concentration camp, we are entitled to consider it significant that Baeck starts by stating history's concern for the continuity of life:

> An equal emphasis is placed upon "life" and upon "continuity." Taking "life" first: this does not merely imply an aimless vegetating, a state of random movement swinging vaguely to and fro at the will of external impulses, but an existence that has become aware of itself, conscious of its yesterdays and tomorrows, of the paths leading up and those leading away from it, conscious of what has gone before and what is still to come, conscious of its course and destiny. [63, p. 1]

Seen together with "continuity," a structure with its own definite lines which are in no ways accidental, Baeck comes to present a view of history which has the most direct relationship possible to his listeners and to himself: What *is* a concentration camp if not a way station to a senseless death where outside pressures move the inmates to and fro in senseless movement? This application can be made with some confidence, without any feeling that something unwarranted is being read into the text, since Baeck's book on Jewish existence, written at that time, applies almost identical words to the Jewish people. [7, pp. 14–17] We would be pressing too much if we tried to read the reference to the tomorrows as a touch of hope; there was too much hope and too little of it among the listeners to make these words of comfort.

Baeck lectured on Herodotus and Thucydides. The first looked out into the wide world, while the other turned within to gain understanding of the forces of history, looking for the underlying reasons of events in the mind of man. When Baeck spoke of Polybius, the captive of the victors, who "personified the problem of a man from a vanquished people who surrenders himself heart and soul to the conqueror" [63, p. 4] we might see this as a reflection of a judgment Baeck passed on Josephus; but when Baeck spoke about Tacitus, of the historian's prejudices, romanticism, and occasional sentimentality, we see once again a clear confrontation with the present. Indeed, toward the end of the lecture, when Baeck stated that we should "pass in silence over all the little Tacitus aspirants, the would-be-great writers of political history who merely perpetuate the weaknesses and defects of the great Roman" [63, p. 7], Baeck is certainly not only talking about men like Treitschke; the scholarly lackeys of the Third Reich were within the reach of this midrash.

Baeck comes to speak of Jewish history at this point. And what he had to say applied to the existential situation of Theresienstadt:

> The prophets . . . turned against every misdeed of history that seeks its vindication in success of expediency. They turned against the sort of politics that creates its own moral code, they objected to any justification of right by victory. . . .
>
> Justice is the ultimate sense of history for Israelite-Jewish historiography. If right were to fail, there would no longer be any sense in dwelling on earth. For living means living for justice, goodness and truth; the ultimate continuity of life is the continuity of this permanent verity; deepest historical awareness is the awareness of this permanency; historical decision is the decision for or against it; the writing of history means to show and present this in all its ways and detours, in its objectives and obstructions. *True history is the history of the spirit, the human spirit, which may at times seem powerless, but ultimately is yet superior and survives because even if it has not got the might, it still possesses the power, the power that can never cease.* [63, p. 6; italics supplied]

We come back here to the "religion of polarity" expressed in the Darmstadt lectures:[12] the awareness of the permanent that undergirds all of life, the assertion of the beyond entering into the now. It would

[12] Cf. Chapter 6, above. But, as indicated there, these statements can be traced back to the 1917 article "Lebensgrund und Lebensgehalt" [21].

be easy to read the italicized lines as a strange and out-of-place idealism in which the speaker had lost all contact with the hellish experience surrounding him. Once they are seen in the context of Baeck's teachings, and as part of the "new midrash," they can be perceived as reaching out to the listeners in the concentration camp and speaking for them in an act of defiance against their persecutors.

They are not words that rally the prisoners into open defiance and rebellion. The miasma of the camp filled the hall; the hopes for food, for one more day of life, for a less sadistic guard—these are the words and thoughts that could create a spark of enthusiasm in that dark underworld. And the interpretations we can give to a text seem far removed from the reality of those days. But if we want to understand Baeck's writings of those days, we still have to deal with the moment of their presentation: a hall packed with almost seven hundred fellow prisoners who quietly listen to a historical lecture and then fade back into the night.[13] Why did they listen? And what did they hear?

They had come to hear Leo Baeck. The topic did not matter. Baeck was not an official member of the camp administration—his position was all the stronger for that reason—but he was known to them. He was the leader of German Jewry and their representative.[14] And when he stood before them they knew that he had not changed. He had given away nothing of himself. Proud, fearless, dispassionate (to the point where this was resented by many), he stood before his community and spoke to them of the universal in which the particular was affirmed. Those who had learned the language of the new midrash saw that the inner irony was there: Was it accidental, for example, for Baeck to characterize the history of the Middle Ages by Dante's *Inferno* and link Dante with the prophetic spirit of Israel? [63, p. 7][15] And when Baeck castigated historians of the past for having kept silent about torture and slavery, for "covering the victor in a mantle of truth beneath which every crime and beastliness were meant to be hidden" [63, p. 8]—was

[13] Eric Boehm [81] quotes Baeck on the attendance and history of these lectures (but must be considered a secondary account).

[14] Selma Stern, *Josel von Roseheim: Befehlshaber der Judenschaft* (Stuttgart, 1959) dedicates book and title to "Leo Baeck Judaeorum Defensori Nobilissimo."

[15] An interesting parallel is Primo Levi's *Survival In Auschwitz* (New York, 1961), pp. 99 ff. "The Canto of Ulysses" where once again we find a discussion of Dante in the concentration camp.

he not speaking about their own situation? The structure of this concentration camp midrash has a curious form: The normal procedure would have followed historical time, and the Jewish historians should have been presented before the Greek thinkers. Baeck placed Greek thought first, and followed it with the presentation of Jewish historiography in what, once again, was a polemical manner. The two are compared; and Greece and Rome are characterized as searching for the meaning and law of history in an earth-bound manner, dependent upon peoples. For the thinkers of Israel, the meaning and law of history "are derived from a single Being, from an eternal, ever-lasting moral justice." [63, p. 6] What is certainly a lecture on history here once again becomes an expression of Baeck's *theologia viatorum*, a statement of theology in which history, even the grim account of the immediate past and present, becomes subservient to the religious vision.

In some ways, it is not inaccurate to think of this lecture in Theresienstadt as the final Darmstadt lecture, a reprise of his talk on "Death and Rebirth." [32] Again, Baeck speaks of the death and life of nations, of the need within the soul of a nation to understand the basic idea and task that is its core, and to act upon it. At Darmstadt, Baeck had warned the German scholars of the death that comes to a nation when it loses its vocation and follows false ideas:

> It is the end of a nation when all true tasks, all ideals die within it, when every connection with the reality of its history has ceased for it. And the worst death takes place when the idea, the spirit, has sunk into the depths and has vanished while the power of existence is still present in that people. The cycle of existence then moves into the senseless, the soulless, into the deficiencies and flaws; the ability to maintain existence is confined to the convulsive shuddering of the sick, the cramps which disintegrate the nation. [32, p. 70][16]

This section is repeated in the lecture at Theresienstadt, where it becomes the most powerful indictment of the German people that has gone astray, where what had been an abstraction of the Darmstadt

---

[16] I surmise this to be an identical text. The original is not obtainable at present; the English translation from which I work states: "And this is a most terrible death, if the mere brute force of existence is then still left to this people and everything, the cycle of existence, the cycle of power, is turned into soullessness, into senselessness, when all the pursuits of existence move as if, in convulsive jerks, in whose coils the people then collapse." With Baeck's excellent memory, we make this a quote.

lecture hall became a reality of the concentration camp, a challenge to the soulless dead guarding the dying. At Theresienstadt, Baeck continues the thought of a nation's rebirth which had been the next topic developed in the Darmstadt lecture; but he now places the stress upon the historian's task to reawaken his people to their task and thus to revive them. The Jewish historian, to Baeck, was the prophet. At this point, he leaves the polemic and becomes the historian, the prophet, who comforts his people by showing them who they are, and why they will not die. It would have been contrary to Baeck's nature to draw the clear Biblical parallel: The lecturer would have been too clearly identified as the prophet. But we would lose a dimension of understanding—that of Jewish experience—if we did not connect this moment and its thoughts to the thirty-seventh chapter of Ezekiel. "Can these bones live?" asks Baeck. And Ezekiel's words, not spoken audibly but conveyed in every nuance of this midrash, assure the people: "Thus saith the Lord God: Behold, I will open your graves, and cause you to come up out of your graves, O My people. . . . And I will put My spirit in you, and ye shall live . . . !"

The universal has brought Baeck to the particular. And the final words of the lecture are the assertion of the particular and its responsibility to the general, in a clear statement of the Jewish mission which is a central category of Baeck's understanding of history. Quoting Ranke, Baeck reminds his listeners that

> "the greatest thing that can happen to man is probably to defend in his own cause a general cause." And that, too, is the greatest thing that can happen to a people, to defend and represent the cause of mankind in its own cause, to fight for itself and in so doing to fight for humanity at the same time. . . . Thus rebirth of many a people could be brought about, a discovery of the great interrelationships of life, a meeting of all to form one mankind. [63, p. 9]

The Theresienstadt midrash is also the quest for Jewish self-definition. In this lecture, and in these circumstances, we find the bridge between *The Essence of Judaism* and *This People Israel: The Meaning of Jewish Existence*. And if this lecture contains quotations from the Darmstadt period, it also indicates, in its basic concepts and purpose, the nature of Baeck's final work that was then coming into form in the darkness of the concentration camp.

III

This People Israel: The Meaning of Jewish Existence [8] can be considered a restatement of Baeck's fundamental teachings in which we have noted, as fundamental to all of Baeck's works, the "religion of polarity." The first volume of *This People* becomes all the more remarkable when we realize that it was written without a library, without any tools of research except its author's own memory, and in the darkness of the death camp. Once more, its antecedents speak out of it; and once again, it has to be understood in the framework of the "new midrash" in which this great apologete of twentieth century Jewry achieves the culmination of his style and method of presentation.

In 1955, when this book appeared in Germany, it received the warmest possible reception (a number of reasons not related to its actual contents readily spring to mind). One periodical placed Baeck alongside Thomas Mann and Berthold Brecht, as well as Martin Buber, designating Baeck as one of the giants of modern times whom the German reader should come to know.[17] The *Merkur* stated that "the day will come when this book, probably the last great Jewish message in the German language, will be prized as an important testimony of Jewish teaching in this age and, no less, as the enduring legacy of a Jew from Germany to the German people." [9, dust jacket, trans. Walter Kaufmann] While this statement says more about itself than about the book, it joins together with a sentence from the *Deutsche Rundschau* as a deeply felt appreciation: "In its beauty, intensity, simplicity and greatness, his language becomes as plain as that of the Biblical patriarchs, as if it came from far away; and yet it welled up in the direst distress in our own midst." [9, dust jacket, trans. Walter Kaufmann] The American response to this book, in 1965, was also extraordinary; but once more the question must be raised whether or not extraneous reasons entered into this; i.e., whether some of the response was not engendered by the legend of Baeck rather than by his teachings.[18]

17 *Die Kultur,* as quoted on dust jacket of Volume II of *Dieses Volk,* [9].

18 *This People Israel* even received the "imprimatur" of *Time* magazine, complete with a picture of Baeck, a full-page review, and the statement that this was "one of the century's most profound and moving attempts to unravel the meaning of Judaism . . . a book that breathes the spirit of peace and hope" (*Time,* February 19, 1965). In the *Saturday Review* (January 30, 1965), Professor Cecil Roth hailed Baeck as a

The key relationship between *This People Israel* and *The Essence of Judaism* is maintained through Baeck's vision of the unity of life in which the people lives in and through its religion; and the religion, just as much, comes to address all the world through this particular people. [4][19] But the integral unity of all Baeck's writings becomes even more apparent when we note that the pattern for this book was already established in the preface to *Aus Drei Jahrtausenden*:

> Three great times encompass the intellectual history of Judaism: the time of the Bible; following that, the time of penetration, the "midrash," which constantly takes hold of the Bible and ever anew emanates from it . . . and finally this new time seen so far only in its beginnings, extending the ways of a newly awakened strength of faith. . . . [5, p. 9]

This is not an attempt to press Jewish history into three separate millenniums and thus to create a symmetrical, artificial historical construction. In the field of Jewish historiography, there has been an increasing wariness of the periodization of history. Baeck has no intention of or interest in rearranging historical events to conform to his pattern. He is not writing history as such, but *theology*. Perhaps there are Hegelian aspects to any historical construction that thinks in thousand-year epochs; but in this case, they are not intended to summarize and evaluate all of man's movements through the world. The epochs here are only evaluated as aspects of Jewish history in which the Divine revelation breaks through and achieves its purposes through the response of the Jewish people.

When Baeck views the Jewish people as being presently within its fourth millennium, which he calls the millennium of hope, [8, p. 290] and labels the three millenniums preceding it as clearly recognizable epochs, he is making a theological statement that carries within it more than a touch of mysticism.[20] God's revelation manifests itself to Baeck

---

prophet and the book as the spiritual testament of the Jewish people: "Seldom if ever has the soul of the Jewish people and the essence of Judaism been better described than in these beautiful, immeasurably moving pages. . . ." Similar reviews appeared in many places. A second edition is now in print. The book is a selection of the Jewish Publication Society, and was also published in England.

[19] Quoted in [8, p. xvii].

[20] Baeck belonged to the representatives of rationalism within mysticism, which had its deep suspicions of those who would "predict the end." Yet both Sanhedrin 97a (quoting Abaye) and an old baraita found in Avoda Zara 9a state that the messianic era comprises two of the six millenniums of the world, while Rabbi Ketina and a baraita see a 6000-year world history with the next millennium as the messianic age (see

through the history of Israel. And each "epoch" is an answer which
Israel gives to God:

> History only lives and becomes fertile if it is able to achieve what may
> truly be called an epoch. . . . Even individual, personal life, the striving
> of man for himself, receives its intrinsic character in breaking through to
> the ordered stages of its own existence, its epoch. [8, p. 290][21]

Baeck equates the beginning of an epoch with a people's ability to be
reborn. The Theresienstadt lecture had ended with the call for rebirth;
and this final work of his intended to show Israel as the people of constant rebirth, of faithful response to the Word and the commandment
that always came to it.

Its first stage, the time of the Bible, saw Israel establish the *oneness of
God* against all the multiplicities of the nations; the second stage, the
time of the Midrash, was the epoch in which Israel learned and taught
the *one way*. Pharisaic Judaism, the sanctification of all of life, the recognition of the task that filled all of life made Israel follow the path which
alone permitted it to fulfill its function as the people of the revelation.
In every country, wherever the Jew peregrinated, the Bible came with
him and found a new interpretation which was part of the one way. The
third millennium, according to Baeck, presented as paramount the choice
and the act of decision between being the *one kingdom* of God or being
one of the many kingdoms of man. And the fourth millennium, now
commencing, became that of clinging to the *one hope* as against the many
hopes that always appeared to be so close to fulfillment.

Each epoch carries over into those that follow: the one God, the one
way, the one kingdom, and the one hope are part of the totality of
Jewish life; but at different times the problems confronting Israel called
for different emphases. There exists again, for Israel, the polarity between
perfection and tension; and the very statement of the epochs is an elucida-
tion of the polarity between the one and the many: one God against many

---

A. Biram, "Millennium" in *Jewish Encyclopedia* VIII, p. 593). The time calculations
at best show accidental resemblances; but the use of the millennium as a measuring de-
vice of God's plan in the universe should at least enter the periphery of our evaluation of
a *baal ha-midrash* who was most at home in the texts, where the millennium is most
frequently employed in the structures of messianic hope.

[21] As we shall see, much of this is an important restatement of Baeck's great
climactic essay of the Darmstadt series, "Death and Rebirth" [32].

gods, one way against all the others, one kingdom different from the rest, one hope against the many hopes of man.

If we bring the Darmstadt lectures to the interpretation of Baeck's final work, we see one other aspect of this system of millenniums which has an organic, almost a physiological content. "Death and Rebirth" [32] looks at the epochs of individual man, seeing them as the caesura of the death and rebirth of the same man as a child who simply takes in the revelation, the young man who meditates on what was given him and seeks his own way, the man established in the world who now seeks to outline the boundaries around his own domain, separate from the world but secure for himself—and the old man who withdraws into himself and finds all creativity dying within himself *unless* he knows who he is and what his hopes for the future make of death, the final caesura which is as little of an end as all the deaths which preceded it. Death itself then comes to reveal rebirth. [32, p. 60]

Baeck's four ages of man directly parallel the four millenniums of Jewish life described in *This People Israel.* The one revelation, the one way, the kingdom, and the hope echo back and forth here. Was it intentional? Or can we take this as one more example of Baeck's consistency that sees the living entity of Israel in exactly the same fashion in which it strove to determine the nature of mankind? The answer lies not so much in Baeck's intentions as in his methods. We cannot forget that he was a psychologist of religion who had adopted Dilthey's pattern of *verstehende Psychologie* for himself. Baeck turns to the experiences of the inner self for his theology, his knowledge of both mystery and commandment. Only then does he turn to history, to the experiences of Israel which bring the revelation of the commandment and of the mystery to all mankind. And so the image of man conforms to the image of Israel, the recurrent rhythm of the great polarity of death and rebirth is found in both, and the universal is found in the particular. But, as Baeck pointed out in Theresienstadt "to find the cause of mankind in its own cause is the greatest thing that can happen to a people."

One final reminder: As we turn to the text of this work, it is important to see it not only as part of the new midrash, as the polemics of the great defender who once defended the faith and now speaks for the people of that faith—but also as the statement of the religion of polarity which, taken together with *The Essence of Judaism,* is to give us a full and complete understanding of Jews and Judaism in the world. It is a book of faith, of theology, written by a modern Jehuda Halevi who absolutely believed in his people as the people of the revelation who have a divinely ordained mission in the world.

IV

The first volume of *This People Israel* starts with the question of one's own origin which every people desirous of rebirth has to ask itself: Who am I? Why am I? And it must not be forgotten that Baeck asked this question in an environment that had crushed his people into a valley of darkness where the one logical question seemed to be: When will it end? But the question is asked, and an answer is given from outside the world, entering the world as part of Jewish history: the covenant with God. The word addresses Israel, and Israel comes to know itself as "a people emerging out of the beyond, as a people of metaphysical existence, a people brought into existence by a revelation of God and on behalf of a revelation of God." [8, p. 6]

In contrast with the *Essence*, where the mystery only slowly took its place alongside the commandment, *This People Israel* starts out with the assertion of the twofoldness of life, of the knowledge that comes from without and that which comes from within, of the relationship between the rational and the nonrational [8, p. 7][22] and their common origin in God. It was also Israel's origin, which thus reached beyond its immediate surroundings and appeared to be "without history to those peoples who had entrapped themselves in self-contemplation and regarded only their own soil and surroundings as having the power to speak to them of history's meaning." [8, p. 8]

This people Israel then presents an approach to religious knowledge which has its special aspects and its particular revelation to be shared with all (this is the mission that rises out of the revelation), but which is also the prototype for every man's encounter with religious truth. To start with, there must be an openness to all aspects of existence: A people (or an individual) cannot let itself be ensnared by its own surroundings and become a victim of what Paul Tillich has called "the gods of space."

---

[22] The translation in [8] I hope will be emended in the third printing. One mistake not caught in the editing was the use of the term "irrational" on pages 7 ff., instead of the clearly indicated "nonrational" called for by the German text.

The transcendent does speak out of the immanent: Each encounter of human experience contains elements of the abiding foundations of existence which stand above the flux of time. The eternity that undergirds the world and the eternal task which is at the core of Israel's existence was seen as one here (the polarity of the Creator and the creature whose ethical action is his creative response):

> The knowledge of God and the knowledge of self became a unity that remains indivisible in this people. Whether Israel lived through bright or dark days, it always knew who was above it and who was before it. It was embraced by the "everlasting arms" (Deut. 33:27), the *branchia sempiterna*. [8, p. 9]

The very data of human experience that impress themselves upon Israel have a transcendent dimension to them which enables Baeck to find the revelation in the immanent: The touch of the "everlasting arms" adds the dimension of the permanent to every experience. The fact that Israel starts its history as a people with that recognition gives it its task and mission.

How does Israel respond to the data of that experience? Part of the teachings of Hermann Cohen still endure in Baeck's emphasis on the idea of the One God which comes to this people with the moment of its creation and receives the full support of human reason which recognizes and gives complete loyalty to the one task which is the necessary correlation to the One God. But human reason no longer stands alone as the creator. Baeck has placed the nonrational alongside the rational. Starting with the insights gained from his other teacher, Wilhelm Dilthey, Baeck explores the dimensions of the human personality, which are just as essential as man's reason in supplying him with true religious knowledge. The feelings of creatureliness, of human dependency and of that human greatness which gives assent to the Divine fundament of its existence—these bring the knowledge of the mystery together with the knowledge of the commandment. The polarity of that religious knowledge as it exists in Israel (read also: in man) is explored in these two volumes which show the rational and nonrational awareness of Israel to its mission (read also: revelation) through the first three millenniums of its existence. The same polarity is contained in the data of human experience: The same mystery and the same commandment emerge from God, the foundation of all being. In Baeck's religion of experience, the sharp split between man and the world is healed. Polarity creates that blurring of all boundaries which is so annoying to the fundamentalist who wants the one clear revelation which is hedged off from all inroads of the world and can only be entered through the particular doorway of his own faith. And so the Kantian critique of Baeck's system of polarity would find an inexcusable blurring between the phenomenon and the noumenon, the *Ding-an-sich* which cannot be known through the Kantian application of the categories of reason which can only fashion the sense impressions of the phenomena into the knowledge of the phenomenal world. The Kantian God exists as a necessary postulate of the mind; and the transcendent cannot be permitted to approach man through the immanent. Baeck's system, by stressing both the nonrational in man and the transcendental aspect of the immanent which comes to man in his existence and is open to this dual awareness which is man's capacity for religious knowledge, here gives us a theory of knowledge which must be taken seriously by philosophy.[23]

It is this theology and this concept of man which are applied to the facts of Jewish history. Baeck's major emphasis is never upon the events, but upon Israel's response to them. And while Israel is always seen as a people emerging out of the beyond, a people of metaphysical existence, its particularity is always seen as expressing the universality of man, God's creature and correlation, who asserts the polarity of existence by the ethical act and the response to the Divine mystery.

Israel's history, then, is an exposition of Baeck's theology, of Judaism. And Baeck once more emerges as the apologete. *This People Israel* is also a restatement of the defense of the faith (read also: people) upon which he had been engaged for more than half a century. Noting the flaws of Israel, Baeck states:

> The saying that the corruption of the best is the worst corruption—*corruptio optimi pessima*—was a palimpset of many a line of this history. Nonetheless, someone who views the whole becomes aware of what might almost be termed a sublimity. That great trait, that trait of ultimate loyalty toward the Eternal and His work, remains in constant evidence. Through each of the many centuries, no matter how this or that person in the House of

[23] I am here in debt to my colleague, the Reverend Lyman Lundeen, whose projected Ph.D. dissertation sketches the implications of A. N. Whitehead's theory of knowledge, and the use of the term "polarity" as applied to sense data, to the linguistic analysis of religious terminology.

Israel acquitted himself, despite every divergent way, including wrong ways and detours, the idea that Israel had to be a people before God continued to shine clearly. [8, p. 10]

Individual and group shortcomings are thus explained and defended in the light of the totality. As long as Israel remained true to its central revelation—that it was a people covenanted to God—it remained bound to the path of life.

The idea of the covenant was also strongly affirmed by Baeck's contemporaries Buber and Rosenzweig, who lived in the language of the Bible. Baeck warns against the misunderstanding of the *berit* ("covenant") by those who would understand it through Greek legalistic terminology. The Biblical word is elemental, alive, pulsating with ever new meaning that unfolds within human life. It is a primary religious word in which the twofoldness again finds its expression:

> The God-given order was to find expression in this term—the here and the beyond, the near and the far, earth and heaven. This order is equally a covenant, for man and his free will are introduced into the covenant so that the *berit* might become the rule of man's domain. Poetry dared even the bolder image that the covenant was also a decision of nature to recognize and to accept this order. [8, p. 12]

The polarity of man is founded upon free will: and all of the immanent, man and the world, freely opens itself to accept the transcendent as the fundamental aspect of its existence.

The Hebrew word *berit* has a meaning for Baeck which he finds absent in Greek and Roman terminology. *Nomos* indicates something functional within a totality, a forming, defining force. *Lex* speaks of something organic, constructive, which coordinates human relations. *Berit*, for Baeck, "encompasses the idea of the living creation through the One, and the living revelation of the One, the idea of the beyond entering the present. Law, creation, revelation—all are fused into a single word." [8, p. 13] The prophets experience the certitude of God and the covenant. From them, it went to their people and became the experience of Israel and to all mankind:

> It became an experience for the people of the world. Within every thing, therefore, there exists an inner reality—unique, one, concealed, unfathomable, infinite, eternal—which is its foundation. It is the all-embracing, so that no one and no one thing can exist beside it or outside it. . . .

This eternal *I* that speaks to us, this I of all I's, from which all emanates, is that which creates all, determines all, beholds all. . . . Everyone can . . . call to it, can elevate himself to it. . . . The eternal, infinite covenant is sealed. [8, p. 14]

The polarity of the outer and inner reality of all things is founded upon the covenant—man's free assent to the universal encounter between man and God. When Israel assented to the covenant as a people, it established its special history which is the exposition of the covenant in the world as it affects all mankind. The covenant with the world is sealed into the covenant of Jewish experience.

As the concept of the covenant is traced through the Bible, it must be kept in mind that, for Baeck, this is not only God's book but also the book of Jewish experience. The basic teachings of Judaism, stated in *The Essence of Judaism,* are repeated here. But they are drawn out of the matrix of Jewish experience, and the mystery is mentioned equally with the commandment:

The true discovery of the law, and thus of God's nearness, is only possible to man if he discovers the mystery at the same time. We cannot experience God Himself; but this people first made the discovery that we are able to experience the eternal mystery that surrounds God, and the eternal law rising out of the mystery. . . . The law assumes its meaning because it is the revelation of the Eternal, the *word* of the One God. Its power and its permanence rise out of the mystery. [8, p. 22]

Ethical monotheism, and its challenge to the surrounding world, became Israel's assertion of that covenant. Its existence became a testimony to the One God; and its history took on meaning. In this way, Israel "found its foundation in the foundation of the All." [8, p. 26]

Next to the concept of the covenant, which was also Israel's first and abiding historical experience, there stands the experience (and concept) of the exodus with which Israel begins its historical existence. Israel has always placed this event into the center of its liturgy, has pondered upon it, has seen it as signifying not only as a beginning in time but also as a beginning of life. The exodus is also covenant, and is therefore law: Baeck points to the great commandment of the exodus—the Ten Commandments—which begins with the exodus. Revelation and the beginning of history are conjoined for this people; and Baeck once again sees history as the teaching of theology which instructs the people in the ways of God and man:

Israel learned through its history to understand humanity. The idea which is revealed to it in its history gives evidence of the wholeness of history, and both illustrates and determines the continuity of law and event. For though each event is particular, so, too, is the law which holds sway over it always and everywhere the same. . . . Israel saw history as the law of a higher will, as the moral law—it encountered a commanding legislation, entering history out of the eternal, infinite beyond. This legislation therefore applies to all; it sets before everyone the commandment of God, the enduring moral task. [8, p. 29]

The exodus marks the beginning of Israel's journey, through all vicissitudes, as God's people and toward all mankind, in its acceptance of the moral imperatives of the covenant that is part of the exodus. History, for Baeck, becomes the self-realization of this people, as it is for all peoples. And the pathos of history itself when a people does not find its idea, its path, and goes astray.

The exodus is a historical experience—but is experienced by every Jew in every generation who listens to his faith. We return here to the point that every law (*Gesetz*) becomes a commandment (*Gebot*) as it comes to be experienced by the new generation. And Baeck stresses that Jewish history is really not *historia*, i.e., the Greek concept of "investigation." It is the Biblical emphasis of *toldot*, the shared experience of the "generations." [8, p. 33] We come here to the "chain of tradition" which is an operative concept for Baeck's principle of the revelation that is manifest in Israel as it moves through history. He notes the tension between the particular and the universal which "plowed the soul of this people," but notes that this polarity has to be recognized as a "law of the soul" [8, p. 34]—again, Jewish history and experience bring us to the experience of every man:

There stands before us that which has become characteristic of this people: Everything which emanates out of the mystery enters the sphere of the moral. The experience of the soul is vital here, for genuine individuality can only develop and genuine universality can only form itself in the moral sphere. Upon the foundation of the moral, difference and community find one another; here they come to be one internally. [8, p. 34–35]

The exodus was a moral decision for Israel, one that said "No" to Egypt and "Yes" to the eternal task of witnessing for God's unity. Baeck notes that Roman history begins with the fortification of a city; Greece had the greatness of vision that saw its people as spectators and authors in a "theater for gods and men"—its history begins with the Olympic games; but Israel began with its redemption from slavery. Finally, it learned to keep its calendar from the creation of the world. "This, too," says Baeck, "arose out of the great decision and the great negation which the exodus from Egypt demanded." [8, p. 43]

Israel here came to recognize that its very existence was its task, in all of its loneliness that was yet no self-exultation above its neighbors. In Israel, alongside with the knowledge that it was different, there also "arose the passion for a great interrelatedness and for the obligation which follows upon it: being different then enters a moral domain, a domain of dignity." [8, p. 46] Again, the picture of Israel is the picture of man: A people, just as every human being, needs to affirm the existence of the *Mitmensch*; and the laws of Israel reach out to the stranger and serf "for ye were slaves in the land of Egypt." In the end, the affirmation of the exodus and of Jewish history is the affirmation of world history, so that Isaiah can speak to Israel and remind them (Is. 19:22–25) "The Lord of Hosts says . . . blessed be Egypt My people and Assyria the work of My hands, and Israel Mine inheritance."

The first volume of *This People Israel* is divided into four sections: The Covenant, The Exodus, The Revelation, and Wilderness and Land of the Fathers. These are the foundations of Jewish thought, found in Biblical man and rediscovered in each generation of this people. All speak of the transcendent that enters into existence—and all are seen in terms of Jewish existence, within the experience of Israel. As we move into the section on revelation, it would seem that a book presenting a theological system would now deal with the details of that revelation. But we must remember that it is the people Israel which is the revelation for Baeck; the details of that revelation must be drawn out of the living experiences of the people. Just as Baeck's system first establishes the mystery and the commandment within man—man senses his creatureliness and experiences both his dependency and his ability to act, and responds to the ethical imperatives with the full assent of his reason which makes the ethical act a concomitant of being alive—so Baeck's system has to present this people Israel as one entity in which the identical process can be discerned.

Israel has experienced the revelation and has become part of that revelation. How could it communicate that experience which "led up to that border which is the outer limit of human sense and feeling?" [8, p.

55] Only through the *Gleichnis,* the language of allegory which can attempt to transmit that which is basically nonlinguistic.

> This people had learned to live in both the visible and the invisible realms. Since it comprehended the two as one, it had to have an expression for that wherein the two touch and merge into one another. This expression is the poetic allegory [*dichtende Gleichnis*]. [8, p. 55]

And Baeck really understands and defines the book of this people, the Bible, as the greatest poem created by humanity, as the poetic allegory that transmits the encounter with the Divine which is the revelation. With trembling, this people wrote about what could not be described. Sometimes, they spoke through eloquent silence; and Baeck would have us understand the silences of the Bible together with the words that bring us into Israel's encounter with God. This listening to the silences of the Bible (Baeck momentarily moves out of the Biblical epoch to speak of the time of interpretation, stressing the mystical element far more than even in the revised edition of *The Essence of Judaism,* but placing it within the boundaries of the commandment) becomes an essential category of understanding the people and the revelation. The Bible must be understood through the people, and the people through the Bible: They need each other to stay alive.

The revelation commences as the history of Israel. The Ten Commandments of the covenant are preceded by the call that goes out to the totality of Israel (Exodus 19:4–6):

> Ye have seen what I did unto the Egyptians, and how I bore you on eagles' wings, and brought you unto Myself. Now therefore, if ye will hearken unto My voice indeed, and keep My covenant, then ye shall be Mine own treasure from among all people; for all the earth is Mine; and ye shall be unto Me a kingdom of priests, and a holy nation.

Baeck sees the emphasis here placed upon the people, upon *all* the people. Throughout this work, he identifies with the prophetic word that "the people . . . is designated to be the servant of Him-Who-Is." [8, p. 62] In these words written in Theresienstadt, one might hear the allegory of the suffering servant. And there follows Baeck's old and constant affirmation of the Pharisees as the men of interpretation who saw the Biblical word so clearly and wanted to sanctify all life as a holy kingdom.

The people are affirmed as one entity here; and, with the people, its

institutions. Baeck's confrontation of the congregation with the Church
[8, pp. 67–68] reminds us that his polemic function as the defender of
his people breaks through all his writings, even in this midrash from
the concentration camp. And alongside the polemic, we also find the
apologetics: Baeck notes those who broke away from the people, who
wanted to assimilate and belong to outer world. But he sees the integrity
of Israel's peoplehood unimpaired. And he speaks for his own, basically
liberal position, when he indicates the various forms of religious life
within Israel:

> Perhaps, for many individuals, religion is otherwise only a matter of dis-
> position? For the men of this people, religion is a problem of inner ex-
> istence. For that reason, the religion has its unconfessional and unorthodox
> aspects. The all-creative force had fashioned this people to take on this
> form. Revelation may here be heard in many tones. It always had its
> breadth and its variety. It may often leave room for question and answer
> if only something is captured from what the prophets heard when they
> could say, when they had to say: "Thus speaks He-Who-Is." [8, p. 73]

The liberal cannot confine himself to the actual Biblical word and make it
his dogma. In the polarities of man and his world, there is an openness
that denies the concretizing of the Biblical allegory into unchanging
ultimates. But the heart of the Biblical revelation, for both liberal and
traditionalist, is the word of the Ten Commandments.

Baeck's treatment of the Ten Commandments reminds us that he was
a master and teacher of exegesis at the Berlin Lehranstalt. He sees them
as an indivisible oneness in which the whole comes before the parts.
Once Israel has been introduced into the revelation, the first and greatest
of the sentences speaks of

> the One God who is God for every man, of the eternal "I," the origin
> and principle of every human "I." In this people's beginning this eternal
> "I," this eternal beginning, revealed itself and pointed out redemption,
> covenant, and meaning to this people. This "I" called it forth through
> the law and for the law so that it now knew what concerned its self, the
> particularity of its "I," and the uniqueness of its way. [8, p. 74]

It speaks to all mankind, but to and through Israel from its beginning.
Separate from the second commandment regarding false worship, the
two are yet linked inseparably:

> The first commandment, as statute and as commandment, gave the aspect
> of greatness to the character of the people and its history. The second

commandment, and with it the third, that of truthfulness, imprinted the deep seriousness of this knowledge of the zealous God. Together they fashioned the belief which formed here for the first time: the determination for the one and complete life, the acknowledgment of the great demand which man is to fulfill in all his days and ways. [8, p. 75]

In the further exposition of the Ten Commandments, Baeck comes to attack the Christian interpretation which saw the Decalogue within the law of nature (to distinguish it from the law of grace). Baeck fights here for the law and for freedom which are not found in the world as something already existent, but which come out of a different sphere: "the realm of law is the realm of revelation and is as such the realm of grace. . . . The eternal enters the finite to fashion and to form it, to complete it in such a way that it may be within the kingdom of God." [8, p. 76] It is the one absolute for Baeck, which gives meaning to everything relative. Once more, the polarities of existence are asserted for the world and for Israel:

There is thus no division between what is here and what is beyond, between what is immanent and what is transcendent, between commandment and grace, the ethical and the mystical, the personal and the cosmic. The same mystery, commandment, and principle rules in the one and in the other; the same reality reveals itself in both. . . . In this, the soul of this people takes its character: an attraction for endless reaches and for the near and tangible are woven together. . . . Idealism and realism become one. Therefore, the dynamic is much more characteristic of this people than the static. . . . That is why the tension between the here and the beyond is so alive in Israel. [8, p. 78]

At the end of Baeck's writings, we have here a summation of his system in which both the Darmstadt lectures and *The Essence of Judaism* are formed into a consistent pattern which is realized through a history of Israel which is no less than a declaration of faith.

Baeck excelled in biography. The vignette of Moses which follows is one of many contained in the two volumes. But the reviewers who lifted these vignettes out of the sometimes involved and baffling text of religious exposition failed to realize that in these vignettes, too, Baeck seeks to show the essence and the character of the Jewish people and of the vision of Israel which he sees as revelation to all men.

One biography is not attempted: The mystery of the Divine Name is maintained as a mystery. But as Hermann Cohen, Martin Buber, and

Franz Rosenzweig all came to their own formulation of the Tetragrammaton and its exposition in Exodus 3:13–14 (אהיה אשר אהיה "I AM THAT I AM"), so does Baeck have to grapple with the force of that verse. "What shall I say?" he exclaims, and continues:

> This one phrase, constantly, doubtingly, almost despairingly, keeps breaking through in speech. Yet something final is spoken which human speech can still receive, to which human speech can still reach. It is spoken in a finality of definiteness and clarity reaching almost beyond the metaphor: "I AM THAT I AM," "I AM hath sent me unto you"—the "I" and the being, the being and the "I" in one, the origin of all being and the origin of every "I," origin and being and "I" in one. [8, p. 83]

There is something new here, according to Baeck. No matter what materials may have been used, language has been enlarged, and a revelation has been given. Something of Baeck's mystic aspect, of the scholar who immersed himself in the *Sefer Yezirah* [36] and in the contention of the *Sefer Ha-Bahir* [36a] that it was the Hebrew alphabet which became the tool of Divine creation, here enters the picture.

Baeck is aware of the mystery and its dangers. When he deals with the theophany (Exodus 34:5–8) it becomes a dialogue between the Creator and man, who is made aware of his own creativity, that breaks through the poetry and is very real. "The mystery itself is forever real. The hidden too can be grasped with certainty, the certainty of intuitive knowledge." [8, p. 90] But Baeck warns against man being led to think that through his concepts he can come to possess everything. The mystery endures, is approached through Jewish philosophy, through mysticism. But when it overwhelms the Jew—for example, the commentators who interpret the verse in Proverbs "A woman of valor" to refer to the Torah and not to woman—then it can destroy religion.

The knowledge of the revelation: Constantly, in his vignettes of the leaders, in his exposition of the text, and in his examination of the Biblical books, Baeck pursues his quest of finding in Biblical man, in this people Israel, categories of understanding that are the universal categories of understanding religious truth. There is a profound exposition of wisdom (*chochma*) literature, of the difference between Job and Koheleth, in which the tension of the Bible and the revelation is exhibited. Job and Koheleth. The fact that Baeck could affirm both the volcanic fury of Job and the calm contemplation of Koheleth while writing in Theresienstadt is a measure of the man. In all of his people's ways and thoughts, Baeck saw the infinite entering into life. The people always heard the revelation, in every time and place, as Baeck heard it in his place and time:

> The way shown by the revelation, indicated by God, the never revealed and always revealing, was to be recognized and taken by this people, clearing the way to God. Thus time and again a voice cried out of the mystery. When the people heard it, it knew in days of confusion where clarity was, and in days of darkness where light will shine. [8, p. 101]

V

The final section of the first volume of *This People Israel* presents us with some problems. So far, in a portrait of his people which is also a depiction of its religion, Baeck's stress upon the metaphysical existence of Israel has placed before us three transcendental incursions into the immanent which molded this people in its response to them. *Berit*, the covenant, was a word that entered the world from the beyond, fusing within itself law, creation, and revelation. Israel had to respond to it, experiencing the covenant as the inception of its history. It had to be a free response to the God-given order (and Baeck noted, in an important aside, that the covenant was also a decision of nature to recognize and to accept this order. [8, p. 12][24] So, too, the *exodus* brought God into history as part of the revelation which infused this people. The same free response by Israel was part of it: the confrontation with the mystery always calls for the moral act—in this case, the saying "No" to Egypt and the acceptance of the task brought by the *revelation*. The Ten Commandments are seen as the one great word of the mystery which speaks in the clearest moral imperatives to man. But now we come to a final category: *The Wilderness and the Land of the Fathers*. To what an extent can we see the mystery emerging from the beyond and entering the now, can we hear the moral imperatives, can we see the metaphysical extension of Israel's history in "the land"?

Part of the answer must be found in the mystic aspects of Baeck's thinking. The gigantic polarity which is the core of this book—Israel as Judaism and Judaism as Israel—is not intended as a rational construc-

---

[24] Compare this with the quotation on page 227, above.

tion, as a theological system. It is midrash. And midrash is poetry, the controlled poetry of the ethical mysticism which seeks to find words for the underlying unity of the universe in which both mystery and commandment speak to man. Dealing with the oldest Kabbalistic text, the obscure and awkward *Sefer Ha-Bahir,* Baeck had hailed it for the fact that

> A grandiose cosmic optimism, the strongest religious emphasis upon the oneness of the world lives in this structure of thought. It contains the most determined opposition against the gnostic dualism with its teaching of the absolute evil, against this tearing apart of the world in which the ancient era dissolved and fell and in which medieval thought received its breach. The mysticism of the Bahir Book . . . is Jewish mysticism: the mysticism of the task and of the return, of the eternal mystery from which there issues the blessing with its commandment. [36a, p. 289]25

In this Kabbalistic text, as presented by Baeck, we find a treatment of *eretz,* "land," which is related to Baeck's final midrash. The *beracha,* the "blessing," is the foundation of all, enters into the world, is also called *eretz.* [36a, p. 281]26 And Baeck translated a difficult passage of the *Sefer Ha-Bahir* thus:

> Since the Shechina is the twofoldness (it is both above and below) so, too, is *eretz* twofold. There exists the upper *eretz,* the place of Gan Eden [the Garden of Eden], and the lower *eretz,* the place of created man and particular of the people Israel. The Gan Eden above is equivalent to the land and the people Israel with its sanctuary. Israel, too, is called *eretz.* When the Temple was destroyed and the people was sent into captivity, God "cast away from heaven the *eretz,* the glory of Israel (Lam. 2:1)." It appeared at that time as though the *eretz* had been destroyed. But just as a king, when sad tidings come, may cast away his crown and mantle in his pain but will pick them up again, since he does not want to be without crown and mantle, so *eretz* remains, above as well as below. [36a, pp. 284–285]27

In his own way, Baeck comes to identify the people with the land and sees them as one: "the people of this land and the land of this people." [8, p. 115]

This can be pressed too far. Baeck always uses the *Gleichnis,* the al-

---

25 On *Sefer Ha-Bahir,* see Gershom Scholem, "Buch Bahir," *Encyclopedia Judaica,* vol. III, col. 969–979.

26 Quoting section 16 of *Sefer Ha-Bahir.*

27 Quoting section 21 of *Sefer Ha-Bahir.* See also [36a, p. 285, n. 1].

legory. But we have to come to terms with the fact that the land itself here begins to speak, to teach, to reveal the mystery and to present the commandment. It is the land that becomes the crowning aspect of Israel and its faith, the final assertion of the transcendent emerging out of the immanent. All data that reaches out to man and leaves its imprint on his sense of mystery and on his rational apprehension already contains within itself that twofoldness. And the land of Palestine, together with the wilderness of Sinai, was a fundamental experience of this people Israel. Israel—and man—never bring the mystery and the commandment into the data of existence through an analysis. It is already there. The Shechina exists in the world as it exists beyond the world. And nothing is static, nothing is devoid of the mystery. The *beracha*, the blessing, supports all of creation and rises out of all creation: and Baeck sees Israel as the people that hears the blessing and hearkens to it, that identifies itself with the land of blessing and becomes one with it.

What is the revelation of the land to Israel? To start with, there is its outer shape, its twofoldness:

> . . . the man of this land looked out upon the wilderness, its approach and its retreat, its familiarity and its awesomeness. . . . The wilderness captivated the very soul of men. It spoke to the people of its time of youth. . . . Here they experienced distance and vista. . . . Here they discovered the drama of the way. . . . Here strength entered its soul. . . . [as they] experienced the unexpected. . . . Thus did this people see the wilderness; remained in its memory. [8, pp. 104–105]

The wilderness as the place of the wide vision, where the far horizon and the distant stars brought man to the knowledge of monotheism, is a familiar concept of Biblical criticism. Renan was probably its chief exponent. Most scholars today counter with the observation that the proliferation of Arab paganism came out of the same desert as Israel's vision of the One God. But while Baeck seems to accept Renan's thought, he does so only within the context of his total construction in which the traces of the wilderness left in this people's character and history (the wilderness poems of Hosea and Jeremiah, the wilderness festival of booths that was to seal the experience of the journey and the openness to the desert into the life of Israel) become part of the teachings of Judaism: Puritanism is a wilderness revelation that enters Judaism. Elijah the Tishbite, the Rechabite tradition, and Essenes lead to a limited asceticism necessary for the polarity of Jewish thought.

The "promised land" itself is lush and rich. Yet it too has a certain purity to convey: Did it not vomit out its defilers and was it not God's word that the land would also vomit out Israel if it came to defile it (Leviticus 18)? Its very geography is a living twofoldness to Baeck: Its mountains and valleys etched differences into the landscape which maintained the individuality of the tribes and made unity a task of history; but its boundaries, of mountain and river, desert and ocean, preserve the totality of its inhabitants.

> When the tribes of this people of chosen talent came, they found a land for the task of unity for which Israel was chosen—here, in this stubborn land.
>
> Again, paradox took hold of this people. The land, divided yet enclosed, nursed a will, often obstinate, for discriminating and sorting out, and a will even more obstinate for unison and unity. This contradiction, too, the people's personality assimilated and transformed into a source of strength, into an inner treasure. [8, pp. 116–117]

The twofoldness of the land is thus impressed upon Israel. And, as Baeck comes to sketch the character of this people Israel, he sees a multitude of polarities within Israel that rise out of its confrontation with the land. Confronting the persistent myths of the rootlessness of Israel, of the denial of the farmer's virtues which was so much a part of the Nazi propaganda surrounding him, Baeck insists that the qualities of the peasant, established in Israel during its stay in the land of Palestine, continued to endure, even if only through the harvest festivals which recalled Israel to its relationship to the land. At the same time, Baeck noted the "unpeasantness" [89, p. 112][28] of the Jew, his readiness to give away things, to make sacrifices, to be mobile upon the earth (the polemic subtly attacks some of the "virtue" of the idolized peasant figure in Nazi mythology). Baeck also notes the joy that comes out of contact with the land, the innocent rejoicing that yet has its check in the contrasting quality of asceticism. As the land leaves its imprint, Israel becomes this people of the polarity:

> It is a people with its paradoxes and its tensions: the most related and the most lonely people, surely the most conservative and perhaps the most

[28] I must here again express my hope that a third printing of this translation will appear, so that the printer's error of "unpleasantness" will no longer plague the text and reader.

radical, the patient and the impatient, the believing and the critical, the people of the fathers and the people of the children, rejoicing in life yet ascetic, the people of receptive humor and of rejecting irony, the people of the way and yet the people of the "fence," the people that . . . looks outward . . . and inward; one could almost say that this is the people of the land and yet of the wilderness. It lives with tension because it lives in two streams at once. It cannot draw its true strength out of the one . . . without the other. [8, p. 113]

Baeck sees a spiritualization of the soil, the transcendent revealing itself in this aspect of the universe as it touches Israel and mankind, that was already an awareness of the Bible and its language: the words "man" and "soil" come from the same source. *Adamah* signifies soil, *adam* signifies man. In the word "soil" the essence of man resounds, and in the word "man" the earth resounds. [8, p. 129] While Baeck rejects all aspects of paganism, he sees the Jew drawing the qualities of rebirth and inner strength from the soil on which he lived when he was young.

In the *Gleichnis* of the land, Baeck's portrait of the Jew reaches its final dimension. The tensions of inner and outer existence are fused together here, and the identity of creation with revelation is once more asserted: The land itself comes to imprint the twofoldness of mystery and commandment upon a people uniquely qualified to reecive it. In this, too, we find a relationship between Leo Baeck and Jehuda Halevi. The poet of the *Kuzari* claimed that the special prophetic qualities of Israel flourish best in the land of Israel; and the poetic midrash of Theresienstadt also looks back to the land of the revelation which merged with the people of the revelation. Both are agreed on land and people, but there is a drastic difference in their concept of revelation. The question we must presently ask Baeck is one raised earlier: When the revelation is asserted to exist in all aspects of life—is there such a thing as a special revelation? And how can it be distinguished? Can the essence of Judaism be clearly represented in the poetic portrayal of Israel?

It had been Baeck's intention to "render an account of this Jewish life, this Jewish people . . . [which] should speak before men and bear witness." [8, p. 3] At the time of annihilation, in the place of utter darkness, Baeck gave his testimony: It was a bundle of pages which took on a life of its own. It became a book for all time and for all places, bringing to all men a vision of Israel in which we can discern a luminous quality. But was it a testimony of life in the concentration camp?

It can be argued that there rests in this work the great silence which Baeck stresses as one of the basic aspects of the Bible's word to man. And we do know of the cold and bitter silence which was certainly one aspect of the "new midrash" written in the Third Reich. But the fact remains that, at the point of death, Baeck did not write a testimony of the suffering and the anguish he and his fellow Jews were then experiencing. The Warsaw Ghetto diary of Chaim Kaplan was a scroll of agony in which Kaplan told of what his eyes had seen, of what his heart had felt. The Ringelblum archives recorded the anguish of the community, the death throes of the Warsaw Ghetto. Elie Wiesel wrote of the night of Auschwitz.[29] Leo Baeck—as we saw in the biographical section—did not let his own personality intrude. His last testament and testimony was the proud proclamation of the metaphysical people Israel, of cosmic man who gains rebirth beyond the caesura of death which is only an incident in his life. Once more, the Darmstadt statement of death and rebirth becomes the framework of thought subordinating the experience of the moment of pain to the greater understanding which sees the underlying reality of the Divine within all existence:

> Man is a cosmic being. He too. Since he thinks, and because he thinks, he meditates upon that. His habitation, his wilderness too, have been placed into eternity. He cannot escape from it. His boundaries are set into this boundlessness; boundary and boundlessness at once are his existence. A birth and a death, a beginning and an end designate his span here, and they are still only part of an extension stretching to the beyond of all distances. They are inside an all. And man's spirit, as if rising to his own beyond, moves outward into the all. He penetrates to an ever-new distance and nearness. But no goal shows itself to him, far or near. Wondrous things are told him by the all, and thus his exploring and meditating are likewise wondrous. But he never hears the answer to his life here; and never is he questioned on this level.

> Only the world of commandment and grace calls him forward and proclaims his vocation. It directs the question to him and bids him answer, lets him ask and gives him the answer. It is injunction and promise in one, always showing the way and revealing the goal. Here, question is answer, and every answer also asks the question. The grace of God proclaims the

29 Chaim A. Kaplan, *Scroll of Agony: The Warsaw Diary*, translated from the Hebrew by Abraham Katsh (New York, 1965); Emanuel Ringelblum, *Notes from the Warsaw Ghetto*, translated from the Yiddish by Jacob Sloan (New York, 1958); Elie Wiesel, *Night* (translated from the French by Stella Rodway (New York, 1960).

commandment, and the commandment of God enfolds His grace at the same time. Purification, reconciliation, and redemption are always the way and the goal. [8, p. 142]

This is Baeck's picture of Israel as of man. In more than one way, it is also an autobiographical statement, in the only way Baeck would permit himself to enter the presentation. Written under the circumstances, it is a last testament aware of itself, consciously deciding to assert the totality of Israel in which the writer is also contained, presenting his personal religion in which all Israel is contained. Baeck's personality comes through here and gives life to the portrait. The young man had written his doctoral dissertation on Spinoza. The calmness of the old man, gazing into the distances with a cosmic view, partakes of Spinoza's temperament and inner strength. But then he discards Spinoza's vision. The answer does not come to man in the contemplation of the beyond, in the vast spaces. Man has to return to the world of human experience, to the world of the commandment and the action. Much of what Spinoza had said was valid for Baeck; but in the end he rejected the philosophical system that did not know the dynamism of the polarity and tried to find in the vast reaches that which he felt could only be known within human experience and in the existence of this people. [8, pp. 306–307][30] And still—the very emphases Baeck places into the portrait of his people come out of Baeck's own philosophical system, inherited from Hermann Cohen. The overriding emphasis upon the ethical act; the assertion of a rational and ethical mysticism (which was certainly part of Baeck but in an historical reconstruction of Jewish thought must be balanced against a darker mysticism which has deeper despairs and an ecstasy ignorant of ethical act or reason); Baeck's use of messianism; the ill treatment accorded to the sacrificial cult; and the liberalism which in the end remains a distinguishing feature of Baeck's Judaism—all these come to tell us that the vision of Jewish existence and of Judaism is best understood as *a* Jewish existence and *a* Judaism, representative of many, but ultimately evoking one life and one faith: Leo Baeck.

[30] [8, pp. 306–307; the second volume, written after the war]: "He [Spinoza] won an answer, but it could not be an answer for his people. An essential polarity, . . . the dynamism, of the commandment . . . and of the social, did not attain its rightful place in the system of Spinoza. . . . [No] driving force . . . emanates from it. . . . He lacks the messianic thrust, for the great 'I AM THAT I AM' and 'THOU SHALT . . .' are not heard. He is rich in fruit, but not in seed."

VI

This first volume of *This People Israel* can be appreciated as a midrash and honored for what we have called the luminous quality of its vision of Jewish existence, but it must also be understood and critically analyzed as a theological statement. Unfortunately, this has not yet happened within the Jewish community. The book was first published in Germany, where there were no longer any Jewish readers. It was read by Jewish scholars scattered across the world; but more as an evocation of a past that no longer lived, as one more aspect of the legend of Leo Baeck, of the indomitable Jewish spirit that rises above all persecution. The midrash of the people was received; the theological contents have had little acknowledgment. When the English edition appeared, in 1965, there were valid editorial reasons for publishing both the midrash from Theresienstadt and its much longer sequel as one book. But in the broad vision of three thousand years of Jewish existence the theological foundations of the first volume receded into the background. Cecil Roth's review[31] recognizes a difference between the first and second volume, but fails to indicate its nature. Perhaps it is the fate of all metaphysical poets that their writings are not understood on all levels until time has passed. Baeck's midrash, certainly, has not yet said everything it has to convey to the Jewish public.

But there does exist a response to, and a criticism of, the theological aspects found in the core of *This People Israel*. Quite logically, this is the response of the Christian theologians. If the polemical core was concealed and is barely noticeable to the Jewish reader, the thoughtful Christian could not but be aware of the barbs. And just as Catholicism, in the person of the scholarly Jesuit Przywara, takes cognizance of the challenges the religion of polarity offers to the Church, so do we find Protestant criticisms. Some of the most thoughtful criticism of Baeck, which has already been noted, is found in the work of Reinhold Mayer [150] who read *This People Israel* with great care. Another critique, which we will now examine in detail, is that of the Lutheran scholar Martin Wittenberg. [193]

Professor Wittenberg shows himself fully aware of the nature of the

---

[31] *Saturday Review,* January 30, 1965.

midrash composed by Baeck. He sees the connection between Baeck and Jehuda Halevi both of whom saw the Jewish people as endowed with unique talent to receive the revelation of God. He notes the tensions and the framework of the religion of polarity in Baeck's presentation. And much of what Baeck has to say—on the relationship of the individual and the community, the courage of Jewish piety, the strength of the Biblical faith, and even the shortcomings of Christianity—is stressed by Wittenberg as worthwhile and important for the Church as much as for the Jewish people.

Wittenberg's first serious conflict with Baeck is prompted by Baeck's polemic against the Christian "misinterpretation" of the Ten Commandments, which states:

> When the church, having achieved dominance, wanted to determine what belong to the legal domain it had entered, many of its thinkers identified the Decalogue with the law of nature, in order to distinguish it from the law of grace. The essence of the law and of the freedom embedded in it was thus misunderstood. . . . The realm of law is the realm of revelation, and is as such the realm of grace. . . .
>
> Later, in the time of the Reformation, when a new justification was to be required for the state, a "loyal-subject theology" placed the Ten Commandments into the domain of the state and its organizing task. The state was declared the "guardian of the two tablets. . . ." But the quintessence of the Ten Commandments . . . is their immediacy; no authority can be the mediator between God and man. Political authority dispenses no revelation. [8, pp. 76–77]

Wittenberg challenges the historical interpretation behind the judgment on the state's role as "guardian of the law"; but his basic objection, naturally, is Baeck's equating of revelation with grace. He realizes that if "a real investigation and illumination of Baeck's concept of law were to take place, it would lead to a genuine controversy" [193, p. 22]; but is satisfied at this point just to indicate that Baeck's equating of revelation and grace overlooks the existence of a revelation of Divine anger. And this leads to four distinct points Wittenberg presents in his attack on Baeck's theology as found in the midrash of Theresienstadt.

Wittenberg's first question to Baeck is "whether his testimony concerning the revelation from God can really be maintained in the light of the Old Testament." [193, p. 23] Wittenberg claims that there is a hidden split within Baeck's definition of revelation which is noticeable from the very beginning. The first page of Baeck's midrash already moves back and forth from the religious experience and conviction of Israel to that speech from the world beyond which comes out of the unending and eternal. [8, pp. 5-6] Sometimes Baeck seems to derive revelation from the Bible, sometimes (particularly the concept of God) from philosophy, and sometimes from the events of nature:

> there is a complete mixing together of the theological validation on the basis of the Divine authority from the beyond with the morphological, religion-phenomenological description of the nature of Israel's soul. Is this, too, to be considered revelation? . . . [Baeck states] that the revelation comes from the One God and therefore embraces all, so that there cannot be a division between the worlds but rather a revelation of the higher world in this world. [193, p. 24]

Why then cannot this revelation be found everywhere, asks Wittenberg. And he feels that Baeck's restatement of Jehuda Halevi's answer (although Baeck seems to replace Halevi's "prophetic sense" with the gift of "poetry") might be an insufficient answer for Jews as well as Christians. Can Baeck really show that his concept of the covenant as "law, creation, revelation . . . fused into a single word" [8, p. 13][32] is found in the Bible? Baeck linked reason and revelation (Wittenberg here draws also on the just published work by Leo Baeck on Maimonides [61a]);[33] and Wittenberg feels that this runs counter to the heart of the Old Testament which knows of the difference between the thoughts of God and the thoughts of man. But Baeck's worst error in Wittenberg's view is that not only is grace always revelation, but revelation is always grace. Again he would remind Baeck of God's anger which is not compensated in the dialectic relationship to God's grace, but within God Himself. [193, p. 26]

This leads to Wittenberg's second question: *How does Baeck understand God?* Baeck's translation of God's name, this use of " 'I AM THAT I AM' the 'I' and the being, the being and the 'I' in one, the origin of all being and the origin of every 'I,' origin and being and 'I' in one"

---

[32] See also page 227, above.

[33] Expressing himself against the "fateful evasion of the twofold truth," Baeck had applauded Maimonides: "For him, truth is one; one and the same in faith and in knowledge, one and the same in the world of revelation and in the world of creation. The oneness of spiritual life, and with it the oneness of the human task and hope, was both demanded and guaranteed with this [p. 26]."

[8, p. 83][34] upsets Wittenberg who sees in this definition more of the neutral God of the philosophers and less of the personal God of the Old Testament. He fears that Maimonides and Aristotle stand behind Baeck's definition—perhaps even Spinoza, although he admits that Baeck's emphasis upon the reality of Jewish prayer mediates against the Spinozistic deity approached through meditation only. And in the same way he is upset by Baeck's translation and explanation of Exodus 33:19:

> "I will proclaim the name of Him-Who-Is before thee: I will be gracious, always; and I will show mercy, always."
>
> Again Moses is granted an answer. "I AM THAT I AM"—I am always —thus had he learned the name of God earlier; now he is addressed in a similar manner and hears the name of God: "I am always gracious . . . and I always show mercy. . . ." This is the categorical grace and the categorical mercy together. [8, pp. 87–88][35]

Those who have read Exodus 33:19 as a statement of predestination must find themselves at odds with Baeck's translation, as well as those to whom grace is a continually renewed activity of God. Wittenberg charges that Baeck's translation of God's name and nature removes the tension of anger and grace from God, and feels that the removal of the dative and genitive from the grammar of the Divine name is paralleled by a flattening out of the God concept through the removal of the dimension of Divine anger. [193, p. 28]

The third charge against Baeck here interlinks with Wittenberg's previous points: *Where does Baeck speak of sin in all of his book?* Wittenberg here uses Baeck's type of presentation against him. If Baeck proclaims the essence of Judaism through the experience of Jewish existence, should Baeck not give due recognition to Israel's awareness of sin which makes the Yom Kippur liturgy the most powerful aspect of Jewish prayer? Wittenberg can—and does—give pages of Biblical quotations indicating the awareness of sin in the Old Testament; but he also notes the great awareness of sin in all eras of Jewish existence. And he specifically challenges "Baeck's Kantian view that the goal of history is the time in which commandment and history become one in the life of

---

[34] See also page 234, above.

[35] But revising the Jewish Publication Society translation in the text. The Buber-Rosenzweig translation for these critical passages: "Ich werde dasein, als der ich dasein werde. . . . Ich-Bin-Da schickt mich" [Exodus 3:13]; "Das ich goenne wem ich goenne; dass ich erbarme wes ich erbarme" [Exodus 33:19].

nations . . . a time which will come to be because it should come to be."
[163, p. 30][36] Baeck's concept of man unimpaired by sin might arrive
at a "should" that is also a "can"; but Wittenberg feels that it must be
grounded in God's will and promise, not in man.

At this point, the fourth challenge is issued: *Does not Baeck ground
his messianism in man and not in God?* Wittenberg joins Przywara here
in the attack upon the emphasis given in Baeck's writing to an ethical
activism which really feels man's ability equal to the messianic task. But
behind it there is the basic polemic between two religions that cannot
come to an agreement on the nature of messianic redemption. Wittenberg tries to use Jewish sources to show that the more fundamentalist
positions within Jewish life are opposed to Baeck's thought, and that
the liturgy (for example, the *birkat ha-mazon* and the *sh'mone esre*)
includes prayers for the messiah, the son of David. But it becomes clear
that Wittenberg is addressing himself to the basic problem of the Christian who wishes the Jew to accept Jesus as the messiah.[37] His greatest
objections are to Baeck's reading of the Old Testament in which Israel's
role as the "suffering servant" replaces the later, Christian interpretations.
And Wittenberg again links Baeck with Halevi's *Kuzari,* as the verses
from Isaiah 53 become applied to Israel as God's servant:

> What the allegory shows here is the way of the man called by God; it is
> also the way of the people when it becomes a personality, when it is a
> people of genuine gifts, or, in the Bible's word, a "chosen people." Every
> people with such powers moves part way down this road. *But this people
> had been designated to walk the whole road.* [8, p. 65; emphasis supplied]

This is indeed the core of Baeck's position. It asserts that superiority for
Israel which he had claimed, half a century earlier, for Judaism. Since
Baeck sees the two as one in this poetic midrash, it is the same claim.
And it must evoke the same polemic response on the part of Christianity.

There are a number of ways in which these four questions addressed to
Baeck can be answered. Some of them lie outside the scope of this book.
Once we have placed the challenge into the context of Jewish-Christian

---

[36] Quoting Baeck's *Dieses Volk* (English translation [8, p. 52]).

[37] It is worth noting here that Wittenberg's study grew out of a lecture he presented
to the Evangelical Lutheran Central Association for Missionary Work within the Jewish
People.

dialogue, we see some aspects of Wittenberg's critique which the dialogue must accept as a permanent disagreement between the two faiths. There are other criticisms which can be found valid, since this examination of Baeck's thoughts is not a defense of Baeck's position but rather its exposition. It is quite clear that *This People Israel* has its flaws as a presentation of Judaism. It does not have the consistency and solid structure of *The Essence of Judaism.* Its use of the *Gleichnis* sometimes leads to an uncertainty on the part of the reader concerning Baeck's position. And the polemic carried out against Christianity does make historical judgments of Church and of dogma which tend to exclude contrary evidence or alternate trends within Christianity. Other aspects of Baeck's apologetics also make their reappearance: Israel's flaws are minimized, and Baeck's own position crowds out other interpretations of Judaism. It is clearly unfair to judge poetry on the same level as philosophic discourse. But in this case, the poetry of this midrash is intended to convey a metaphysical structure which lives in every aspect of Jewish existence. One only does full justice to Baeck's work by coming to terms with the underlying concepts.

Wittenberg fails in this. The philosophic position inherent in Baeck's religion of polarity has escaped him. And while that position also runs counter to Christian fundamentalist thought and to some areas of Orthodox Judaism, Baeck can be found to be perfectly consistent in the context of the Bible and of philosophic discourse. In these final writings of Leo Baeck, we can find answers to this critique which help us to understand the religious thought of Leo Baeck after he had emerged from the concentration camp.

Wittenberg's first challenge dealt with Baeck's concept of revelation. Wittenberg saw a hopeless muddling of Biblical revelation with the inner workings of the mind of man, a revelation that could be found everywhere. He felt that Baeck had broken the barrier between reason and revelation which Wittenberg considered essential to the nature of religion. But it is just that relationship between reason and revelation, expounded in the essay on Maimonides quoted by Wittenberg, which shows the consistency of Baeck's system. Baeck viewed Maimonides as one of the few persons who was a master of science (e.g., his works on medicine), of the law (his *Mishne Torah*, his *Guide to the Perplexed*, etc.), and of philosophy. And he stated the problem and gave its ramifications for Jewish thought:

An unavoidable problem presented itself to thought . . . : where is the border of knowledge which science procures, and where does that knowledge begin which is given by religion, by faith? And this also contains one other problem: the mystery.

For science, the mystery is a border concept; as Aristotle said, science "must come to a stop" some place. For religion, mystery is the center; the revelation comes out of the mystery. Unendingness and eternity, which basically say the same thing, are a question to science which cannot be rejected here or there. For religion, they are both part of the mystery that supports the world. It is significant that the Hebrew word "olam," which indicates both eternity and unendingness, also includes the meaning of mystery in its roots. And furthermore: what is eternal—unending? Is it just God? Is it the spirit which comes from God, the force which creates and orders and forms? Or is it matter as well . . . ? Who gives the final answer? Both science and religion? Does each give it in its own way, in its own area? [61a, pp. 23–24]

The answer that Baeck saw for Maimonides and for himself was that there was one truth that enters all realms. One aspect of that truth is the Bible and the prophetic vision, which remains open to the examination of philosophy and continues to speak to man: "The doors of investigation are not closed (Moreh Nevuchim, Book II)." And the certainty of religious vision which is the heritage of Israel should not be considered a complete possession to which nothing need be added. The knowledge of the world around us enlarges our revelation; and the prophetic revelation of the moral cosmos, of the messianic task, of the Divine commandment is just as essential: religion, science, and philosophy are all aspects of the revelation of the One God which brings metaphysical questions into the domain of the psychological:

It is the particularly Jewish religious problem—and out of it rise all questions and all demands here—faced by Maimonides: this problem of the entrance of the eternal, the unending, the mysterious, the unconditional, the commanding into this world of the finite, the limited, the terrestrial, the natural, the knowable—this problem of creation and of revelation was grasped here. . . . And he understood it in what was essential and decisive and therefore enduring. [61a, p. 25]

Creation and revelation are also united for Baeck; and there is one truth that manifests itself in all.

Moving on from Maimonides to Baeck's own system, we find that

Baeck's definition of revelation depends on this structure of polarity in which a distinction is made between the data of revelation and the system of revelation. In logic, all evidence depends upon the rule of evidence (proving this rule could only lead to an infinite regression); and just so, it would be impossible to use the term revelation if it were not recognized that man has to confront the data of revelation with a structure in which the rational is just as basic as that nonrational sense which responds to the mystery. Baeck's view sees the transcendent in all that is immanent, and all human beings can discern it—"except that this people has been designated to walk the whole road." This use of the term "revelation" actually unites Christianity and Judaism with all other religions who would use the term "revelation." The data of revelation, the infinite manifesting itself, is here part of a common language. Only at the next stage, where the figure of Christ encounters the personality of this people Israel, do we find an unbridgeable gap. Baeck deals with this concept of revelation in an essay written almost immediately after he had come back to the world of the living, out of Theresienstadt. In 1947, he returned to Ascona, where he had previously attended the round-table conferences of the Eranos association, to participate in a discussion on the nature of man. It is indicative of Baeck's system that his concept of revelation is contained in the definition of man: the *individuum ineffabile*, as he named this essay. [54]

Baeck sees the form of life and knowledge as individuality. We do not know abstractions like "tree": We know the individual fir tree or birch tree. There is a unity to existence which is indivisible, and individuality may be termed the one a priori: "a long-ranging view from the all-embracing, most distant beyond . . . would be presented by all of this existence as by a gigantic Milky Way of individualities, of onenesses." [54, p. 386] The individual cannot be defined, only stated: *individuum est ineffabile.* This is the Talmudic image of God whose imprint does not create men like coins, but fashions every creature individually, but all in God's image. God's attribute is creation: He is *deus creator*, just as man knows the use of tools and is *homo faber*. But there can awake within man the creative spark—he *is* fashioned in God's image.

The fact of existence, then, is individuality—but individuality within a system. All concrete individuality enters our life as a construction. It is the individuality of the system: Unity only exists as totality. And behind a system there is the dynamism of a law: "Individuality, system, law are thus the different designations for this unity and totality which is the form in which all existence appears." [54, p. 389] And Baeck pursues this further: there is an underlying universality to law, to system, and to individuality. The conclusion follows that

> All individualities, all systems, all laws are terminated and find their unity and totality in a final . . . totality and unity . . . system, . . . law . . . individuality . . . continuity . . . in which all existence has its essential existence, all form of life has its basic form and thus finds its total form. [54, pp. 389–390]

Here is where we return to Wittenberg's plaint. Seeing the transcendent in every totality and individuality, are we not reduced to a kind of pantheism? And Baeck acknowledges that pantheism in religion—and pancosmism in metaphysics—is part of the point he has made. But its insight is only valid if it moves on from that position: "pantheism often becomes a passageway to monotheism, perhaps a necessary one." [54, p. 390] Just so, the Talmud stated:

> "God is the place of the world, but the world is not His place" . . . but the two Hebrew terms which repeat themselves are really not translatable. The first, the Hebrew word "makom". . . contains also "the existent," "the given," "the enduring"; "olam" not only means "world," but originally "eternity": it designates in one the unendingness of space and the unendingness of time. A more proper translation of this sentence would be: "God, the One, is the existence of all unendingness; but all unendingness is not His existence," i.e., he gives the totality, the unending its unity, but all the unending does not give him his unity. It has its continuity in him, but he does not have it in it; it is in him, but he is not in it. Pantheism and pancosmism only know the first half of this sentence. [54, pp. 390–391]

A line, a development has been drawn. But it is characteristic of the "later" Baeck that this line must be continued in the realm of experience. Human existence contains the fact of individuality and the fact of the system. It contains a third fact: the caesura of human existence which Baeck first stressed in the lecture on "Death and Rebirth" and which was again emphasized in his concentration camp lecture; this fact of the caesura has come to assume major proportions in Baeck's system at this point. The tension of human existence is seen here, the polarities of the relationship between individualities to systems in the framework of human existence with its caesura. In biology, as in physics, man is confronted with the laws and systems of polarity. Thus, the polarity of male-female establishes every human individuality in relationship and opposition to the other individuality:

> Expressed anthropologically, fate enters here into existence, the man- and wife-fate, the father- and mother-fate—this *fatum*, this *destinatum originale*. The individuality becomes dualistic and has a fate. Historically, every concept of fate has its roots in a dualism. [54, p. 392]

In trying to understand the individual and his relationship to the revelation of the One who undergirds all facets of existence, Baeck makes the biological dimension of man basic to the process of understanding. Consciousness, self-awareness, man's ability to make himself both subject and object create an internal tension just as the male-female tension is part of his exterior relationship in which the individuality asserts itself; and the psychological tensions join the biological polarities within *individuum ineffabile*. And out of the tensions of the inner confrontation, there emerges man's intellect. [54, pp. 395–396]

Man's intellect creates another polarity: that between life and intellect's picture of that life. Life splits into the existent and into the imagined. And the outer world of the system splits in the same manner. The immediacy of the relationship between the individuality and the system is thus disturbed, and uncertainty and doubt become aspects of human existence. Instinct, man's previous relationship to the system, becomes damaged and is pushed back into the subconscious. The very fact of man having become self-aware (Baeck relates the "nudity" of the Garden of Eden story to "knowledge" [54, p. 397]) means that he has separated himself from the underlying unity of the universe, and must find his way back to it. It is not that man *may* come to know the revelation, but that he *must* come to know it in order to heal the split. Here Baeck's vision of man is determined by the statements of Judaism: Man has freedom. He can give his assent or his rejection to the task of coming fully into his individuality:

> Individuality, the form of existence, the oneness and the totality here is that which is created, given, but it is also that which has been assigned and is commanded. To the "I am" is added the "I should." Man should also be a creator, his own creator. . . .

A law presents itself to man here, in the form of a demand, an imperative, a commandment; and man has the pause, the possibility of the decision in which he recognizes the commandment and acknowledges it, or denies and rejects it. As all law, this law has reality in the system, and the system, as all system, has reality in the law. But at the same time a demand directs itself to man. It speaks of what is and also of what man should do. Just as man confronts himself, so does he confront the law which he is to make the law of his life. He is to order himself, his own existence into this law, thus to become a creator. It only becomes a reality for him when it becomes, through him, the forming law of his life and individuality, when his existence, his individuality thus receives its form in a higher, moral system through a higher, moral law. The individuality becomes the demand. [54, pp. 400–403]

Creation in human life then means the response by the individuality to the commandment which man can answer because he has the quality of freedom and the ability to create, i.e., to move toward the full attainment of his individuality, beyond the ceasura which are contained in the form of human existence.

Baeck builds the knowledge of man's relationship to the universe out of the data of human experience. But he is aware that "things encountered in the domain of our experience reach beyond this":

The moral law which man attains through a decision, through freedom, precisely because man first has to arrive at it, is something different and belongs to a different sphere as the given law of human existence and human individuality. By nature, in his given form of existence, man is not yet moral . . . not yet selfless, just, truthful, loving. In nature . . . ethics . . . could only indicate how it might be useful . . . in adding nobility to egoism and guiding it to a useful purpose. When ethics wanted to be more . . . it always had to recognize the higher law. Only with the recognition of that which stands beyond the created and given existence . . . did ethics become possible. [54, p. 405]

Ethics and religion here link together while maintaining their respective autonomy (reminding us of Hermann Cohen). But the total picture is more of an allegory of the nature of religion as found in the *verstehende Psychologie* Baeck derived from Dilthey: that aspect of man, the fullness of his as yet unachieved individuality, comes to him with the commandment that he realize himself. And this picture is enlarged until we see every individuality confronted by the ground and goal of all being— but it is man who has the dimension of freedom and can respond.

That is why pantheism fails, even though it notes the universality of revelation. Hippocrates' alleged saying, "All is divine, and all is human," fails to take full account of the tension and the potential split between the human and the Divine. The pantheistic method only leads to cosmology, not to psychology; it arrives at the cosmic law, but not at the psychical and the ethical law. The fact of the moral "Thou shalt," the fact of the moral decision, of the creative pause and autonomy has no place in pantheism, but is only grasped in monotheism.

Finally, one more aspect of man's nature is noted by Baeck. Man has the abilities of genius in the fields of knowledge, of art, and of morality. In the first two areas, the full dynamism of this genius is found in only a few. But every man can find himself in the dynamics of the moral sphere, can be *homo creator*:

> Individuality, in its genius, creates what is individual, whether in the formation of knowledge, in the works of art, or in the moral action. Something individual is here created, i.e., something unique and therefore inexplicable, something which religion says has its roots in the mystery, and which possesses its relationship with the spirit of all spirits, with the original basis of all unity and totality.
>
> The circle of experience, its observations, and the lines moving outward from it come to a stop here. Wherever they have come, they stand before the individual, his system, and his law, the *individuum ineffabile*, the recognizable in which there yet remains the mystery, the beyond. [54, p. 410][88]

Baeck, then, discovers both man and God in the realm of experience. In the world, there lives the commandment which goes out to all; in man, there is the creative genius which can respond. The mystery of God cannot be known: but his will is open to every individual, who can move toward self-attainment in the moral realm. But in man, too, there is the mystery of his individuality which links up with the underlying foundation of all existence. The beyond makes itself known in man as in the world around him: All data of revelation come out of the experience, as all reality has experience. But the creativity of man is an avenue for life to achieve itself, for new facts and for new reality which can emerge out of the moral task. *The individuum ineffabile* contains the *homo creator*.

---

[88] The second section of the essay, entitled "Rebirth," is a restatement of the Darmstadt lecture and once again stresses man's ability for rebirth, overcoming the caesura: "man can be fulfilled individuality," the closing words, again express the optimism of faith in man.

Drawing together Baeck's more important postwar statements (i.e., *Maimonides* and "Individuum Ineffabile") has been of help in supplementing our view of the theological structure that is implicit in *This People Israel*. His definition of revelation is seen to be completely consistent in a religious structure that starts within human experience but analyzes both man and the world in terms of the trancendental that breaks into the immanent and offers the experience of the tension which can be resolved by the ethical act. Here, too, we found confirmation for Wittenberg's surmise that Baeck's God is more the God of the philosophers, of Maimonides. But as Wittenberg also noted, Baeck's God is not the distant First Cause, but a personal God who can be addressed by man. Baeck's awareness of the mystery had changed his concept of God in an appreciable way. Yet Baeck would not go along with those who would define aspects of that mystery in terms of God's anger, or God's withdrawal from the world. God's will, the ethical command, could be known clearly; the mystery could be experienced and encountered: but just as the individual has an ineffable quality, so, too, has God.

Wittenberg's wonder at the absence of sin in Baeck's religion is overstated; and it is no fundamental challenge to the system. But it is a matter of interest to the student that sin is muted in Baeck's presentation. It is not denied; man's failings are stated. Nevertheless, they are bracketed by a fundamental optimism which permits Baeck, two years after he has come out of the concentration camp, to present a statement on man that emphasizes the fullness of his powers and his ability for greatness. In *This People Israel*, Baeck's defense and praise of his people was apologetic writing. But Baeck here shows himself as the great apologete who is utterly consistent: he also defends man, after Auschwitz and Dachau, from those who would see the human failure of the past decades as the final proof of man's inability to make his way in the universe. This is, of course related to Wittenberg's final charge that Baeck's messianism differs from traditional Christian (and perhaps traditional Jewish) emphasis. It is grounded in Baeck's hope in man.

As we have seen, this cannot be identified with humanism, just as his emphasis on the revelation in all existence was not pantheism. The deepest faith in God stands behind all of Baeck's teaching; his optimism deals with the way in which God operates through human beings, with Baeck's hope for the dimension of freedom to turn men to creation and not to destruction. It would be easy to identify this optimism with

Baeck's inheritance from Hermann Cohen. But while the optimistic appraisal of the messianic task may have originated there, Baeck's thoughts are very different from the teachings of early Reform Judaism at the turn of the century.

We would call Baeck's approach that of millennial messianism. There is no short-term hope here (Hermann Cohen was hopeful the next century would see a fairly complete achievement of the better world); Baeck looks into the vast reaches of the millenniums. The messianic task is never fulfilled, and it is always fulfilled: Men who occupy themselves with it—and peoples, as well—achieve their own individuality and stand in the world as creators. And Baeck asserts that man can be *homo creator* in the midst of all the darkness of our days. In the tension of human existence, messianism sees the goal at the end of an unending way. But the way is to be walked. And the Divine grace which Wittenberg requires as a special, almost visual intrusion into man's world is already given in the creative genius that lives in the *individuum ineffabile*.

VII

The postwar writings of Leo Baeck are no longer part of a polemical literature—the "new midrash"—which maintained itself against a hostile environment. They belong to a new era that is yet old in Jewish life: The temple has been burned to the ground, the people have been killed and dispersed, and the survivors wander about the ruins and ask their questions. When the feeling is strong that man has failed, the questions are asked of man, who is often redefined as powerless if not evil. When there is a suspicion that God has withdrawn from the world or has revealed a lack of power, the question is asked of God; and religions without God flourish. Baeck had not lost his faith in God or man. "Individuum ineffabile" upholds both aspects of his faith in an affirmation of man fashioned in God's image with his task and with his freedom. *This People Israel*, particularly the second part, written in his last years, expresses his faith in one special individuality within the family of man, Israel, in its movement through the millenniums of history. Indeed, it is in this area that Baeck pursues the quest for answers. He turns to history, to the experience of the generations and to the experience of his generation, and tries to come to terms with it.

We have noted the shift between his early concern for the essence of Jewish thought and his final pondering upon the meaning of Jewish existence. But this is a shift in emphasis, not a change of the system. At a public lecture in 1949, Baeck was asked about his attitude to the schools of existentialism. In a few words, he rejected the theological existentialism which originates from man's deep anxiety in a dismal world and equates the despair of life confronting death with the core of existence. He noted that one aspect of philosophical existentialism places the greatest stress upon the existential character of the individual framed by the here-and-now. But he concluded:

> On the other hand, the philosophy of existentialism emphasizes the responsibility of the individual resulting from his existence, from the "call to eternity," which summons him by the voice of conscience to make a human value of existence. This existentialism is genuine philosophy, and certainly we have here an interrelation, a common ground with Judaism. [57, p. 17]

It is this "human vale of existence" which stands out in Baeck's writings of the final years. The eternal verities are sought out in human experience and are affirmed in the facts of Jewish history. Once again, Baeck pursues the middle way of the polarities which places him outside the existential thinkers, yet no longer with the idealist group.

But if the emphasis has shifted, Baeck's basic teachings continue unchanged. Some modifications may be noted in his evaluation of Paul;[39] yet his historical writings of these years are once more the exposition of the *theologia viatorum,* in which the path that has been traveled is once again surveyed through the application of those values Baeck had identified as the essence of Judaism half a century earlier.

In 1946, Baeck gave one of the first postwar radio lectures broadcast from London to Germany. The mood of the new era is part of it: The historian walks through the places that have been destroyed—*et perire ruina* ("even the ruins have perished"). [52, p. 9] But all pessimism is rejected. These are curious lectures. The first one, entitled "The Sense of History," repeats part of the concentration camp lecture on Herodotus and Thucydides, and ends with a similar statement of the possibility of the rebirth of individuals and nations who preserve the moral task. The

---

39 "The Faith of Paul" [59] contains a much milder appraisal of Paul. See also [62].

task and the goal endure: "And that is the meaning of history, that is the answer to the question: what endures in the course of time? The law and the spirit, these are eternal—on earth, too." [52, p. 12] "Culture and Man," the second lecture, deals with *homo faber*, with man in the new world where his tools have been perfected and the world has become smaller. And Baeck reminds his listeners that the strongest reality of existence is still man, his soul, his life. [52, p. 18] The final lecture discusses "The State and Civilization" which are defined in this manner:

> Civilization is the permeation of a community [*Gemeinschaft*] by a spirit so that a moral idea stands before the law and history and can point the way for the law and the history; community is thus not only given through soil and fate but by a shared, true spirit. Only thus does a people and a state win their inner value, their particular dignity. Just as individual man can become a personality, that is, can unfold in himself a spiritual, intellectual, and moral possession, . . . so that he has meaning not just through what he achieves . . . but through what he is . . . so is this the lot of the people and the state. They too can have a moral, a spiritual civilization —for this alone is truly civilization—and can therefore give something to mankind just through the fact of their existence. [52, p. 22]

But civilization is found in human beings, in individuals who assert the values of existence. Speaking to a Germany emerging from the period of *ein Volk, ein Reich, ein Fuehrer,* Baeck spoke of the individuality of human beings which gives meaning to the state, of the "ten righteous people in the city" who can preserve the community. Man can define the state, but the reverse leads to destruction. And man stands in history, but gives it the meaning which time places upon space: "Man stands in history. It has been granted him that he can know those from whom he came, that he can think of those who will proceed from him. He has been placed into the frame of generations. He stands within the people and the state, giving fate and receiving it." [52, p. 24] Once more, we are within the theology of history.

The exegete once again moves to the foreground in these last writings. Human history, the history of the nations, can be understood by looking at the one people who discerned the underlying meaning of that history, Baeck's people Israel. And Jewish history can also be understood and interpreted by looking at the lives of the individuals who stand out within the generations. In his final lecture series, given in Germany in 1956 some months before he died, Baeck once more tried to come to terms with the history of modern Judaism, with that German-Jewish community which had been entrusted to him at the moment when its thousand year history was coming to an end. Baeck saw this history through the "types of Jewish self-understanding in the last two centuries"—the men of modern German-Jewish history he found most significant: Mendelssohn, Hess, Rathenau, and Rosenzweig. [63a]

In a significant way, these lectures form one totality with *This People Israel: A Second Part.* [8, 9] In the larger work, Baeck reflected upon the full course of Jewish history; here, in the lectures, the reflection is turned upon his own self. When we consider the two works together, a weakness of the second volume of *This People* comes into view: There are areas of Jewish life which are touched only lightly, i.e., the Middle Ages and the full development of Eastern European Jewry. They are not ignored, and Baeck does not display the prejudices of Graetz and others. But the somewhat cursory treatment ultimately serves to make Baeck's judgment upon the last two hundred years of European Jewish life one that draws too much upon Western sources and misses some nuances introduced through Eastern European sources.[40] Baeck was not attempting to write a full-scale history of Jewish life, but to see in the events of Jewish existence the proclamation of the essence of Judaism. Yet there is an autobiographical aspect of the historian who has to exercise selectivity in searching out his people's history: He gives assent to himself in his selections. And there were darker aspects to Jewish life, and deeper weaknesses, which this autobiography of a man and his people notes but does not plumb to the depths.

This People Israel is always scholarly and often brilliant in its appraisal of Jewish history. Its special value to our study is that it shows us the final dimension of Baeck's thinking. The self-reflecting theology here tests itself on the material of history, and the religion of polarity finds evidence for the twofoldness of human existence in the oneness of Israel's life. This is not pressed too far; and it does lead into new historical insights; namely, the polarity within European Jewry that becomes evident in the interplay between Ashkenazim and Sephardim. The *haside ashkenaz,* the "pious of Germany," and the *hakhme sepharad,* "the

[40] That is, the Eastern European aspects of Haskalah (the revival of Hebrew thought) find sufficient treatment, and the more rational mysticism of Germany (Sefer Hasidim) is seen as more characteristic of Judaism than the powerful forces of Eastern European mysticism.

wise, the philosophers of Spain," come to portray the inner response of
Israel to the mystery and the commandment. [8, p. 265] And Baeck's
distinction between the "piety of culture" and the "culture of piety" is
not a play on words but a profound insight into the forms of Jewish life:

> The individual uniqueness resulted from the different answers given the
> question about the permanency of a culture. It was the question of whether,
> in the human world, there existed preconditions . . . for the great order
> and harmony, for the kingdom of God, whether the many avenues that
> truly approach [the kingdom] . . . exist there. When the religion of this
> people and the philosophy of the Greeks met for the first time, this ques-
> tion was answered in the affirmative [and was now also affirmed by the Se-
> phardim]. . . . Ways leading to religion, areas of the "preparation,"
> were found in culture. One would become even more conscious of one's
> own truth, so went the credo, when one saw the totality. The word "har-
> mony," "order," *tikkun,* was now also used for culture. Religion, in a
> sense, was a religion of culture. [8, pp. 267–268]

The Ashkenazim had a different fate. Isolated from the outside culture, its
affirmation would have been self-betrayal. Instead,

> For the Ashkenazim, only where Torah is could there be *hokhmah.* Piety
> engendered culture. . . .
> The problem of the culture of piety and of the piety of culture raised
> itself in this people continually, and continually drove toward new formu-
> lation. This question is rooted in its faith as a task without end. This faith
> wants to be both, and only where it is both can it live. It must be *torah,*
> the revealed, with its commandment that is ever anew to be fulfilled, with
> its teaching of what this people is; and *hokhmah,* the artistic power granted
> to man, constantly realizing, constantly vitalizing, with its moral demand
> of what this people is to be. They belong together, and together they give
> this faith its totality and its unity . . . Both *hokhmah* and Torah are pos-
> sessed by the Ashkenazim and the Sephardim, and only together do they
> represent the spirit and the existence of this people in its third epoch. The
> Bible has been one great epoch, the Talmud a second. Now, together, the
> Ashkenazim and the Sephardim, each in their special historical manner,
> interwoven with the other in one creative unity, created the third great
> movement and let the Bible and the Talmud be reborn in it. This achieve-
> ment of the two, in its totality and unity, then became both heritage and
> task to a succeeding millennium. [8, pp. 268–269]

As we sift through a key passage such as this one, the old themes of
mystery and commandment, of death and rebirth, of what is and what

is to be, are all sounded together. But in reading them again and again, one parallel passage after another throughout this survey of Baeck's books, we are not just retracing the same ground. One reviewer of *This People Israel,* David Goldstein, has rightly noted:

> The intrinsic message of Leo Baeck is one with his style. Here is no logical thread consistently maintained and followed through 400 pages. His words are written as if for orchestral performance. A theme is announced. It is developed. Another theme is announced and developed. The two themes become intertwined, and slowly the work progresses, gaining in intensity, while the conviction and confidence of Baeck himself remains always in the background, providing an unshakable bass for the many variations played upon it. [126, p. 15]

This pattern has been followed in our study; like Baeck's work, it has the intrinsic character of midrash which takes its form out of the material it has to explicate.

But why had Leo Baeck found it necessary to add a second volume to the midrash of Theresienstadt, this book that was a self-contained testament and testimony? In his preface, Baeck indicates that the man to whom history has spoken cannot cease his testimony, that his books have to continue as well. The first volume spoke of the basic forces Baeck sees as the foundations of Jewish existence, of the special task and the special way that belongs to Israel within world history. And now, Baeck wants to know whether Israel followed the pathway set for it. Did its youthful vision die? Or was there a rebirth in every generation, a transmittal of the ancient revelation which has to speak to every generation? He affirms the rebirth, the people, and its faith. But there is a special poignancy as he turns to the bright hopes of his own time, and to the destruction of these hopes.

Baeck saw the entrance of the Jew into the modern world as that of *homo mysticus* whom the world of the Enlightenment would only admit as *homo rationalis*:

> That was the difficult task of those days . . . for in this mysticism, at that time, Jews all over the world found their consolation. The higher world began at the gates of the ghetto; "Jew-street" went up into the higher spheres. One lived there, in the higher spheres; through all the doors of the houses, through all the windows of the houses, this mystic spirit pushed its way in. [63a, p. 19]

The German Jew, according to Baeck, is founded upon mysticism—his own brand of mysticism, of mystic experiences. In contrast to the Sephardic mystic systematizing, Baeck sees the Ashkenazim stress the mystic personality, and not the system. Living in a culture of piety, they were confronted with an enormously difficult task in terms of entering the outside culture.

Moses Mendelssohn, whom Baeck takes as the first type of Jewish self-realization in modern times, was not a hero; but he acted heroically. He was not a great thinker; but he found a way for the *homo mysticus* to enter the world of rationalism. Baeck describes this way by an analysis of Mendelssohn's *Jerusalem,* in which Mendelssohn fights for the right of existence which belongs to those noble particularities which have received God's grace. There is a universal religion of reason in which all—particularly the Jews—can join. But Mendelssohn then claims that within that framework

> there exists the fact that *one* people, a tiny people . . . stood at Sinai, that the task to remain true to iself was set for it . . . until the end of time. Nothing rational can explain it. The fact exists, this fact of this people as the carrier of the revelation. And therefore . . . a Jew should be a man of reason, but completely a Jew, completely within his particularity, living completely in the tradition without which there would be no history. [63a, p. 23]

Baeck sees Mendelssohn as proclaiming a style of life which is a basic aspect of a people of rebirth. And by making this style of life his own, he showed the Jew of his time that the problem of the Jew in modern times had a solution that was not self-betrayal but affirmation. [63a, p. 24][41]

The second of Baeck's lectures is puzzling when set against the book that is its counterpart: In moving from Mendelssohn to Hess, he by-passed at least a dozen prominent German Jews (Zunz, Graetz, R. S. Hirsch, etc.) whom he could have selected as types of German Jewry. But Baeck had something specific in mind with these lectures. He spoke in post-Hitler Germany; and the exposition of Hess made it possible for

---

[41] In *This People Israel* [8, p. 345] Baeck expands his appreciation of Mendelssohn. Some of his sentences of praise could be applied to Baeck himself: "In his being, his humanity, there is already fulfillment. His personality is his most individual accomplishment; . . . it is an historical achievement."

him to attack that mythus of the state which had proved fatal to his people: "A myth arose in the national state, a myth that had two faces, the myth of the nation and the myth of the state. Myth distinguishes itself from the idea in that the myth only promises man something; the idea demands something from man." [63a, p. 25]

More than that, Baeck could stress the relationship of Hess to Marx, and see both of them in the framework of a religion which "entered the world as a religious revolution, but just as much as a social revolution." [63a, p. 26] Yet his main purpose must have been born out of the realization that the modern Jew could not be understood without Zionism; that there was a way leading out of Judaism and into general culture that is walked by the many who have lost the sense of the mystery but would still listen to the ethical commandment that rises out of life. There is a type of Jew—Baeck saw this clearly—who does not leave Judaism even when his departure seems clear to all those around him:

> Gabirol's word: "I flee from Thee, O Lord, to Thee" . . . One fled from God because the doubts of the day or the disappointments of the years drove him away, but he returned to God: Heinrich Heine. In a certain sense, this was also the life of Moses Hess. He never forgot his Judaism, let alone left it. But other, new ideas captured him completely; and for the sake of these new ideas he wanted to remain a Jew. Now he recognized that it was for the sake of his Jewish people that these ideas were to be realized. A place, a domain, a land on earth, the old promised land, was to belong to them so that the prophetic ideal could be realized. [63a, p. 30]

Baeck also claims the secular Jew who understands himself and his task for authentic Jewish existence. And in Hess he gives assent to that aspect of Jewish hope and striving which his critics saw as a suspicious teaching within his own Judaism:

> The present is conquered . . . by being rooted in the future. The future will signify the right of the present; the future will give its testimony for what the present really is.
>
> This was the idea of Moses Hess. Something of the messianic came to life in him. The flaw of his time, and of the Jews in his time, was that the messianic had grown weak in them. [63a, p. 31]

In Hess, Baeck saw the great hope of man that had not yet been realized.

Walther Rathenau is not mentioned in *This People Israel*. That he is part of the presentation of these lectures seals them as a spiritual autobiography. There is a personal dimension here: Baeck was an intimate of the Rathenau family, and Rathenau's widow presented the slain statesman's library to him. Baeck inherited more than that from Rathenau; in a very real way, he filled the position of leadership for German Jewry which would eventually have come to Rathenau. Baeck wrote:

> He sought his Judaism. Had he lived—it can well be said that he would have found it. It is the tragedy of this man that he was upon the way, and that he died on that road, at the edge of it. He could have given much to Jewish thought and hope if he had found the Judaism for which he searched. [63a, p. 41]

If this is speculation, we can turn to the fact that Walther Rathenau, as the "crown prince" of the AEG[42] was a personification of that German Jewry which had risen to wealth and power, had felt itself to be part of the German nation, and yet had fully realized that it did not belong to it. Rathenau shows us that aspect of German Jewry which is all too easily dismissed as the "assimilated Jew" by those who do not examine the inner together with the outer aspects. Baeck sees Rathenau inheriting Jewish qualities from his nonreligious home: pride from his father, feeling from his mother. And he is essential to Baeck's typology of the German Jew; his life contains the pathos of German-Jewish existence:

> Walther Rathenau did not show the Jews a new path like Moses Mendelssohn from Dessau and Moses Hess from Bonn. But in his person— and that person, in the decisive hours, was always personality—in his personality there stands the struggle and hope, the disappointment and expectation, the search of Jews in that time; in that time, when a generation with its hopes had dropped out, and a new generation saw much evil ahead. In his searchings of that time he was as a symbol for many within Judaism. He may not be passed over in the history of German Jewry. [63a, p. 42]

The final lecture in this series speaks of Franz Rosenzweig. It is warm, generous, open in its praise and perceptive in its assessment. Nevertheless, there is something impersonal about it—perhaps the life and death of German Jewry is too clearly limned in Rosenzweig's personality and life to make this a personal exposition. Baeck saw in

[42] AEG: Allgemeine Elektrizitaets-Gesellschaft, a huge industrial complex established by his father Emil Rathenau.

Rosenzweig that German-Jewish community which had sent Freud, Marx, and Einstein into world history, but which had preserved its own garden as well. The millenniums had broken through the centuries, a rebirth was evident:

> This is the "Jewish Renaissance." It shows itself in everything: in a religious orthodoxy and in a religious liberalism, in a Jewish enthusiasm for Zion and in a Jewish universalism. The millenniums found their way, the outlet needed, and a great inner certainty came to man. This is the time into which Franz Rosenzweig was born. And it is his life that he sought to understand, this rebirth. [63a, pp. 44–45]

Rosenzweig wanted to return his people to the paths of Jewish learning which were now opening up. And he wanted them to live within the Jewish law. Once again Baeck notes that aspect of law which is the style of life and the poetry of life, which distinguishes the religious person from his opposite—the philistine. And he characterizes Rosenzweig's *The Star of Redemption* as "the poetry which endures." [63a, p. 47] Baeck feels that Rosenzweig's concept of law was not rigid; it was not a Reform law, but law somehow re-formed, with new life given to the old vision. Rosenzweig brought the insights of modern culture into Judaism, in order that his people might find new expression for their special heritage. Mendelssohn is the first modern Jew, assenting to both Judaism and the outside culture. In him were both the mystery and the commandment. Moses Hess followed the commandment which ultimately brought him back to the people; but the mystery remained closed to him. Walther Rathenau showed us the anguish of a Jewish community in search of its identity, blessed with the gift of poetry and vision, but finding the great rejection from the outer world even in its moments of temporal success. And in Rosenzweig the Jewish rebirth breaks through; the promise of Mendelssohn is fulfilled, and German Jewry sees, for one clear moment, what it can be. And so "Rosenzweig will maintain his place as long as there is a Jewish people, as long as there is a Jewish faith." [63a, p. 50]

Baeck walked away from the rostrum at that point. The lecture had ended. An account had been given, to himself as well as to his listeners, of the rise and fall of German Jewry. This was not true, of course. The way from Mendelssohn to Hess to Rathenau and to Rosenzweig leads inexorably onward—to Leo Baeck. Something of that was sensed by the chairman of the Franz Delitsch Lecture Series, Professor D. Johannes Herrmann, who indicated that the framework of the presentation the group had been privileged to attend was the personality of a great man in whom "a pure and mature intellectuality . . . join with a pure and unlimited goodness." [63a, p. 52]

A greater, deeper, fuller statement is found in the final pages of *This People Israel*, which Baeck would prefer as his last testament to a lecture in which he himself must have sensed an autobiographical quality which was not his manner of address to the public. But the two works should be read together, just as all of his writings form one full statement. The quality of rebirth he noted in his people, the ability to let the past break through into the present, is also evident in Baeck's writings. He never ceased speaking of the essence of Judaism, with which he began his task as a teacher to his people. But commandment and mystery become joined as the later teachings clarify his early thoughts. And these last writings of Baeck, from the "new midrash" of the thirties to the teachings in the concentration camp and beyond, also bring Baeck to the restatement of his earliest concerns: Once more, he is the apologete. *This People Israel* is a noble statement of his people, and so is the lecture series where the greatness and hopes of German Jewry receive a final poetic statement in the recalling of great personalities. The statement on the *individuum ineffabile* then is one final and great work of apologetics for man in the ruins of a world which now doubted whether man could do more than create ruins. Baeck's vision was clear: Man is greater. God can be encountered in the human dimension.

The man who wrote that was a rabbi, a teacher. But when we close the book of his teachings, and the book of his life, we are aware that what he had to say goes out to all men.

8

The End of the Matter

Can there be theology today? We live in the post-Auschwitz world, the Age of Brutality, the time of uncertainty. Western religion flounders in its attempts to deal with today's theodicy. A divided Christian establishment gains minor ecumenical victories while major minds leave the Church and find their tasks in "religionless Christianity" and in "death-of-God" theology. Jewish thought parallels its outer environment, and many of the younger theologians have become estranged from the testimony of Jewish history in their espousal of contemporary thought. An anguished awareness of the existing moment has shattered their knowledge of "this people Israel" and has made their faith the proclamation of the individual in a darkened world. But as long as questions of ultimate concern are asked, theology continues to be relevant; and when these questions are asked of contemporary life, the teachings and testimony of Leo Baeck take on a fundamental importance: Traditional theology was tested here in today's furnaces of affliction; and it survived.

Christianity has to listen to Leo Baeck. For Baeck was a Jew: a witness of God to the world. The whole enterprise of Christianity is bound up with the truth of that statement. Professor Rylaarsdam of the University of Chicago recently lamented the fact that the Christian world has never really overcome its assumption that the only good Jews are either dead ones or Christians.[1] Unless Christianity comes to know the Jew for what he was, is, and will be—the Jew as himself, and not as a Christian stereotype—the true nature of its own existence will be unknown to Christianity. And if there is indeed a waning of the Western world, and we are living in the "post-Christian era," Christianity may yet have to draw upon its Jewish heritage, which finds an eloquent statement in Baeck's works. Baeck is the paradigm of the Jew drawn for us in Berkovits's essay on the "post-Christian era":

> We are here at the threshold of the new age. We who were there when the Christian era began; we in whose martyrdom Christianity suffered its worst moral debacle; we in whose blood the Christian era found its end —we are here as this new era opens. And we shall be here when this new era reaches its close—we, the *edim*, God's own witnesses, the *am olam*, the eternal witness of history. [77a, p. 84]

Christianity can no longer live under the illusion that it is the Church militant, sword in hand, determining the future of the world. The sword has been broken, together with many illusions. And the Jew who stands before the Church in this world is no longer the cathedral image of the blindfolded synagogue, its staff broken, renouncing this world. His testimony is to the world and in this world; Israel is *not* a metahistorical people. Through the teachings of men like Leo Baeck, we see Israel performing the ancient task of God's witness and prophet. And this is healing for Christianity. For the sharpness of Baeck's polemic rises out of a love for Christianity: The parent still loves the child and would have it turn to ways in which the fullness of its heritage can come to flower. Dialogue between Judaism and Christianity is possible. It has to begin on the level of life, with the shared experience of one humanity. It has to continue on the level of theology, with the shared vision of God's sovereignty. Baeck's life and teachings open both areas to the Christian who is truly in search of his fellow man.

And Judaism has to listen to Leo Baeck. Only the few can take upon themselves the full yoke of the commandments, can live outside of history and thus outside its problems and its anguish, occupied with the

---

[1] Quoted by A. Roy Eckardt, "The Perennial Effrontery" (review of Cardinal Bea's *The Church and the Jewish People*), *Midstream*, January 1967, p. 66.

testimony as the one task. Most of us must come to terms with recent history and ask the questions of our time. A tradition which does not know the specifics of our age, the inner and the outer dimensions of Jewish existence (where the reality of the state of Israel is also a theological statement), which does not know that the earlier centuries and their teachings have been surmounted—cannot speak to us. The younger theologians of today are the disciples of the theologians of the nineteen twenties, Jewish and Christian, who taught in Germany before thought ceased there. But where the teachings of Rosenzweig and Buber have been assimilated into their language and formulations, Leo Baeck has until now been ignored.[2] His life obscured his teachings: He was viewed as the spokesman of a community. Since that community had adopted the language of Hermann Cohen and of nineteenth century optimism, Baeck was viewed as one more spokesman of that liberal Judaism. Yet Hermann Cohen said far more than the German-Jewish community realized; and Leo Baeck said far more than the American-Jewish community has realized. As the insights of Martin Buber come to be incorporated in the fields of epistemology and sociology, his relevance for the study of universal human experience becomes much clearer; but we also discover that he is not the guide for the particular Jewish experience which theologians and laymen seek. Rosenzweig and existentialism have left their impact—but the individual has somehow become separated from the community. Baeck's religion of polarity here moves to the foreground. It is the child of neo-Kantianism, informed and raised by the twentieth century. A subtle and competent intellectual framework supports it. This has caused many to reject Baeck's teachings. Our theologians are afraid of classic philosophy; existentialism has brought a peculiar type of anti-intellectualism into modern theology. But Baeck's teaching of a style of life, of the ancient traditions and customs and their role, also finds opposition among philosophers who feel themselves emancipated from religion. Baeck's is the middle way, always opposed by both sides. Yet the excesses on either side run their course, and the

---

[2] Most of the "younger Jewish theologians" were taught by Baeck: including Emil Fackenheim, Eugene Borowitz, Stephen Schwarzschild, Arnold Wolf, Bernard Martin, and Jacob Petuchowski, among others. And many examples could be given where the teachings, if not the teacher, are in evidence. One clear acknowledgment of Baeck's stress upon the ethical action and the mystery is found in Arthur A. Cohen's writings on the "natural and supernatural Jew" [95].

middle way may well be the path which will endure. And Baeck's teach-ings rise not only out of Jewish thought, but out of Jewish life. Baeck was a rabbi. Once secularized intellectualism has overcome that fact, it becomes a source of strength for his teachings. Baeck was a Pharisee. Once Christian thought has overcome its ancient prejudices, it may well come to learn from Baeck how to sanctify all of life and come to terms with its current problems.

II

A final review of our findings is necessary for an assessment of what Baeck means to modern thought. That Baeck was a rabbi must be stated again and again; not because a rabbi differs from the Jewish layman, but because he emphasizes the goals of all Jewish life. Jewish life unfolded Baeck's existence from birth to death; the rabbinical heritage of his ancestors guided him and directed him. When we consider his theology and its roots in experience, we cannot ignore the experience of traditional Jewish observances which filled every day of Baeck's life. From the beginning, Baeck stressed ritual observances which express religious thought and are necessary to establish these teachings within human existence. Baeck stressed Jewish law. As we have seen, this was a liberal's stress which loved the law without feeling the need for self-subjugation. Baeck was not a *baal ha-Halacha*, but a *baal ha-midrash*. The allegories, mystic allusions, and proud proclamation of Jewish life which form the midrash formed Baeck.

Baeck was the final leader of German Jewry, epitomizing its greatness, not free from some of its flaws. There were times when people felt a distance, a certain coldness, between themselves and Baeck. On one occasion, when Martin Buber discussed Leo Baeck with a young Abraham Heschel, he expressed his opinion that the one adjective which fitted Baeck most closely was *adlig*—"aristocratic." [198] The greatness and its flaws are both sensed in this expression. And the details of Baeck's biography which have come to us: the "new midrash" of resistance against the oppressors, the strong internal life of the Jewish community and Baeck's refusal to leave it, his life at Terezin, his actions in the last years—all testify of the character of German Jewry while giving us a true image of Baeck.

The German background of Baeck has not yet received its full evaluation. Jewish scholars in this field have to remember too much; and the new German scholars forget too much. For the Jew, the anguish of the German-Jewish relationship has had to be resolved on a personal basis. As far as the Jewish community is concerned, it is quite clear that the old "metaphysical love" for German culture has not survived; and we have noted the argument within Jewry on the possibility of German-Jewish dialogue.[3] Yet Baeck's life, through the darkest days, shows us a reaching out toward the better elements within the German community; and Baeck's teachings grow out of German soil. The ethical rigorism is rabbinic, but it is expressed in the language of neo-Kantianism. And Baeck can be seen as the logical outcome of German theological thought (we have noted the impact of Schleiermacher and Dilthey). He shared more with Harnack than he realized. But it is easy to overgeneralize. Comparison could then be made with other empirical philosophers of religion of our time, men like Hocking and Brightman—a comparison which breaks down when we distinguish between the German and American backgrounds, and those aspects of idealism and transcendentalism which keep Baeck on the middle way. Baeck's appeal to experience, to a certain immanentism, and a stress on man's ability to discover God outside the traditional framework do not place him in any one school but rather show his openness to the *Zeitgeist*. And it is this very openness which makes him an effective defender of the Jewish tradition in our times.

Our broad sketch of Baeck's theological developments enables us to see how Jewish reactions duplicated those of the outside environment. Baeck's attack upon Harnack parallels Loisy's championing of liberal Catholic thought against Harnack. But where Loisy is forced out of the framework of his religion, the different pattern of Jewish thought and community life established Baeck as the foremost defender of twentieth century Judaism. Yet *The Essence of Judaism,* set alongside *The Essence of Christianity,* is more than the defense of an established position. The concept of a dynamic and developing faith is built into it through the use of "the paradox" which comes to open Baeck's idealistic system to the

---

[3] Gershom Scholem's "Wider den Mythos vom Deutsch-Juedischen Gespraech" [171] opened a new phase of this argument, carried on by Scholem and others; the most interesting challenge to Scholem has come from Salo W. Baron, "Jews and Germans: A Millennial Heritage" [76a], recording an optimistic speech Baron delivered in Brussels at a World Jewish Congress meeting.

area of human life as the place of validation, a first stage toward Baeck's "religion of polarity."

Baeck's polemic against Christianity is central to his teachings. To the extent that what he challenges is the perversion of classic Judaism into a romantic faith, the polemic reaches beyond Christianity and challenges aspects of Jewish thought and Jewish community life. Even more challenging, in some ways, is the restoration of Jesus and the Gospels into the Jewish tradition. But what is most relevant to Christianity today is the warning against making the dogmas of Calvary the boundaries of the revelation; the searching questions asked of an ecclesiastical structure which demands obedience within and seeks alliances with secular powers without in order to maintain itself; the fear of overstressing the emotional experience of the encounter with revelation; and the warning against making the ethical act subservient to inner feeling and sentiment. Baeck was harshest—and unfair in a number of ways—in his attacks upon Luther (which he balanced with qualified praise for Calvin). But the attack rests not only upon Luther's teachings, but upon the way these teachings have evidenced themselves in the life of the German community. The life of Dietrich Bonhoeffer indicates that Lutheran life can be righteous testimony; but it is not a full answer to Baeck (and there have been German studies on Bonhoeffer stressing the Calvinist strain in which Baeck also found the stronger ethical strain of Protestantism). Christianity can no more be summed up as *fides quae creditur* than one can make *fides qua creditur* the total statement on Judaism. Judaism is often less than the faith which believes; Christianity is more than a faith demanding belief in its dogmas. But there is body to Baeck's attack, both in terms of Christian thought and in terms of Christian life. The romantic dream and the Greek concept of the "finished" man have deferred, delayed, and impeded the fashioning of the better world; holiness, when trapped inside the Church and accessible only to the true believer, can serve as a terrible prison;[4] and the record of Christian institutions during the years of the Holocaust is at best ambiguous. The twofoldness of Baeck's polemic demands clarity and intellectual responsibility in the realm of ideas; but it also demands that all ideas receive their validation within human experience. As Baeck sees Judaism and the

[4] The case of Charles Davis, the prominent Catholic theologian who defected from the Church recently (cf. this writer's brief discussion of Davis's *God's Grace in History* in *Saturday Review*, February 4, 1967, p. 49) underscores this point.

Jewish people as a totality, so does he approach Christianity as a unity in which tragic errors of thought have torn the fabric of human experience itself. Theology in our time can only ascend into the realm of ideas through the torn fabric of twentieth century existence. Baeck stands before Christianity as an ancient prophet: If Christians would re-enter their sanctuary, there must first be acknowledgment of sin; there must be atonement. The way to God leads through fellow man.

III

As Leo Baeck summarized the essence of Judaism for Jew and for Christian at the beginning of our century, the emphasis on rational thought and on optimism were not its sole characteristics. From the beginning, he stressed that "Judaism has no dogmas," no clearly enunciated statement of a revelation which had to be guarded and passed on by an ecclesiastical structure. Baeck spoke of the dynamism of the Jewish faith which kept open the future as the place for attainment. And so he did not present a set of beliefs, but an ongoing task, an ethical task, found in the categorical "Ought." There was the commandment. Behind it, still in concealment, there stood the mystery. And a foreknowledge of sufferings to come, not clairvoyance but the experience of the past two thousand years, began to bring Israel into focus as the individual and collective martyr. *The Essence of Judaism* is dominated by the call for ethical action; and the clarity and distinctiveness of its intellectual framework are derived from Hermann Cohen and earlier philosophic forebears. Yet Cohen's excessive optimism is already tempered here, in a work which presupposes faith in God but finds its emphasis in faith in man. Idealistic ethical optimism is already in movement toward the later religion of polarity which draws upon human existence, with its tragedy and anguish alongside its affirmations, upon Jewish history as a revelation of the Divine, and places these twofold data of religion into the condition of the *individuum ineffabile.*

The primary message which Baeck's theology brings to our times is the definition of man, the *individuum ineffabile,* within the religion of polarity. Man's religious knowledge is based upon the polarity of his nature, and upon the polarity of religious data. Hermann Cohen's concept of the correlation, with Cohen's knowledge of God and of the ethical act, are central here. Baeck inherited Cohen's sense of the integrity of the intellect, the assertion of that world of intellect where God and man as religious concepts are genuine logical abstractions standing in necessary correlation to one another, leading to the concept of the *Mitmensch* and his basic claim upon our ethical actions which needs no appeal to sentiment. But Baeck had to go beyond the world of ideas; the correlation between God and man had to be apprehended in existence, where man not only acts in response to the commandment but also reaches out toward the mystery with the nonrational aspects of his being. We come to the "new thought" of twentieth century Jewish life here. Baeck did not move from the thesis of Cohen to the antithesis of Buber and on to a new synthesis. Instead, he placed both insights into his framework of polarity where the commandment and the mystery exist within each other.

Baeck starts with the data of experience and with their polarity: The infinite appears in the finite, and whatever is finite bears witness to the infinite. The life of man leads from God to man and from man to God. In the pattern of Baeck's theology (seen most clearly in the Darmstadt lectures) this twofoldness has its own life within the ethical action. The authority of the ethical act is derived from the transcendent but the way to the transcendent is through the human experience. And in this pattern Israel occupies a special place as the people of the revelation and therefore of the mission. Its path through history is a paradigm of man in the universe, confronting commandment and mystery. The beginning of the path is faith in God, but man's knowledge of the way is drawn out of the human experience. This is not immanentism. It is not humanism. The *individuum ineffabile* has a divine dimension; the divine has a human dimension: With Franz Rosenzweig, Baeck believes that "God is *at least* personal." Baeck teaches the theology of those on the path of life: Awareness of the interpenetration of the human and the divine is realized in existence. Man acts justly. God's love comes to be known. And the testimony of a life which did not falter in the concentration camp gives evidence that what Baeck taught was not a textbook exercise of what religious men might say; it was the way in which Jews are to live, the way in which Jews have lived.

The nouns of the age of ontology have become the verbs of the age of empiricism for Leo Baeck. His stress is that of activism: not love but the act of loving, not justice but the just act loom out of his teaching.

But the just act is not relativistic. In the framework of Baeck's polarities, it is the content of life established upon the foundation of life. And Baeck's teachings and actions blend together here in witness of this truth of human existence.

IV

When Baeck moved from the essence of Judaism to the existence of the Jewish people, he came to the expression of a modern Jewish theology which has a profound significance for the Jewish community. It is theology for the synagogue, finding in the rich ceremonies of the house of prayer the style of life. And it is not limited to the synagogue, since the totality of Jewish life contains the revelation which is not confined to one place or one approach. Yet because the new insights are said in the old language, they are suspected or ignored. It is a sad truth of contemporary Jewish life that the majority of pulpits use the old language—but without the old insights. Scriptural verses are recited like magic incantations, but are not placed into life; the theology is glib and shallow. Gresham's Law applies here: the bad product drives out the genuine good product, and Baeck's profound theology is lost among the banalities and mean visions which present themselves to the public as contemporary religion.

The fault lies not so much in the men as in the institution. Dedicated rabbis are often discouraged because their congregants come to the synagogue for social and economic gains and not for the answers to vital questions. *Almost all* the "young Jewish theologians" mentioned earlier have left their pulpits and have become academicians. Sometimes it seems that they write more for one another than for the community. Yet the synagogue cannot survive without theology. And theology, too, must be rooted within the total community if it is to survive. It needs the traditions and the poetry of life, together with the disciplines of academia. The life and teachings of Leo Baeck, reaching out to academia with the integrity of philosophy and to the synagogue with the affirmation of religious existence, appear here as a middle way accessible to all.

Changes must first take place within the synagogue. It must again present ritual as the embellishment of life and not as its surrogate.

Where is the pulpit today which looks at the anguish of personal existence and speaks to human needs? The midrash of today, the language which is heard, is found in films like Antonioni's *Blow-Up*. The pulpit must match this language: it must be able to tell us what we are today, and what we can be tomorrow. Only then will theology and life once again interlock. And only then will our generation begin to appreciate the wide vision of Leo Baeck which affirms aspects of human existence blocked out of contemporary awareness by a cybernetic culture which has lost its sense of religion.

Changes must take place within the Jewish academic community. The standards of the university are often established by those who have not grasped the richness of Jewish life; and Jewish scholars follow their colleagues far too uncritically. Bernard Martin writes:

> Tillich's recognition that theology must start with the doctrine of man is an insight of capital importance which, I believe, Jewish theologians would do well to adopt, and . . . Tillich's analysis of the nature of reason and revelation and their relation to each other should prove helpful to Jewish theologians. [152a, pp. 186–187] See also [152b].

The truth of that statement is only an underscoring of the fact that Baeck's *individuum ineffabile* and his religion of polarity have not been evaluated by Baeck's own students. In search of what is new, the Jewish theologian can learn much by putting these two men of religion into juxtaposition. Both Tillich and Baeck instruct the modern mind. Baeck's language of polarity brings an openness to the language of theology not unimportant to linguistic analysis. The rational aspect of the revelation and the revelatory aspect of reason rise out of Baeck's analysis of man which stresses the twofold openness to the revelation; and this same polarity is found in the data of human experience where the immanent and the transcendent have an interrelationship noted by both Baeck and Tillich. A common language can be spoken here by different religions. More, religion and philosophy can talk to each other—a rare possibility which must be explored by both disciplines.

Baeck's teaching is placed into *toldot*, into the dynamic movement of Jewish life. It is a theology of history which encompasses Auschwitz and its despair and makes allowance for the euphoria which followed the Six Day War of 1967. It does not permit the people Israel to cancel one experience with the other, but forces it to view both as stations upon its way of life. But these way stations and this experience is part of the continuous revelation. In the days to come, when theologians and psychologists ponder together upon the stirrings within the Jewish people, engendered by the results of the Six Day War, the middle way of Leo Baeck can provide us with answers which would otherwise be lost to us. The hidden religious dimensions of Jewish secularity will become clearer. Baeck's concept of the twofoldness of Jewish existence will find new affirmation; and new tasks will present themselves to the people which rise out of his ethical dynamism.

Leo Baeck did not leave us a systematic theology. He did leave a way of life. That life conveys the overriding imperative of the ethical commandment, and the teachings convey the knowledge of the Divine mystery. Baeck was a metaphysical poet of his people who spoke out of the reality of Biblical man—which could not be reduced to a symbol —and moved from the revelation which is the people Israel to the tasks which link Jew and non-Jew. Judaism was a missionary task for Baeck, a revelation and a testimony which had to be shared. It was also an eternal flame within the people, leading from rebirth to rebirth. In our time, when many find themselves frozen in the darkness of that knowledge which has Auschwitz in its past and personal death in its future, Baeck's way becomes an affirmation of man who reaches beyond the caesuras of existence. Holiness is rediscovered, and man comes to find the *foundation* of his being in the eternal mystery and the *contents* of existence in the ongoing commandment of the ethical task with its messianic horizon.

That teaching could surmount the nights of Terezin. It may well serve to lead man through the flames of the Atomic Age. For as the dimensions of man are enlarged to the point where the divine mystery can be discerned, man also comes to the knowledge of his fellow man. Mystery and commandment are joined here: "Thou shalt love thy neighbor as thyself—I am the Lord."

Bibliography

PRIMARY SOURCES: WRITINGS OF LEO BAECK
(*in chronological order*)

PRINCIPAL AND COLLECTED WORKS

1. *Das Wesen des Judentums.* Schriften der Gesellschaft zur Foerderung der Wissenschaft des Judentums. Berlin, Nathanson und Lamm, 1905.
2. ———, 2nd rev. ed. Frankfurt am Main, J. Kauffmann, 1923.
2a. ———. Fourth edition. Frankfurt, 1926.
3. *The Essence of Judaism,* rev. ed. Rendition by I. Howe, based on the translation from the German by V. Grubenwieser (*sic*) and L. Pearl (London, 1936). New York, Schocken Books, 1948.
4. *Wege im Judentum. Aufsaetze und Reden.* Berlin, Schocken Verlag, 1933.
5. *Aus drei Jahrtausenden. Wissenschaftliche Untersuchungen und Abhandlungen zur Geschichte des juedischen Glaubens.* Berlin, Schocken Verlag–Juedischer Buchverlag, 1938.
6. ———, in *Nachdruck des Werkes* (ohne die Beitraege ueber die Pharisaer und das Evangelium). Introduction by Hans Liebeschuetz. Tuebingen, 1958.
7. *Dieses Volk. Juedische Existenz.* Frankfurt am Main, Europaeische Verlagsanstalt, 1955.

8. *This People Israel: The Meaning of Jewish Existence.* Translated and with an introductory essay by Albert H. Friedlander. New York, Holt, Rinehart and Winston, 1965. This translation contains both the 1955 edition of *Dieses Volk* and the Second Part of *Dieses Volk* published in 1957.

9. *Dieses Volk. Juedische Existenz. Ein zweiter Teil.* Frankfurt am Main, Europaeische Verlagsanstalt, 1957.

OTHER WRITINGS

10. ———. See [8].

11. *Spinoza erste Einwirkungen auf Deutschland* (doctoral dissertation, Friedrich Wilhelms University, Berlin). Berlin, Mayer und Mueller, 1895.

12. Review of *Dreizehnter Bericht ueber die Lehranstalt fuer die Wissenschaft des Judenthums in Berlin,* Von Martin Schreiner (Berlin, 1895), *Juedische Chronik,* vol. II (1895), pp. 90–91.

13. Review of *Die Staatelehre Spinoza,* by Josef Hoff, *Juedische Chronik,* 1895, pp. 188–189.

14. ———. Reprinted in [124].

15. "Orthodox oder ceremonioes?" *Juedische Chronik,* vol. III (1896), pp. 237–243.

16. ———. Reprinted in [14].

17. "Harnack's Vorlesungen ueber das Wesen des Christenthums," Monatsschrift fuer Die Geschichte und Wissenschaft des Judentums. September 1901, pp. 97–120.

18. ———. Sonderabdruck aus der Monatsschrift fuer Die Geschichte und Wissenschaft des Judentums. Zweite vermehrte Auflage. Breslau, W. Koebner, 1902. This edition was seven pages longer and had a number of new footnotes.

19. "Die Schoepfung des Mitmenschen," in *Soziale Ethik im Judentum,* Zur fuenften Hauptversammlung in Hamburg, 1913. Frankfurt am Main, Verband der Deutschen Juden, 1913, pp. 9–15.

20. "Griechische und juedische Predigt." Inaugural Lecture at the Lehranstalt fuer die Wissenschaft des Judentums. May 4, 1913. *Lehranstalt,* vol. XXXII, pp. 57–75. Reprinted in [5, pp. 142–156].

21. "Lebensgrund und Lebensgehalt," *Der Jude,* vol. II (1917), pp. 78–86.

22. ———. Reprinted in [4, pp. 134–150].

23. "Heimgegangene des Krieges. Ueber den preussischen Staat" (1917). In [4, pp. 382–400]. Page references are to [4].

24. *Die Lehren des Judentums nach den Quellen.* Herausgegeben vom Ver-

band der deutschen Juden. Unter Mitwirkung von L. Baeck (and others)
. . . bearbeitet von S. Bernfeld (and Fritz Bamberger) Berlin. C. A.
Schwetschke und Son, 1920–(1929). (An anthology of Jewish teachings published by the outstanding teachers of the German Jewish community.)

25. "Geheimnis und Gebot," *Der Leuchter*, 1921–1922, pp. 137–153. Re-
    printed in [4, pp. 33–48].
25a. ———. In *Judaism and Christianity;* see [28].
26. "Nehemia Anton Nobel. Ueber schoepferische Empfaenglichkeit." In
    [4, pp. 357–361].
27. "*Romantische Religion.* Ein erster Abschnitt aus einem Werke ueber
    "Klassische und romantische Religion," in *Festschrift zum 50 jaehrigen
    Bestehen der Hochschule fuer die Wissenschaft des Judentums.* Berlin,
    1922, pp. 1–48. Reprinted (With three additional chapters) in [5].
28. ———, in *Judaism and Christianity: Essays by Leo Baeck* (1958),
    translated by Walter Kaufmann. Meridian Books, 1961, pp. 189–292.
29. "Bedeutung der juedischen Mystik fuer unsere Zeit," *Die Tat*, August
    1923, pp. 340–344.
30. "Die Spannung im Menschen und der fertige Mensch," *Der Leuchter*,
    vol. IV (1923), pp. 117–141.
31. "Vollendung und Spannung." In [4, pp. 9–32].
31a. "Judaism in the Church," HUCA (1925).
32. "Tod und Wiedergeburt," *Der Leuchter*, vol. VI (1925), pp. 195–218.
    Reprinted in [4, pp. 49–71]. Page references are to [4].
33. "Zwei Beispiele midraschicher Predig," *Monatsschrift fuer Die Ges-
    chichte und Wissenschaft des Judentums*, vol. LXIXX, pp. 258–271.
    Reprinted in [5, pp. 157–175].
34. "Besitzt das ueberlieferte Judentum Dogmen?" *Monatschrift fuer Die
    Geschichte und Wissenschaft des Judentums*, vol. LXX (1926), pp.
    225–236.
35. "Hat das ueberlieferte Judentum Dogmen?" In [5, pp. 12–27].
36. "Sefer Yezirah." In [5, pp. 256–271].
36a. "Sefer Ha-Bahir." In [5, pp. 272–289].
37. "Das Judentum," in *Die Religionen aer Erde, ihr Wesen und ihre
    Geschichte*, with F. Babinger, L. Baeck (and others). Munich, 1927,
    pp. 401–422.
38. *God and Man in Judaism.* New York, Union of American Hebrew
    Congregations, 1958.
39. "Die Pharisaer," *Lehranstalt*, vol. XLIV (1927), pp. 34–71.
40. *The Pharisees and Other Essays.* Introduction by Krister Stendahl. New
    York, Schocken Books, 1947.

41. "Die Mystik im Judentum." In [4, pp. 90–95].
42. "Neutralitaet" (1929). In [4, pp. 215–223]. First published in *Blaetter des Deutschen Roten Kreuze.*
43. "Franz Rosenzweig; Ueber Bildung" (1930). In [4, pp. 362–373].
44. "Geist und Blut." (vortag, gehalten auf der Jubilaeumstagung der Gesellschaft fuer freie Philosophie in Darmstadt), *Der Morgen,* vol. VI (1931), pp. 583–590.
44a. "Zwischen Wittenberg und Rom." In [4].
45. "Theologie und Geschichte," *Lehranstalt,* vol. XLIX (1932), pp. 42–54.
46. "Theology and History" (translated by M. Meyer), *Judaism,* Summer 1964, pp. 274–285.
47. "Schoepfungsordnungen," *Juedische Allgemeine Zeitung,* vol. XVI (1936), No. 22, Beilage, p. 3.
48. "Nachruf auf Felix Warburg," *Der Morgen,* vol. XIII (1937–1938), pp. 358–371.
49. "Der 'Menschensohn' " *Monatsschrift fuer Die Geschichte und Wissenschaft des Judentums,* vol. LXXXI (1937), pp. 12–24.
50. *Das Evangelium als Urkunde der juedischen Glaubensgeschichte.* Berlin, Schocken Verlag–Juedischer Buchverlag, 1938.
51. ————. In [28, pp. 41–139].
52. *Der Sinn der Geschichte.* Drei Vortraege aus der Sendereihe "Lebendiges Abendland" des Deutschen Dienstes des Londoner Rundfunks: 1. Der Sinn der Geschichte; 2. Die Zivilization und der Mensch; 3. Staat und Kultur. Berlin, C. Habel, 1946.
53. "The Task of Progressive Judaism in the Post-war World," Presidential Address, World Union for Progressive Judaism, in *Report of the Fifth International Conference held in London.* London, 1946, pp. 70–73.
54. "Individuum ineffabile," *Eranos-Jahrbuch,* vol. XV (1948), pp. 385–436.
55. "Why Jews in the World? A Reaffirmation of Faith in Israel's Destiny," *Commentary,* vol. III, pp. 501–507.
56. "A People Stands before its God." In [81, pp. 284–298].
57. *Two Series of Lectures:* "The Interrelation of Judaism, Science, Philosophy and Ethics," the Dr. Samuel Schulman Lectures at the Hebrew Union College–Jewish Institute of Religion, Cincinnati, 1949; and "Judaism, the Jew and the State of Israel," the Dr. Nathan Krass Lectures at the Hebrew Union College–Jewish Institute of Religion, New York, 1950. New York City, Congregation Emanu-El, 1950.
58. "Jewish Mysticism," *Journal of Jewish Studies,* vol. II (1951), pp. 3–16.

59. "The Faith of Paul," *Journal of Jewish Studies*, vol. III (1952), pp. 93–110. Based on lecture delivered to the Society of Jewish Study, London. Reprinted in [28]; page references are to [28].

60. "The Psychological Root of the Law," *Hebrew University Garland* (London), 1952, pp. 11–17. Wingate Lecture at the Hebrew University, 1951.

61. "Wanderer zwischen zwei Welten. In memoriam Eugen Taeubler," *Aufbau*, vol. XIX, no. 35, p. 9.

61a. *Maimonides*, Duesseldorf, 1954.

62. "Some Questions to the Christian Church from the Jewish Point of View," in *The Church and the Jewish People*, Goete Hedenquist, ed. London, International Missionary Council, 1954, pp. 102–116.

63. "Survival: An Address at the Concentration Camp (Academic Address given on June 15, 1944, at the Community House, Theresienstadt)," *The Synagogue Review* (Journal of the Reform Synagogues of Great Britain), November 1962, 9 pages (unnumbered).

63a. *Von Moses Mendelssohn zu Franz Rosenzweig* (1956). Stuttgart, 1958.

64. "Letters from Berlin 1942 (The Last Days of the *Reichsvertretung*)," *Leo Baeck Institute Yearbook II* (London), 1957, pp. 309–315.

65. Two excerpts from an unpublished manuscript: "Wandlungen der Weltanschauung und der Parteien"; "Das Wiederauflaben im Judentum." *Leo Baeck Institute Yearbook III* (London), 1958, pp. 361–375.

OTHER SOURCES

66. The Archives of the Leo Baeck Institute. These archives contain unpublished letters of Leo Baeck, written over a span of forty years, including the Baeck-Jaser correspondence (1946–1956) from which Dr. Kreutzberger of the Leo Baeck Institute has permitted some citations for this study; sermons; and other unpublished writings of Leo Baeck (see [65]).

67. Personal conversations with Rabbi Leo Baeck; during the winter months of 1950–1951 and 1951–1952, at the Hebrew Union College–Jewish Institute of Religion, Cincinnati, Ohio.

68. ———. Class notes taken during the period noted in [67].

SECONDARY SOURCES: WRITINGS ABOUT LEO BAECK AND BY HIS
CONTEMPORARIES

PUBLISHED WORKS

69. Adler, H. G., *Theresienstadt 1941–1945*. Das Antlitz einer Zwangsgemeinschaft. Geschichte Soziologie Psychologie. Tuebingen, 1955.

70. Altmann, Alexander, "Hermann Cohens Begriff der Korrelation." In [184a, pp. 377–400].

71. ———, "Theology in Twentieth Century German Jewry," *Leo Baeck Institute Year Book I* (London), 1956, pp. 200 ff.

72. ———, "Zur Auseinandersetzung mit der 'dialektischen Theologie,' " *Monatsschrift fuer Die Geschichte und Wissenschaft des Judentums*, vol. 79 (1935), pp. 345–361.

73. Alexander, Kurt Ansprache. *Gehalten bei der Trauerfeier der American Federation of Jews from Central Europe*. New York, September 9, 1956.

74. ———, "Die Reichsvertretung der deutschen Juden." In [160, pp. 76 ff.].

75. Bach, Hans E., "Leo Baeck (1875–1956)," *Synagogue Review* (London), January 1957. Reprinted 1959.

76. Bamberger, Fritz, "Leo Baeck: The Man and the Idea," *Leo Baeck Memorial Lecture No. 1*. New York, Leo Baeck Institute, 1958, unpaged.

76a. Baron, Salo W., "Jews and Germans: A Millennial Heritage," *Midstream*, January 1967.

77. Baumann, Julius, *Neuchristenthum und reale Religion*. Bonn, 1901.

77a. Berkovits, Eliezer, "Judaism in the Post-Christian Era," *Judaism*, Winter 1966.

78. Bergman, Samual Hugo, "Das Dennoch des Glaubens" (translation from Hebrew article "Leo Baeck" in *Davar*, Tel Aviv, December 11, 1956). In [59].

79. ———, *Faith and Reason: Modern Jewish Thought*, Alfred Jospe, trans. and ed. New York, 1961. Schocken paperback, 1963.

80. ———, "The Problem of Christianity in Jewish Thought," *Prozdor* (Tel Aviv), 1965. Review of Jacob Fleishman, *The Problem of Christianity in Jewish Thought from Mendelssohn to Rosenzweig* (Jerusalem, 1965).

81. Boehm, Eric H., *We Survived*. New Haven, Yale University Press, 1949.

82. Brodnitz, Friedrich, "Die Reichsvertretung der deutschen Juden." In [184a, pp. 106 ff.].

83. Bollnow, O. F., *Wilhelm Dilthey: Eine Einfuehrung in seine Philosophie*, 2nd ed. Stuttgart, 1955. First edition, Leipzig, 1913; page references are to first edition.

84. Bonhoeffer, D., *Widerstand und Ergebung. Briefe und Aufzeichnungen aus der Haft*. Muenchen, 1952.

85. Bousset, W., "Das Wesen des Christentums," *Theologische Rundschau,* vol. 4, (1901), pp. 89–103.

86. Brod, Max, *Heidentum—Christentum—Judentum,* 2 volumes. Munich, 1921.

87. Buber, Martin, *Reden ueber das Judentum.* Gesammtausgabe. Frankfurt am Main, 1923.

88. ———, *Ich und Du. Um ein Nachwort erweiterte Neuausgaba.* Heidelberg, 1958.

89. ———, *Die Stunde und die Erkenntnis, Reden und Aufsaetze, 1933– 1935.* Berlin, Schocken Verlag, 1936.

90. ———, *Dialogisches Leben.* Gesammelte Philosophische und Paedagogische Schriften. (Gregor Mueller Verlag, Zurich, 1947).

91. ———, *Eclipse of God.* New York, Harper Torchbooks, 1957.

91a. ———, "Der Mensch von heute und die juedische Bibel." In [93].

92. ———, *Two Types of Faith.* New York, Harper Torchbooks, 1961. First published as *Zwei Glaubensweisen* (Zurich, 1950).

93. Buber, Martin, und Rosenzweig, Franz, *Die Schrift und ihre Verdeutschung.* Berlin, Schocken Verlag, 1936.

94. Cohen, Arthur A., *Martin Buber,* London, 1957.

95. ———, *The Natural and the Supernatural Jew.* New York, Pantheon, 1962.

96. Cohen, Hermann, *Juedische Schriften.* Veroeffentlichungen der Akademie fuer die Wissenschaft des Judentums 1, Introduction by Franz Rosenzweig, Bruno Strauss, ed., 3 volumes. Berlin, 1924.

97. ———, *Deutschtum und Judentum.* Giessen, 1915.

98. ———, *Die Religion der Vernunft aus den Quellen des Judentums.* Published after Hermann Cohen's death by his wife. Berlin, 1918.

99. Dienemann, M., "Besprechung von L. Baeck's Das Evangelium als Urkunde der juedischen Glaubensgeschichte," *Monatsschrift fuer die Geschichte und Wissenschaft des Judentums,* vol. 82 (Neue Folge 46), 1938, pp. 353 ff.

100. ———, *Midraschim der Klage und der Zuspruchs.* Schocken Buecherei, No. 36. Berlin, 1935.

101. Dilthey, Wilhelm, *Das Erlebnis und die Dichtung.* Berlin, 1905. 12th ed. Goettingen, 1921.

102. ———, *Das Wesen der Philosophie* (1907), vol. V. *Gesammelte Schriften,* vol. V, Berlin, 1957; pp. 339–416.

103. ———, *Die Biographie,* vol. V, *Gesammelte Schriften.* 1957.

104. ———, *Einleitung in die Geisteswissenschaften.* Leipzig, 1883.

105. ———. *Die Entstehung der Hermaneutik,* vol. V, *Gesammelte Schriften.* 1957.

106. Dubnow, Simon, *Welgeschichte des juedischen Volkes*. Berlin, 1925.
107. ———, *Nationalism and History: Essays on Old and New Judaism*, trans. by Koppel Pinson. Philadelphia, Jewish Publication Society, 1958.
107a. Fabian, Hans Erich, "Dis Letzte Etappe." In [160].
108. Fackenheim, Emil, "Jewish Existence and the Living God," *Commentary*, August 1959.
109. Friedman, Maurice, *Martin Buber: The Life of Dialogue*. Chicago, 1955.
110. ———, "Christianity and the Contemporary Jew," in *Rediscovering Judaism*, Arnold Jacob Wolf, ed. New York, 1965, pp. 240 ff.
111. Friedlander, Albert Hoschander, "The Arendt Report on Eichmann and the Jewish Community," *CCAR Journal*, October 1963.
112. ———, "A Final Conversation with Paul Tillich," *Reconstructionist*, November 12, 1965.
113. ———, "Rolf Hochhuth's 'Deputy' on the College Campus," *CCAR Journal*, June 1964.
114. ———, "Umbra Vitae: Zum 10. Todestage Eugen Taeublers," *Ruperto Carola* (Jahrbuch der Universitaet Heidelberg), 1963.
115. ———, Introduction to [8].
116. Freier, Recha, "Who Are the Guilty?" *Jewish Quarterly* (London), Spring 1965.
117. Fritz, Kurt von, "Greek Prayer," *Review of Religion*, November 1945.
118. Geiger, Abraham, *Allgemeine Einleitung in die Wissenschaft des Judenthums*, Ludwig Geiger, ed., Berlin, 1875.
119. ———, *Judaism and Its History*. New York, 1865.
120. Geiger, Ludwig, *Geschichte der Juden in Berlin*. Berlin, 1871.
121. Geis, Robert Rafael, *Maenner des Glaubens im deutschen Widerstand (Baeck, Bonhoeffer, Delp)*. Muenchen, 1959.
122. ———, "Leo Baeck," *Frankfurter Haefte*, Jahrgant 12, Heft 1, January 1957.
122a. Goldschmidt, F., "Der Anteil Deutschen Juden an der Gruendung und Entwicklung des Ordens B'nai B'rith." In [160].
123. Goldschmidt, Hermann Levin Frankfurt am Main, *Die Botschaft des Judentums*. Europaeische Verlagsanstalt, 1957.
124. ———, *Leo Baeck Heft und Achter Jahrsbericht*. Zurich, Juedisches Lehrhaus. September 1959.
125. ———, *Das Vermaechtnis des Deutschen Judentums*. Frankfurt am Main, Europaeische Verlagsanstalt, 1957.
126. Goldstein, David, "The Jewish Spirit: Review of *This People Israel*," *Pointer* (Quarterly Journal of Union of Liberal and Progressive Synagogues, Winter 1965.

127. Glatzer, Nahum N., *Franz Rosenzweig, His Life and Thought*. New York, 1953.

128. Gruenewald, Max, "Leo Baeck: Witness and Judge," *Judaism*, Autumn 1957.

129. ————, "Theology and History," *Leo Baeck Memorial Lecture No. 3*. New York, Leo Baeck Institute, 1960.

130. ————, "The Modern Rabbi," *Leo Baeck Institute Yearbook II* (London), 1957.

131. Guttmann, Julius, *Philosophies of Judaism*. Translation by David W. Silvermann. New York, Jewish Publication Society and Holt, Rinehart and Winston, 1964.

132. Hahn, Hugo, "Die Gruendung der Reichsvertretung." In [184a].

133. Harnack, Adolf, *Das Wesen des Christenthums*. Leipzig, J. C. Hinrichs'sche Buchhandlung, 1900. Page references are to 1913 edition.

134. ————, *What is Christianity?* Translation by Thomas B. Saunders. London and New York, 1901. This translation is used in citations from Harnack, except where antiquated language suggested a retranslation of the original. In those instances, the 1913 edition of *Wesen des Christenthums* was used.

135. Heschel, Abraham Joshua, *Man is Not Alone*. New York, Farrar, Straus, and Cudahy, 1951.

136. ————, *The Sabbath: Its Meaning for Modern Man*. New York, Farrar, Straus, and Cudahy, 1951.

137. ————, *Who Is Man?* Stanford, Stanford University Press, 1965.

138. Horton, W. M., "The Development of Theological Thought," in *Twentieth Century Christianity* (revised American edition), Stephen Neill, ed. New York, 1963.

138a. Italiener, Bruno, "Der Rabbiner." In [160].

138b. Jacob, Walter, "Leo Baeck and Christianity," *Jewish Quarterly Review*, October 1965.

139. Kaplan, Mordecai M., *The Meaning of God in Modern Jewish Religion*. New York, 1937.

140. Kaufmann, Walter, Biographical Sketch and Preface to [28].

141. ————, *Critique of Religion and Philosophy*, New York, 1958.

142. Klausner, Joseph, *Jesus von Nazareth*, 3rd ed. Jerusalem, 1952.

143. Kluckhohn, P. *Die deutsche Romantik*. Leipzig, 1924.

144. Leschintzer, Adolf, "The Unknown Leo Baeck," *Commentary*, May 1957.

145. Liebeschuetz, Hans, "Jewish Thought and its German Background," *Leo Baeck Institute Yearbook I* (London), 1956.

146. ————, Introduction to [6].

147. Loisy, Alfred, *L'Evangele et L'Eglise*. Paris, 1902.

148. ———, *The Gospel and The Church*. 1904.
149. Losie, John P., "Biblical Religion and Ontology: Has Tillich Established a Point of Identity?" *Journal of Bible and Religion*, July 3, 1965, pp. 223–229.
150. Mayer, Reinhold, *Christentum und Judentum in der Schau Leo Baecks*. Stuttgart Studia Delitzschiana, 1961.
151. Maybaum, Ignaz, *God's Face After Auschwitz*. Amsterdam, 1966.
152. Mackintosh, Hugh Ross, *Types of Modern Theology: Schleiermacher to Barth*. New York, Scribners, 1958.
152a. Martin, Bernard, "Paul Tillich and Judaism," *Judaism*. Spring 1966.
152b. ———, *The Existentialist Philosophy of Paul Tillich*. New York, Bookman Associates, 1963.
153. Martin, James Alfred, Jr., *Empirical Philosophies of Religion*. New York, 1945.
154. Perles, Felix, "Was lehrt uns Harnack?" *Juedische Skizzen*. Leipzig, 1912, pp. 208–232. First published 1902.
155. Petuchowski, Jakob J., "Faith as the Leap of Action," *Commentary*, May 1958.
156. ———, in *Rediscovering Judaism*, Arnold J. Wolf, ed. Chicago, 1965, pp. 35 ff.
157. Przywara, Erich, S.J., *Ringen der Gegenwart*, Aufsaetze II. Augsburg, 1929.
157a. ———, *Gott*. Munich, 1926.
158. Reichmann, Eva G., "Symbol of German Jewry," *Leo Baeck Institute Yearbook II* (London), 1957.
159. ———, ed., *Worte des Gedankens fuer Leo Baeck*. London, 1959. This is the basic collection of Baeck studies.
160. ———, *Festschrift zum 80. Geburtstag von Leo Baeck am. 23. Mai 1953*. London, 1953.
161. Rengstorf, K. H., "Leo Baeck als Theologe und im theologischen Gespraech." In [159].
162. Rosenzweig, Franz, *Der Stern der Erloesung* (1921), 3rd ed. Heidelberg, 1954.
163. ———, *Kleinere Schriften*. Berlin, E. Rosenzweig and Schocken Verlag, 1937.
164. ———, *Understanding the Sick and the Healthy*, Nahum Glatzer, ed. New York, 1953.
165. ———, Introduction to [96].
165a. Schleiermacher, Friedrich, *On Religion—Speeches to the Cultured Despisers*. New York, 1958.
166. Schmitt, Carl, *Politische Romantik* (1922), Zweite Auflage. Munich und Leipzig, 1925.

167. ———, *Stastsgefuege und Zusammenbruch des zweiten Reiches.* Hamburg, Hanseatische Verlagsanstalt, 1934.

168. ———, *Verfassungsgechtliche Aufsaetze.* Berlin, 1958.

169. Schoeps, Hans Joachim, *The Jewish Christian Argument.* New York, 1963.

170. Scholem, Gershom G., *Major Trends in Jewish Mysticism.* New York, Schocken Books, 1946.

171. ———, "Wider den Mythos von Deutsch-Juedischen Gespraech," *Bulletin of Leo Baeck Institute*, No. 27, 1964.

172. ———, "Zur Literatur der letzten Kabbalisten in Deutschland." In [184a].

173. ———, "Martin Buber's Hasidism: A Critique," *Commentary*, October 1961.

174. Schwarzschild, Steven, "To Recast Rationalism," *Judaism.* Summer 1962.

175. ———, *Franz Rosenzweig. Guide for Reversioners*, London, Education Committee of Hillel Committee, undated.

176. ———, "The Democratic Socialism of Hermann Cohen," *Hebrew Union College Annual*, vol. XXVII (1956).

177. Simon, Ernst, *Aufbau im Untergang.* Tuebingen, 1959.

178. ———, "Geheimnis und Gebot. Zu Leo Baeck's 75. Geburtstag," *Aufbau*, May 21, 1948.

179. ———, *Bruecken: Gesammelte Aufsaetze.* Heidelberg, Verlag Lambert Schneider, 1965.

179a. ———, The Jew as God's Witness to the World" (address delivered at Deutscher Evangelischer Kirchentag, Cologne, 1965), *Judaism*, Summer 1966.

180. Strack, Hermann L., *Einleitung in Talmud und Midrash*, 5th ed. Munich, 1921.

181. Strauss, Leo, *Spinoza's Critique of Religion.* New York, 1965.

182. Strich, Fritz, *Deutsche Klassik und Romantik* (1922). Vierte Auflage. Bern, 1949.

183. Tillich, Paul, *Die Judenfrage, ein christliches und ein deutsches Problem.* Vier Vortraege, gehalten an der deutschen Hochschule fuer Politik. Berlin, 1953.

184. Taeubler, Eugen, "Heimat." In [160].

184a. Tramer, Hans, ed., *In Zwei Welten.* Tel Aviv, Bitaon, 1962.

185. Troeltsch, E., "Was heisst 'Wesen des Christentums'?" (1903), in *Gesammelte Schriften*, vol. II. Berlin, 1913.

186. Weltsch, Robert, "Trag ihn mit Stolz, den gelben Fleck!" *Juedische Rundschau* (Berlin), vol. IV, no. 4 (1933).

187. Weltsch, Robert, ed., *Leo Baeck Institute Yearbooks.* London, 1956–

1966. These yearbooks are a primary source for this period of German-Jewish history.

188. Wilhelm, Kurt, "Der Zionistische Rabbiner." In [184a].

189. ———, "Leo Baeck and Jewish Mysticism," *Judaism*, Spring 1962, pp. 123–131.

190. ———, *Das Erbe des deutschen Judentums*, 1957.

191. Wiener, Max, *Abraham Geiger and Liberal Judaism*. Philadelphia, Jewish Publication Society, 1962.

192. Wiener, Theodore, *The Writings of Leo Baeck, a Bibliography* (*Studies in Bibliography and Booklore*, vol. I, no. 3). Cincinnati, Hebrew Union College Press, 1954. This is an almost complete bibliography of Baeck's writings up to 1954.

193. Wittenberg, Martin, *Juedische Existenz nach Leo Baeck*. Neuendettelsau, 1955.

194. Wolf, Arnold J., "Leo Baeck's Critique of Christianity," *Judaism*. Spring 1963, pp. 190–194.

195. Wolf, Arnold J. (ed.), *Rediscovering Judaism*. New York, 1965.

196. Wolfsberg, Oscar (Jeschajahu Aviad-Wolfsberg), "Zu Leo Baecks Gedaechtnis." In [159].

197. van der Zyl, W., "Memorial Tribute," *In Memoriam Leo Baeck*. London, 1957.

OTHER SOURCES

198. Personal Interview, with Professor Abraham J. Heschel, Jewish Theological Seminary, New York City, December 17, 1965.

199. ———, with Dr. Max Kreutzberger, Leo Baeck Institute, New York City, various times during 1964, 1965, 1966.

200. ———, with Professor Ernst Simon of Hebrew University; in New York City, December 23, 1965; December 27, 1965.

201. ———, with Professor Paul Tillich, in Easthampton, Long Island, August 14, 1965; see [112].

202. ———, with Professor Hannah Arendt, New York City, January 7, 1966.

203. Unpublished material from Dr. Alfred Jospe, National B'nai B'rith Hillel, Washington, D.C.

INDEX

289